D1577043

WHITE DEBT

WHITE DEBT

The Demerara Uprising
and Britain's Legacy of Slavery

THOMAS HARDING

W&N
WEIDENFELD & NICOLSON

First published in Great Britain in 2022 by Weidenfeld & Nicolson
an imprint of The Orion Publishing Group Ltd
Carmelite House, 50 Victoria Embankment
London EC4Y oDZ

An Hachette UK Company

1 3 5 7 9 10 8 6 4 2

A CIP catalogue record for this book is
available from the British Library.

ISBN (Hardback) 978 1 4746 2104 5
ISBN (Export Trade Paperback) 978 1 4746 2105 2
ISBN (eBook) 978 1 4746 2107 6
ISBN (Audio) 978 1 4746 2108 3

Printed in Great Britain by Clays Ltd, Elcograf S.p.A.

MIX
Paper from
responsible sources
FSC® C104740
FSC
www.fsc.org

www.weidenfeldandnicolson.co.uk
www.orionbooks.co.uk

To my agents Sarah Chalfant and James Pullen,
and my editors Alan Samson and Jenny Lord,
who were steadfast in their support of this project

CONTENTS

PART 1

ARRIVAL

PART 2

UPRISING

PART 3

THE TRIAL

THE ATLANTIC WORLD c.1823

N

NORTH AMERICA

ATLANTIC OCEAN

BERMUDA

1 DEMERARA-
   ESSEQUIBO*
2 BERBICE*
3 SURINAME (Dutch)
4 FRENCH GUIANA
*(*Estimated southern border)*

CUBA

HAITI

JAMAICA

ST LUCIA

BARBADOS

TOBAGO

TRINIDAD

GRAN COLOMBIA

1

2 3 4

PACIFIC OCEAN

SOUTH AMERICA

PERU

EMPIRE OF BRAZIL

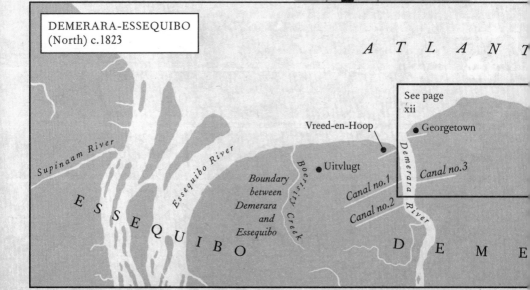

DEMERARA-ESSEQUIBO
(North) c.1823

ATLANT

Supinaam River

Essequibo River

Boeriny Creek

Boundary
between
Demerara
and
Essequibo

Vreed-en-Hoop

Uitvlugt

See page
xii

Georgetown

Demerara

Canal no.3

Canal no.1

Canal no.2

Demerara River

E S S E Q U I B O

D E M E

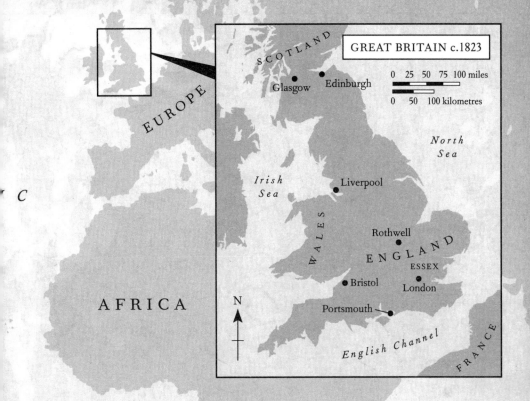

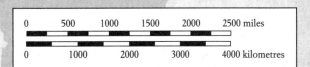

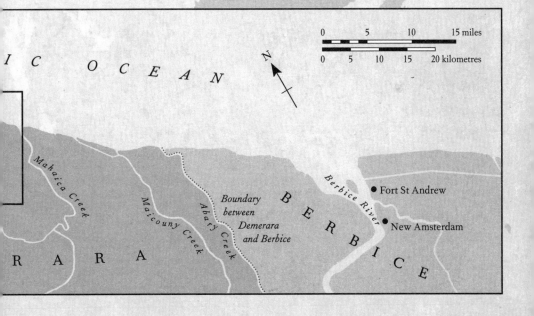

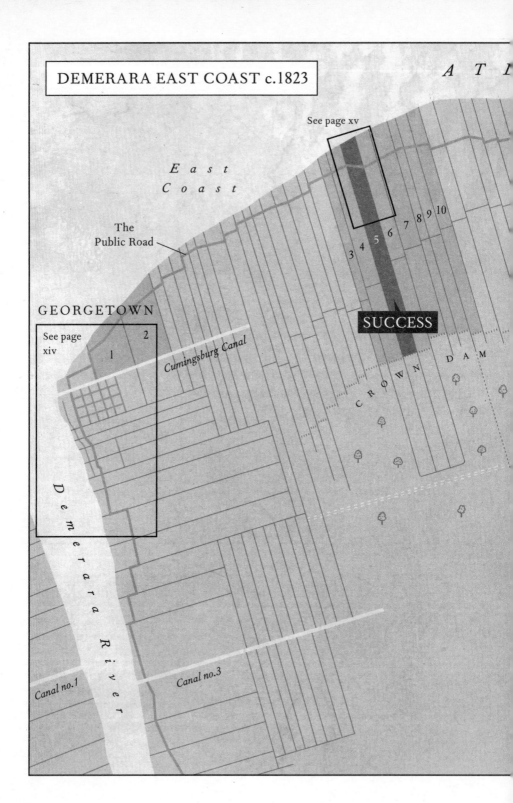

DEMERARA EAST COAST c.1823

A T L

East
Coast

See page xv

The
Public Road

3 4 5 6 7 8 9 10

GEORGETOWN

SUCCESS

See page
xiv

1 2

Cumingsburg Canal

C R O W N   D A M

Demerara River

Canal no.1

Canal no.3

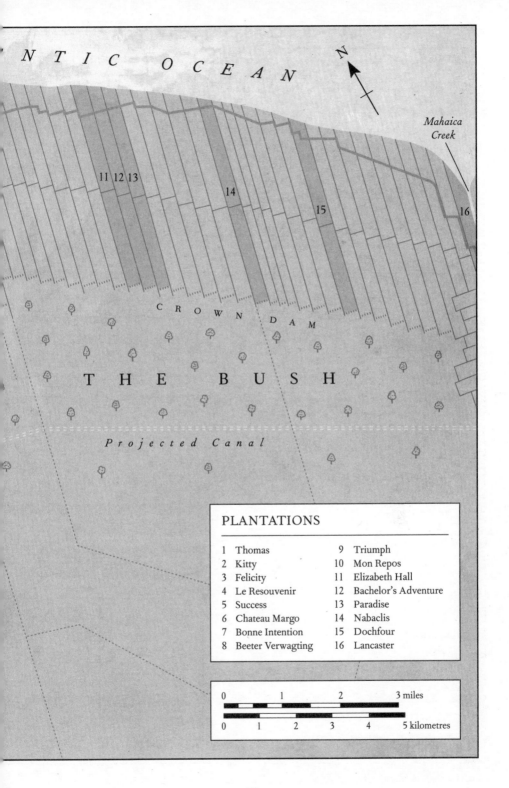

PLANTATIONS

1	Thomas	9	Triumph
2	Kitty	10	Mon Repos
3	Felicity	11	Elizabeth Hall
4	Le Resouvenir	12	Bachelor's Adventure
5	Success	13	Paradise
6	Chateau Margo	14	Nabaclis
7	Bonne Intention	15	Dochfour
8	Beeter Verwagting	16	Lancaster

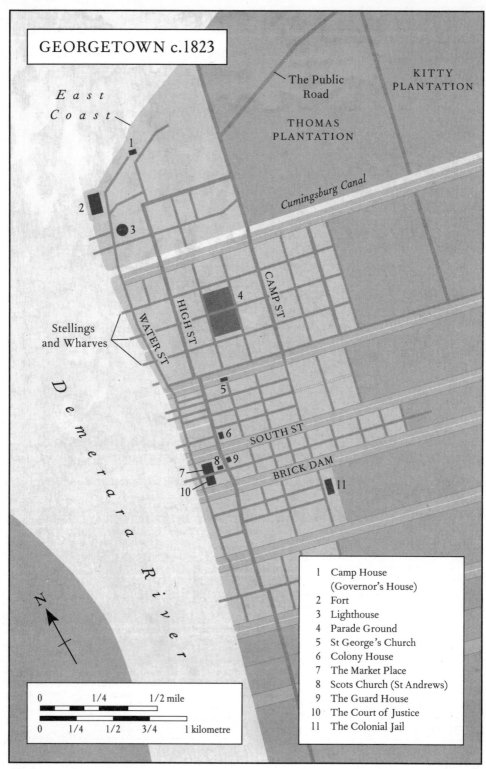

GEORGETOWN c.1823

East
Coast

The Public
Road

KITTY
PLANTATION

THOMAS
PLANTATION

Cumingsburg Canal

1

2

3

CAMP ST

HIGH ST

WATER ST

Stellings
and Wharves

4

Demerara River

5

6

SOUTH ST

8   9

7

BRICK DAM

11

10

N

0   1/4   1/2 mile

0   1/4   1/2   3/4   1 kilometre

1   Camp House
    (Governor's House)
2   Fort
3   Lighthouse
4   Parade Ground
5   St George's Church
6   Colony House
7   The Market Place
8   Scots Church (St Andrews)
9   The Guard House
10 The Court of Justice
11 The Colonial Jail

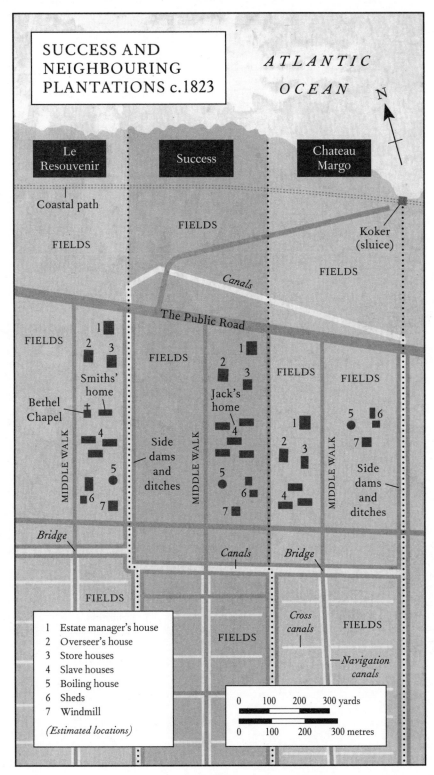

SUCCESS AND NEIGHBOURING PLANTATIONS c.1823

ATLANTIC OCEAN

N

Le Resouvenir

Success

Chateau Margo

Coastal path

FIELDS

FIELDS

Koker (sluice)

FIELDS

Canals

The Public Road

FIELDS

FIELDS

FIELDS

FIELDS

FIELDS

1

2 3

Smiths' home

Bethel Chapel

4

5

6 7

MIDDLE WALK

Side dams and ditches

1

2

3

Jack's home

4

5

6

7

MIDDLE WALK

1

2 3

4

MIDDLE WALK

5 6

7

Side dams and ditches

Bridge

Canals

Bridge

FIELDS

Cross canals

FIELDS

FIELDS

Navigation canals

1 Estate manager's house
2 Overseer's house
3 Store houses
4 Slave houses
5 Boiling house
6 Sheds
7 Windmill

(Estimated locations)

0   100   200   300 yards

0   100   200   300 metres

ILLUSTRATIONS

CAST OF CHARACTERS

JACK GLADSTONE ringleader of rebellion, enslaved on Success plantation

QUAMINA father of Jack, enslaved on Success plantation

JOHN SMITH missionary at Bethel Chapel, lives at Le Resouvenir plantation

JANE SMITH married to John Smith, lives at Le Resouvenir plantation

JOHN MURRAY governor of Demerara

ELLEN MURRAY married to John Murray

JOHN STEWART estate manager at Success plantation

JOHN CHEVELEY store clerk, militiaman, works for Pattinson brothers

WILLIAM PATTINSON merchant, brother to John Pattinson

JOHN PATTINSON merchant, brother to William Pattinson

JOHN GLADSTONE merchant, politician, estate owner, slaveholder

ROBERT EDMONSTONE merchant, slaveholder, court interpreter

MICHAEL M'TURK owner of Felicity plantation, member of Court of Policy, captain in militia

FREDERICK CORT lawyer/agent for John Gladstone in Demerara

JOHN HAMILTON estate manager at Le Resouvenir plantation

SUSANNAH 'housekeeper' for John Stewart, enslaved on Le Resouvenir plantation

DANIEL secretary to Governor John Murray, free man

BRISTOL deacon at Bethel Chapel, enslaved on Chateau Margo plantation

AUTHOR'S NOTE

In writing about this period of slavery, I have tried to include words that maximise comprehension and authenticity whilst minimising offence. I have therefore replaced the use of the N-word with 'slave'. I kept the word 'Negro' only if quoting someone else, say a newspaper, for the sake of historical authenticity. If the word was not included within a quote, I replaced it, even it was the contemporary usage; so 'negro house' became 'slave house'. In general, I have tended to use 'enslaved men and women' rather than 'slaves', because slavery was a situation not a trait. I have also translated quotes that have been written in the local creole, to assist those unfamiliar with the vernacular, and I have used the names of streets, towns and plantations from 1823, although some of the spellings have now changed.

What is the impact of racism on those who perpetuate it?

Toni Morrison

Abolitionist: Applied specifically, and probably originally, to persons seeking the abolition of negro slavery.

Concise Oxford English Dictionary, 1973

INTRODUCTION

In June 2020, hundreds of protesters gathered around the statue of Edward Colston in Bristol, England. The statue was made of bronze and stood eight feet high on top of a white Portland stone plinth. Colston was a British slaver. He sat on the board of the Royal African Company for twelve years, during which time the company transported over 84,000 kidnapped women, men and children from West Africa to the Americas and the Caribbean, of whom it is estimated over 18,000 died en route. The protesters did not believe that this man should be venerated. Two men climbed up the statue and tied a rope around its head, and to much cheering and applauding, the figure was pulled down. The crowd then dragged the statue through the streets and dumped it in Bristol Harbour.

Over the next few days, the media was full of stories about the tearing down of the Colston statue. It kicked off a fierce debate in Britain about empire and slavery. About history and memory. About accountability and responsibility. Some said that the removal of Colston was 'erasing history'. Prime Minister Boris Johnson was one of these. 'We cannot now try to edit or censor our past,' he declared. 'Statues teach us about our past, with all its faults. To tear them down would be to lie about our history, and impoverish the education of generations to come.' Others, such as the historian and broadcaster David Olusoga, argued differently. 'The toppling of Edward Colston's statue is not an attack on history,' he remarked, 'it *is* history.'

The demonstration in Bristol was part of a wave of global protests that followed the police killing of George Floyd, an unarmed Black man in Minneapolis, Minnesota. Around the world, people marched in the streets, chanting slogans and carrying signs declaring 'Black Lives Matter' and 'No Justice No Peace'. Strikingly, those taking part were not only Black and Brown, but also White. It felt to many that we were at a moment of profound historic reckoning.

The pulling down of Colston's statue and the global protests triggered something in me. An urge to find out more about Britain's role in slavery. Recently, while researching the book *Legacy*, I had learned that my mother's family had made money from the slave system. In the nineteenth century, they had sold tobacco from plantations worked by enslaved people of African descent. They were not themselves slaveholders, but like millions of others – bankers, insurance brokers, sugar dealers, shipbuilders, cotton mill workers – they were part of a broader economy that profited from slavery. I began to feel increasingly uncomfortable about the choices made by my ancestors.

Over the past eight years, the shoe had been firmly on the other foot. I had been working in Germany to restore a lake house that the Nazis had stolen from my father's Jewish family, who had fled Berlin in 1936. Some had found refuge in England, but others were killed during the Holocaust. I had received money from the German government as a token of restitution. It was not only an official admission of guilt; it was something material. This was part of the process of reconciliation. So if I was willing to identify as a victim in my father's family, to receive reparations from the German government, then surely I had better understand Britain's role in slavery.

As a child, I was taught that Britain had been the first nation to abolish slavery, that the effort had been led by the politician William Wilberforce, that we were the 'good guys', the great emancipators. I began reading articles and books and was quickly shocked at how little I knew. That it had been British captains commanding British boats operated by British sailors who had transported around 2.8 million captive Africans to the British Caribbean. That it was British families who owned plantations in the Caribbean run by British managers and overseers where hundreds of thousands of enslaved men, women and children were forced to work and die. That it had been British businesses that had transported the cotton, tobacco, sugar and other crops cultivated by the enslaved people to the consumers back in Britain

How was it possible I didn't know any of this? It was like a national amnesia. In my experience, if White British people spoke about slavery, which was rare, it was about the plantations of the southern states of the USA. The world captured in the films *Gone with the Wind*, *12 Years a Slave* and *Django Unchained*. And we tut-tutted about how evil they were, those American slavers, those American plantation owners. As for the Caribbean, it was treated as 'over there', not our responsibility. Even though in the next breath, we proudly talked about the British Empire and all that we had accomplished.

When I told people I was looking into the history of British slavery, some responded negatively. A few questioned why I was focusing on events that took place two hundred years ago. Others were more direct. 'You are a White person,' they said. 'How is this your story to tell?' I thought hard about this, wondering if they were right. But the more I researched the subject, the more I realised that Britain's role in slavery is not only Black history, it is also White history – all of our history. More than this, as a member of a family that profited from slavery, I felt I had an additional responsibility to explore the period. So I went back to the archives and continued my reading.

I wanted to find an example that captured what British slavery was like in a microcosm. An event that could reveal the complexities of a British slave society in granular detail, the ambiguities involved. A set of characters who reflected different points of view. A colony in the Caribbean was the obvious place to start, the heart of the British plantocracy, one that could shed light on the trade links with the mother country. Preferably somewhere that could explore whether the abolition of slavery was brought about not just by humanitarians in Britain but also – through information-gathering, organising, protest and rebellion – by the enslaved people themselves.

Which is how I learned about the insurrection that broke out in Demerara in 1823. I had never heard of Demerara. That is, beyond the brown crystallised sugar that I sometimes spooned into my tea. I soon learned that back in the early nineteenth century, it was a British colony, located above Brazil in South America. Today it is called Guyana. In the National Archives in London and online, I found enormous amounts of primary source material about the 1823 insurrection. Most importantly, and quite exceptionally, the records included the voices of enslaved women and men, contributing tone and texture to the story. I was gripped.

To tell this story, a story of non-fiction, I have relied on archival records, including court testimonies, judicial complaints, journals, memoirs, photographs and letters. Many of these documents were collected during the trials and inquiries that took place soon after the incidents described in this book. In addition, as part of my effort to find out how Britain's legacy of slavery impacts society today, I spoke with academics, researchers, writers, campaigners and the descendants of both enslaved people and slaveholders. All quotes included in this story are taken verbatim from sources such as letters, diaries, newspaper articles, court testimony and my own interviews.

A brief note about this book's title. I hope that by the final chapters you will agree that considerable harm has been done, that a debt is indeed owed. The question then becomes, who caused this harm and who should bear the cost of restitution? For a long time, I danced around this question and when I found the answer, it made me a little nervous. I am someone who until recently did not enter 'White' on the census form because it made me feel uncomfortable.

I didn't want the label. It wasn't the government's business. But then, having spent two years researching Britain's role in slavery – which was built on the classification and brutalisation of people according to their skin colour – and after the murder of George Floyd, it became obvious to me that I had to give a name to those primarily responsible: White people.

After all, the vast majority of those who transported the captured Africans to the Caribbean were White. Similarly, the vast majority of those who 'purchased' these enslaved men, women and children and made them work on the appalling sugar, cotton and coffee plantations were White. The same is true of the shipowners and sailors, bankers and insurance officers, traders, dock-workers, shopkeepers and countless others including my family who were employed transporting, processing and selling the commodities back in Britain. As to the general population who gained from the enormous wealth that poured into Britain on the back of slavery, again the vast majority were White.

Of course, there were some Black and mixed-race people who helped capture the African men and women who became enslaved by the British. Indeed, the presidents of Benin and Ghana have both acknowledged and apologised for their ancestors' culpability in the slave trade. There were also some Black and mixed-race sailors, traders, plantation owners, even slaveholders. But this was on a small scale compared to the systematic brutality of the White-supervised Caribbean slave societies.

More than this, from my conversations with people descended from those enslaved, it is clear that the legacy of slavery is very much alive in Britain today. You can see it in the higher arrest rates for Black British people, the differentials of economic opportunity and health outcomes, the widespread racism. Clearly, other groups experience social and economic hardships in Britain, including members of the White working class, but this does not preclude the specific challenges facing those of African and Caribbean descent.

So while Britain today is a far more diverse society than it was in the 1820s and 1830s, surely it is reasonable to say that the White population has an additional responsibility when it comes to the legacy of slavery. In an article entitled 'White Debt' for the *New York Times* magazine in 2015, the writer Eula Biss pointed out that the German word for debt, *Schuld*, is the same word for guilt. Not 'guilt' in the sense of emotional burden, of self-indulgent introspection. But 'guilt' in the sense of acknowledged wrong-doing, an obligation to redress an offence, of something owed.

This is the White Debt. A cultural debt, acknowledging and apologising for the horror that was British slavery. A financial debt, compensating for the economic losses endured by the men, women and children enslaved and the generations of their descendants. And a debt of gratitude, to the freedom fighters, who not only won liberty for themselves, through bravery, courage and organisation, but for everyone, all humanity, including White people. To be clear, I am not saying that White people alone have a debt, I am saying that White people have an additional or special responsibility. In the same way that by affirming that Black Lives Matter it does not mean that everyone else's lives don't matter, but that special attention needs to be paid to Black lives as they are disproportionately suffering inequality and abuse.

This, then, is the story of everyday industrialised cruelty and damaging legacies that still devastate the lives of the descendants of enslaved Africans, despite the ending of slavery almost two hundred years ago. It is the story of a group of people, almost entirely White, who benefited from this system of slavery and whose wealth, both economic and cultural, continues to be enjoyed today. It is the story of courage, of a small group of people who, out of sight of empire, increased freedom not just for themselves, but for all humanity. And it is an attempt to answer the question: what is the impact today of Britain's historical involvement in slavery and what, if anything, should we do about it?

PROLOGUE

The Vendue Office was located off the main street in Georgetown, the capital of Demerara. It was an immense two-storey stone building that had been built by the Dutch when they ran the colony. Today was auction day, and around its entrance milled a large crowd of Black, White and mixed-race people. Some were customers on their way inside. Others were hawkers and street pedlars, trying to make a few guilders in the hubbub. Still more were simply curious, with little else to do on this balmy tropical spring morning than sit on a wall and watch what was going on.

It was easy to find the sale; all one had to do was follow the noise. A great heaving cacophony of auctioneer babble, shouted bids and, for those victorious, raucous cheering. There were also, if you listened hard, cries of anguish and fear, but these were easily lost in the hullabaloo. Through the two large wooden doors and along a shadowed passageway was an expansive inner courtyard crowded with buyers and sellers, their agents and lawyers. For this was an auction of enslaved people, where men, women and children were sold and bought, where money changed hands in return for human 'property'.

Up on a platform stood a man with black skin, nearly naked except for a cloth cast about his loins. Half a dozen White men were examining his torso and limbs. A few steps back, standing in a semicircle, were another fifty pink-faced men. Some were dressed in linen suits, others in cotton trousers and jackets. Most wore panama or other straw hats to keep the blazing sun off their fragile heads. To lighten the atmosphere, ham sandwiches were handed out, along with glasses of rum or sangaree, a strong liquor made from brandy and nutmeg.

On one side of the platform stood the auctioneer, hammer in hand. 'Capital slave, gentlemen, named Joe, good carpenter, age twenty-eight,' he yelled. 'Oh, you needn't look there, hasn't had the whip often. Now who bids?' The auctioneer now looked at the enslaved man : 'Walk about, you, and show yourself.' After a brief flurry of raised hands, Joe was 'purchased' for 600 guilders.

A woman and her three children were next. 'Here's a good lot, gentlemen. Capital washer, Polly,' shouted the auctioneer to the crowd. 'Stand up, girl, and show your legs, let people see what you are made of.' The crowd laughed and the auctioneer continued. 'Three handy boys, gentlemen, must be sold with the other, six, eight and ten, grow bigger and better every day, will make capital fellows by and by. Look smart, you young rascals. You, Sam, mind yourself. If you look sulky, you catch licks. Come, gentlemen, we can't wait, what do you say? Knock 'em off, there's plenty more to come.' This 'lot' went for 1,000 guilders.

For the enslaved women and men, being sold at the Vendue was brutalising, terrifying, humiliating, heartbreaking. It meant a lifetime of servitude, unrelenting years in which they would have to perform back-breaking work and receive punishment for even the smallest of transgressions. For the slaveholders and the people who supported them, it meant profit and luxury and power. In other words, business as usual.

PART 1

ARRIVAL

When you make men slaves you deprive them of half their virtue ... above all, are there no dangers attending this mode of treatment? Are you not hourly in dread of an insurrection?

Olaudah Equiano

The only place where Negroes did not revolt is in the pages of capitalist historians.

C. L. R. James

CHAPTER 1

Jack, January 1817

The British colony of Demerara was situated to the east of Gran Columbia (today Venezuela) and to the north of the Empire of Brazil. Sitting near the equator, it had two rainy seasons – late November to late January and early May to mid-July – and was mostly dry the rest of the year. 'Discovered' by Europeans in the sixteenth century, it had long held allure for adventurers and those wishing to suddenly improve their economic situation. Indeed, the British explorer Sir Walter Raleigh believed that the mythical city of El Dorado was located alongside a lake hidden somewhere within the colony's interior.

Demerara had been farmed by Dutch settlers until the 1780s, when British colonists took charge. Control was exchanged between London and Amsterdam multiple times over the next two decades, until the matter was finally settled in 1814 and the colony of Demerara-Essequibo, to use its full name, came permanently under Britain's authority. The Dutch legacy, however, persisted. Demerara continued to use the Dutch currency, the guilder, and the justice system was based on Dutch law.

Though Demerara was approximately the same size as Great Britain in terms of square miles, it had 1 per cent of Britain's population. Around 89,000 people lived in the colony, comprising approximately 2,500 White settlers, the same number of free Black men and women, 7,000 Indigenous people and 77,000 enslaved people. As such, those enslaved outnumbered the colonists by a factor of thirty to one.

In the previous century, cotton and coffee had been the main crops, but since 1800, the fastest-growing business in Demerara was sugar. Though its population was tiny compared to Britain's other colonies, it produced a sixth of British Caribbean sugar. Indeed, its sugar business was so productive that the price of enslaved people was higher here than in any other British colony. As a consequence, men, women and children were regularly transported from plantations in Barbados, Jamaica and other West Indian islands to be sold at the Demerara slave auction. For despite the British Parliament passing a law in 1807 that prohibited the Atlantic slave trade, the shipping of enslaved people between British colonies was still permitted.

The Success sugar estate was located seven miles east of Georgetown. It was one of sixty-five plantations that hung down from the northern Atlantic coast like tinsel on a string. Each of the estates was four hundred yards wide and between two and three miles long. In the previous century, the Dutch colonists had reclaimed this area of wetland by building a grid of drainage ditches and earth embankments. Success was owned by an absentee landlord who lived in England, and was home to an estate manager, a handful of overseers, a small number of free Black men and women, and two hundred and thirty enslaved people.

According to the colony's meticulously kept slave register of 1817, the enslaved population at Success included 102 men, 70 women and 58 children. Such a gender imbalance was typical for Demerara, where estate owners preferred to 'purchase' men over women. Three quarters of the enslaved adults worked in the fields. Other roles on the estate included domestic servants, carpenters, coopers, nurses and boatswains. Most of the children aged between seven and thirteen were also listed as employed. They worked as 'jobbers', doing odd tasks around the estate. The register also recorded that more than 80 per cent of those over sixteen years old had been born in Africa. This meant that the vast majority of the enslaved adults living at Success remembered what life was like back in their home countries, when they were free.

One of those enslaved on Success was Jack Gladstone. His mother had died shortly after giving birth to him. Since she was enslaved when Jack was born, according to colonial law he was also enslaved. In the spring of 1817, Jack was twenty-two years old and worked as a cooper on the plantation. He spent his days making and fixing the enormous hogshead barrels that were used to transport sugar to Liverpool, Bristol and London. Six feet two inches tall, he was charismatic and widely considered handsome. He lived with his father, Quamina, his grandmother, Tonisen, and Quamina's new wife, Peggy (a free woman) in one of the communal slave houses on the estate.

At an early age, Jack had been told by Tonisen how she had ended up in Demerara. As a young woman, she had been kidnapped from her village in West Africa and transported to the colony by ship. A few days after landing in Georgetown, she had been sold at the dreaded Vendue slave auction. Luckily, when her son Quamina was born, they had been kept together. Not all families were so fortunate. When Quamina turned ten years old, he had been assigned to work as a houseboy in the estate manager's home. During the next nine years, he had carried out assorted duties, including waiting at table, during which he listened to many conversations between the gentlemen. He had also sometimes been obliged to fetch young enslaved women for the colonists to have sex with. Later, he was reassigned to the carpentry shed, where he learned the skills of the trade including joinery, turning and furniture-making.

That was more than twenty years ago. Tonisen was now in her sixties, and frail. She was no longer able to work and spent most of the day at home. Peggy, though free, completed tasks around the plantation, allowing her to earn some money. Quamina was now in his mid-forties and was the head carpenter at Success. It was he who had taught Jack how to make casks and barrels, bending the hardened wood to his will.

Like everyone else, Jack's family had to rely on the rations provided weekly by the overseers. These varied according to the season and what was available at the stores and markets in Georgetown, but a typical supply might consist of fifty saltfish, half a cask of barley, a handful of tobacco and a bunch of plantains. To supplement their meals, Peggy also maintained a small vegetable patch. Around Christmas time, they received additional supplies. This was mostly clothing, the quantity of which depended on the age and gender of the recipient. Jack and his father, for instance, might be given four yards of osnaburg (a coarse-woven fabric), a new hat or a blanket.

Towards the northern end of the plantation, near the coast, was the home of John Stewart, the estate manager. It was a two-storey house, with painted wooden shutters, an outhouse and a small, pretty garden. Next came the overseers' houses and various estate buildings, including the storehouse where supplies and weapons were kept. Further down the estate, away from the coast, stood half a dozen slave houses; within each, five or more families slept. About 100 feet long and 20 feet wide, these huts were built of bricks made of baked mud, thatched with cane grass and had dirt floors. There were no windows or furniture. Outside the entrance of each structure were the fire pits where meals were prepared. A few steps away, behind some rough fencing, were the latrines.

Next, continuing south, came the windmill. This is where the sugar canes were crushed and the juice piped to the boiling house next door. Here the syrup was clarified, crystallised and poured into the barrels that Jack delivered each week. Beyond the farm buildings and the slave houses lay many acres of cane fields stretching away from the coast. Criss-crossing this land were a series of canals. On these floated shallow-bottomed punts, which were used to transport the felled sugar canes to the windmill. Along the edges of the fields ran deep ditches, draining the water away from the fields to the ocean. Even further on were the backlands, where Jack rarely went. This was the far edge of the plantation, marked by the Crown Dam, an earthen dyke six feet high, on the other side of which lay the swamp and then the bush.

The rules on the estate were as simple as they were clear. Do what you are told and do not talk back. Turn up for work on time and work hard. Do not gather with others before sunrise or after sunset. Do not leave the estate without permission. Failure to stick to these rules was met with severe punishment. For minor violations, offenders were placed in the stocks, their ankles held between two wooden boards, and deprived of food and water for a day or more. For greater misdemeanours, they were lashed. Some of the overseers and drivers used the bush whip, or carracarra, a short leather instrument that was sometimes doubled up to increase the force of the blow. Others wielded the tarred rope, a cord coated with oily tar. A few used the cart whip, which was worst of all. Designed to spur along horses, it sliced the skin open upon impact. According to the colony's law, an overseer or driver was not allowed to give more than thirty-nine lashes and a doctor was meant to be at hand in case of need. In practice, these guidelines were rarely followed.

In Jack's experience, the list of crimes that could result in such beatings was long. What was known as 'bad work' was the most typical. This could be failure to gather enough sugar canes, or incomplete weeding of a field. The next most common transgressions were disobedience and insolence. This included laughing at the overseers or singing songs that caused upset. Other misdemeanours that frequently resulted in punishment included quarrelling, refusing to work, and absence from work – even if caused by injury, sickness, pregnancy or exhaustion. What the managers called 'theft' or 'stealing' were the next most repeated offences. Frequently these were the result of misunderstandings. For instance, one man was whipped for keeping a handful of iron nails (bent and old) that he had thought would be otherwise thrown away. Other crimes that resulted in vicious beatings included adultery, harbouring runaways, carelessness in regards to a fire, ill-treatment of wives, and drunkenness.

Life at Success was brutally hard. It is not surprising, therefore, that it made for fertile ground for those who imagined a world without hardship: the missionaries.

Eight years earlier, when Jack was fourteen years old, a man called John Wray had arrived at Le Resouvenir, the estate immediately to the west of Success. It was owned by Hermanus Post, a Dutchman who believed that enslaved men and women should have access to religious instruction. A few days after his arrival, Wray visited Success and announced that he was from the Missionary Society in London and had come to preach the word of the Lord.

Over the next few months, Jack and his family saw a new building constructed on Le Resouvenir, only a few hundred yards away and clearly visible from Success. It was built of wood, had a cross on top and was large enough to seat more than six hundred people. Wray called this the Bethel Chapel. Next to it was built a small dwelling house and garden for the missionary, both paid for by the estate owner.

After the Bethel Chapel was completed, Jack had witnessed his father undergo something of a transformation. From contemporary sources – journals, registers, letters – we know that Quamina was one of the first to be baptised there. He also learned to read, and as his confidence grew, he began taking on more responsibilities at the chapel, eventually becoming the missionary's deacon. Inspired by his father, Jack also learned to read, and soon was teaching Bible stories to the other children.

Every Sunday, Jack and Quamina would arrive at the chapel at 10 a.m. to attend the 'morning prayer'. Another service was held at 2 p.m., called the 'noon', which was better attended and therefore rowdier. Whilst most of the congregants came from Le Resouvenir, Success and their adjacent estates, plenty travelled from further afield, walking many miles each way. The vast majority were enslaved, but not all. One of those who regularly took a pew was named Mary Chisholm. She was a free Black woman, who worked as a baker on Success and 'owned' five enslaved people. A handful of local plantation owners, managers and overseers also attended the chapel, but they tended to come to the later service, if at all. During Communion, Quamina and the other deacons handed out the wine and bread, and when Wray made it clear that things were getting too noisy, they encouraged everyone to quieten down.

In addition to their chapel duties, Jack and Quamina had helped Wray get accustomed to his new surroundings. They taught him some of the local words. *Matty*, for instance, meant friend, *sopie* was a dram of spirits, while *buckra* referred to a White boss man or woman. They provided information about the local plantation owners and background on the enslaved people who lived nearby: who could be trusted, who might be interested in baptism. And they encouraged everyone to attend the services.

During his sermons, Wray had often spoken out against how the enslaved people were treated on the sugar estates. He also asked Quamina and the other deacons to read Bible stories that mirrored the situation experienced by the congregation. One of these was Exodus, Chapter 14, which told of how the Israelites suffered as enslaved people in Egypt, and Moses encouraged them to flee in order to escape bondage. 'Fear not, stand still, and see the salvation of the Lord,' he told his people, 'for the Egyptians whom you have seen today, you shall see them again no more forever. The Lord shall fight for you, and you shall hold your peace.' And with God's help, so the story went, Moses parted the Red Sea, trapping Pharaoh's soldiers, and the Israelites found dry land and freedom. According to Wray's reports sent back to England, those who heard such readings were greatly affected.

When colonists learned about what was going on in the Bethel Chapel, many grew angry. They didn't appreciate the missionary encouraging his flock to imagine life without bondage. 'It is dangerous to make slaves Christians,' proclaimed the *Demerara Royal Gazette*, one of the main newspapers in Georgetown. 'Will not the Negro conceive that by baptism, by being made a Christian, he is as credible as his Christian White brethren?'

Following such attacks, Wray doubled down. 'There is no truth, nor mercy, nor knowledge of God in the land,' he boomed from the pulpit, quoting from Hosea, Chapter 4. 'Therefore shall the land mourn, and every one that dwelleth therein shall languish.' Such provocation did not go unnoticed. By June 1813, and following intense pressure from the governor, John Wray had been forced to move to Berbice, the British colony sixty miles to the east, and the doors of Bethel Chapel were locked shut.

Following Wray's departure, life for Jack on the estate had continued unaltered for a while, and then three things happened. First, he was made head cooper, giving him the additional responsibility of managing the other barrel-makers. It also meant that he now travelled without escort or supervision to Georgetown when he delivered the hogsheads to the shipping houses. Sometimes he would load them onto a sloop or schooner tied up at the dock and then return directly to the estate. On other occasions, if he had time, he might meet with friends and acquaintances who hung out around the shore and the marketplace, picking up the latest news and gossip from the colony and beyond.

The second change took place in June 1817, when Jack's grand-mother Tonisen became ill. For some time she had been experiencing severe pain in her abdomen, but now it grew worse. Her stomach became unnaturally swollen and sensitive to the touch. Leaving his post without permission – which was risky – Jack rushed to a nearby plantation to find a doctor and begged him to visit as soon as possible. When the physician arrived at the family's hut, he examined the elderly patient and removed excess fluid from her abdomen by a process known as 'tapping', but it was no use. A short while later, Tonisen took her last breath, watched over by Jack and his father.

Death for Jack was not new, but seeing his grandmother pass away must have been difficult. His father had been born in Demerara, so Tonisen was Jack's only link to where his family was originally from; the only person who could tell him stories from the old country. With her death, his connection with Africa was effectively broken.

The third change took place in the next-door estate of Le Resouvenir. The chapel had been quiet for years, but at last the Missionary Society had sent out a replacement preacher. Hopefully he would improve life at Success. The missionary's name was John Smith.

I have grown up knowing about the horrors of slavery in the USA. But I had no idea that British people and British companies ran slave plantations in the Caribbean, or how terrible these places were. Honestly, I'm embarrassed by my ignorance.

Now, almost two hundred years later, I wonder about the legacy of this slavery. How does it impact people in today's society?

To try and answer this question, I make contact with Kehinde Andrews, who is Professor of Black Studies at Birmingham City University and is of African-Caribbean descent. He tells me that little has changed in the Caribbean since the time of slavery. He lists the issues: poverty, mass incarceration, violence, lack of social mobility. 'White supremacy and economic inequality still exist,' he says.

After we speak, I look up some statistics. Black people in England and Wales are stopped and searched at least five times more than White people, arrested three times more often than White people and are five times more likely to be imprisoned than White people. Black households are twice as likely to be living in poverty than White households. The median total wealth for households with a Black African head (£34,000) is roughly a tenth of that owned by White British households (£314,000). Black Caribbean and Black African households are far less likely to own their homes (40 per cent and 20 per cent respectively) than White British households (68 per cent). Youth unemployment (ages 16 to 24) is two and half times higher for Black British people than White people. Whilst in England, Black women are four times more likely to die giving birth than White women.

I have a conversation with David Lammy MP, the shadow secretary of state for justice, and ask him about the legacy of slavery. His family is from Berbice, Guyana. 'The legacy of slavery is real,' he tells me. 'You can't tear millions of people away from their homes and cut them off from their cultures, religions and languages and not expect some deep scars. We see it across communities, in the USA, in the West Indies and here in Britain.' He pauses before continuing. 'Only when the European countries that did this acknowledge their role and we have a process of truth, reconciliation and repair will we be able to move forward.'

Next I have a call with the writer and former ambassador for Guyana, David Dabydeen, who has lived in Britain for more than five decades. 'Slavery is still etched into the memory of Caribbean peoples,' he says, 'the slave forts and ruins of sugar mills and the drainage canals dug by Black muscle and shovel being visible reminders of that dark past. At the same time, being steeped only in memory can be a hindrance to progress.' Dabydeen then adds, 'In Britain today, slavery is only now being remembered. Because of Black Lives Matter, we are now acknowledging the ways that revenues from slavery built great wealth in Britain, which still exists.'

Each of those I speak to make one thing clear: there is a direct link between historic slavery and problems besetting society today.

CHAPTER 2

John Smith, February 1817

John Smith was born on 27 June 1790 on Ponder Street in Rothwell, a small market town in Northamptonshire, England. When he was a young boy, his father died while fighting Napoleon's forces in Egypt. John was brought up by his grieving mother, in poverty and without a formal education. They belonged to the Independent Church, and it was there, at Sunday school, that he learned to read. At fourteen, he travelled to Clerkenwell in central London and became a baker's apprentice, where he remained for the next five years. By nineteen, he was a fully grown man, slender, with a ginger widow's peak, a square jaw and compassionate blue eyes. The course of his life changed when he attended the Silver Street Chapel and heard a priest's passionate sermon on the value of public service. John Smith was so inspired that he immediately applied to join the Missionary Society.

Formed in 1795, the Missionary Society supported evangelical missions around the world. By the 1810s, they had missions on four continents, with three hundred and twelve stations (or sub-missions) in India alone. There were missions in South Africa, Russia, Singapore, China and Malaya. And spread across the Caribbean, there were forty-one stations. The Missionary Society's 'sole object', according to their founding document, 'was to spread the knowledge of Christ among the heathen and other unenlightened nations.' Their membership was varied, including Congregationalists, Methodists, Baptists and other Protestant denominations. John Smith applied to join the society's foreign service and was accepted. But before he was posted overseas, he would have to attend the Gosport Academy on England's south coast.

The academy's task was to train Missionary Society novices. It had been established following a series of failed missions to South Africa and the South Pacific. Either the missionaries had been unable to cultivate a long-term congregation or they had found the post unbearable and returned home in disgrace. According to the Society's *Report on Missionary Training*, the aims of the academy were to foster 'the communication of knowledge' and the 'strengthening of good dispositions'. One of the key classes was called 'Missionary Instructions', in which would-be clerics learned about the history of the organisation and about mission strategy. This included a clear admonition not to become involved in local politics. 'Some of the gentlemen who own the estates, the masters of slaves, are unfriendly towards their instruction,' John was warned. 'Not a word must escape you in public or private which might render the slaves displeased with their masters or dissatisfied with their station.'

Normally the training course lasted for three years, but word had arrived from Demerara that a new missionary was urgently sought following the relocation of the previous representative, John Wray. So it was that the twenty-six-year-old John Smith was ordained at Somers Town, London, on 12 December 1816. Before he left, there was one more task to accomplish – a wedding. It had been something of an arranged union, hastily put together by the Missionary Society, who viewed a married man as emblematic of Christian values. John had met Jane Godden, a calm, God-fearing woman, just weeks earlier. Neither of them had lived outside of England. A few days later, John Smith and his new bride set sail on the *William Neilson*.

Amongst John Smith's belongings stored in his cabin below decks was a letter from George Burder, the secretary of the Missionary Society, which included the following admonition: 'The Holy Gospel you will preach will render the slaves who receive it most diligent, faithful, patient and useful servants; will render severe discipline unnecessary, and make them the most valuable slaves on the estates, and thus you will recommend yourself and your ministry, even to those gentlemen who may have been averse to the religion instruction of Negroes.' Clearly the secretary had felt it necessary to repeat the lesson taught at the academy. His instructions were clear: the objective of the mission included maintaining the slave system in Demerara and keeping the planters happy. John Smith was not to cause any trouble.

Eight weeks after leaving Portsmouth, the *William Neilson* approached Demerara. Unlike the becalmed turquoise waters of the Caribbean islands, the sea here was dark grey and turbulent. Out on deck, John and Jane saw the South American shoreline for the first time. It was edged with black mangroves and foxglove trees and populated by flocks of scarlet ibis, white egrets and orange-billed cormorants. The closer they drew, the busier became the traffic: merchant ships and packets on their way to London and Liverpool; schooners heading north towards Barbados, Jamaica and other British colonies; sloops and brigantines sailing westwards to Essequibo or eastwards to Dutch Guiana.

After hugging the coast for a short while, the *William Neilson* turned sharply left, leaving the Atlantic Ocean and entering the Demerara River. Known to the Dutch as the 'Demerary', the river at this point was a mile wide, its water browny-orange and brackish. To the right, on the west bank, the shore was a mass of lush green vegetation, but on the left, the east bank was more developed. They passed a fort that boasted eighteen large iron cannons pointing out to sea, a lighthouse warning of the sand bars upon which ships might go aground, and then the signal station, a low block building with a wide view of the ocean, able to flash communications to the neighbouring British colony of Berbice.

Now they came to the start of Georgetown proper, marked by a long ribbon of white wooden wharves known as stellings. It was alongside one of these that the brig finally anchored. There was some waiting around while the customs paperwork was completed, with the captain growing increasingly irritated, followed by an inspection by the surgeon of health. Finally they were cleared, and John, Jane and the other passengers were allowed to leave the vessel.

As they stepped ashore and onto the stelling's wide wooden planks, they were immediately hit by a rich smell of sawdust and horse piss long heated by the sun. A few steps on and they were surrounded by hucksters and pedlars eager to sell their wares: bars of soap, lengths of cotton and leather belts; bunches of plantains, pineapples, sapodilla and mangos. The offerings that were waved towards them were varied and enticing, but this was not the right moment to purchase anything.

The Smiths were tired, disorientated and needed to settle in before engaging with local commerce. Others offered to find them transport and accommodation. But this too was of no interest to them. Instead, having asked directions, they proceeded away from the docks in search of their lodging. As they walked, the couple took in their surroundings. The houses were of small dimension, wooden-framed, roofed with shingles and covered by white-painted siding. None was above two storeys and their windows went unglazed; instead the openings were covered by shutters. To avoid perennial flooding, the buildings near the river were built upon wood and brick piers, their lower levels serving as stores or warehouses accessible from the street.

The road, or dam, as the locals called it, was wide and dusty, its edges lined with scrubby orange-flowered bucayo trees that offered welcome shade. Through the middle ran a canal dotted with pink, white and yellow water lilies. Away from the warehouses and storefronts, the houses became more residential, with picket fences enclosing small well-tended yards planted with pink-flowering oleander shrubs, sweet-scented cannonball trees and large-leafed plantains. Occasionally a wooden bridge spanned the canal, allowing a person living on one side of the street to cross to the other.

Given that Demerara was located near the Equator, it was extremely hot. In Gosport it would likely have been below forty degrees Fahrenheit, perhaps even freezing. Here it was well into the nineties. The bite of the unmasked sun was barely softened by the breeze blowing off the sea. Yet the sweltering heat didn't seem to repel the locals, who were out in force. They were mostly Black pedestrians. The attire of many would have gone unremarked in London, Paris or New York: for the men, cotton shirts, jackets, trousers and shoes; for the women, cotton skirts and blouses, their hair tied up with colourfully patterned cloth. These were either free men and women or enslaved people who worked as domestic servants. Others wore rougher clothes more suitable for the fields, while a third, smaller group were barely dressed at all, wearing little more than loincloths.

There were also colonists going about their business. Some of these were more expensively dressed and were transported comfortably by horse and buggy. But not all. A good number journeyed by foot, dressed in work clothes. These were shopkeepers, innkeepers, dock workers and the like. And from those they passed, the Smiths heard a rich array of languages. Dutch, French, Spanish and English they recognised. But there was another language, a local creole, spoken fast and difficult for them to understand.

By the time they reached their accommodation, they found themselves bathed in sweat and thirsty. Their host – a friend of a friend referred to them by the Missionary Society – welcomed them inside, which was, to their great relief, far cooler. They were offered a glass of water, which was wonderfully refreshing. It was rainwater, collected in a wooden cistern and filtered through a stone. Then, having exchanged a few pleasantries, they were directed to their room, where they collapsed on the bed. They had arrived.

*

Two days later, John managed to secure a meeting with the governor, John Murray. As the representative of His Majesty King George IV, Murray had near-absolute power in Demerara. Not only did he collect the local taxes, appoint the judges to the courts and control the British armed forces in the colony, he was also in charge of all licensing. If John Smith wished to run a mission anywhere in Demerara, he first needed the governor's approval.

John Murray was very much of the British establishment. Born on 4 June 1777 and the eldest son of a brigadier general who had also been a colonial administrator, Murray had enlisted at the age of sixteen. He first served in the 58th Regiment and then, during the Napoleonic Wars, in the 96th regiment, where he rose to Lieutenant Colonel. He married Elizabeth Hume, an English woman three years his junior, who gave birth to two children. Then, around 1805, he was posted to Newfoundland, to oversee the brigade at St John's. It was there, according to one of his descendants, that Murray 'became enamoured' with a certain fourteen-year-old girl from Newfoundland named Ellen Butler O'Connor, who he made pregnant, and together they 'fled' to the Caribbean. What happened to Elizabeth and the two children is unclear. Shortly after arriving in the Caribbean, Murray was promoted to Colonel and served as a general's adjutant during various campaigns, including the capture of the island of Guadalupe. In 1813, he had been appointed as governor to Demerara-Essequibo and promoted to the rank of Major-General. Over his long career, Murray had proven that he was a man who knew how to climb the ranks, who was not afraid to face danger and who was capable of making quick decisions that, while serving his interests, might hurt others along the way.

By the time of John Smith's arrival in the colony, John Murray had been in post for the past four years, during which time the Netherlands had officially ceded the colony to Britain. He was now forty years old, father of two more offspring (in all he and Ellen would have sixteen children) and, in addition to his public duties, he was proprietor of three sugar estates, one here in Demerara and two in Berbice. This included the 'ownership' of over 540 enslaved women and men. As such, the treatment of the colony's enslaved people was important to the governor both professionally and personally.

John Smith met Governor Murray in an anteroom off the main reception hall at Committee House, a barn-like wooden building overlooking the Demerara River and opposite a large market square dominated by a Scottish church. In his diary, the missionary recalled that when the governor asked what he hoped to achieve while in the colony, he explained that he planned to instruct the enslaved people by 'teaching them to read' and by 'preaching the Gospel in plain manner'. Murray did not take this well. 'If you ever teach a Negro to read and I hear of it,' he yelled, 'I will banish you from the colony immediately.' Despite this frosty reception, several days later John managed to secure a second audience with the governor, during which he assured him of his tranquil intentions. He was then given permission to run the mission.

John and Jane spent the next few days preparing for life on the plantation. First, they acquired a chaise and two horses, which would be necessary for moving around the mud-rutted countryside. Then they set about picking up provisions from various stores around Georgetown, enough to subsist on for a few weeks. From one supplier they collected a barrel of flour, some boxes of soap and a firkin of butter. From another, a cask of wine and a crate filled with dried fruit, salt and candles. At a third, a bag of nails, a few hams and several rounds of cheeses.

Finally they were ready. On 6 March 1817, a little after lunch and almost two weeks after arriving in Demerara, they set off for their new home. The route took them eastward, out of Georgetown and along the coast, with views of mangrove trees and crashing surf. They were now on what was known as the public road, which had been fabricated from shells and shingle taken from the beach, packed hard as granite.

After about fifteen minutes, they came to a dusty path heading away from the coast. This was the entrance to the Thomas estate, the first of the coastal sugar plantations. Fifteen minutes further along the public road was the next plantation, Kitty. Then came Blygezight, followed by Bel Air, Sophia and Leliendaal. From the names, the Smiths could guess at the current owner's nationality. Every few hundred feet they crossed an irrigation ditch or canal, and from the condition of the bridges that spanned these water-ways, they could also guess at the estate-owner's prosperity. Some were in good repair, recently painted white – presumably to improve visibility at night – while others were rough-looking and blackened from dust and dirt, shaking dangerously as their cart wheels rumbled over.

As they continued, they overtook groups of enslaved people known as task gangs, who were on their way to work. They 'belonged' to a planter, who then hired them out to someone else for a particular job or project. They carried papers with them stating their purpose, as travel outside of an estate was forbidden without written permission. Occasional traffic came from the other direction: men on horseback on their way to do business in town; carts ferrying barrels of sugar and molasses to the docks; an assortment of free Black men travelling by foot in pursuit of some errand or other, along with various female hucksters. These last sold goods to the plantations up and down the coast.

Around 5.30 p.m., John and Jane arrived at the twentieth plantation, Le Resouvenir, about seven miles from Georgetown. The track leading in towards the estate was lined by tall palmetto trees. Their tops held green balls of vegetation that looked like large cabbages. As a matter of courtesy, they stopped by at the house of the estate manager, Adrianus Van der Haas, who gave them a cold welcome. Apparently, like the governor, der Haas was not in favour of religious instruction being given to the enslaved men and women. After a few moments, he pointed John and Jane Smith towards a structure that stood a few hundred yards further down the track. It was the object of their journey: the Bethel Chapel. 'This is our appointed station,' John wrote later that day in his journal. 'The place has been forsaken more than 12 months. Everything appeared very gloomy, but we hoped that God would make us happy in our new station.'

The next day, a Friday, John was woken by a bell. It was just getting light outside, and from his front doorstep he could see the chapel standing stolidly a few paces away. He was looking forward to exploring the building, to see what he had inherited from the previous custodian, but for now, he was eager to become acquainted with the geography of his new home. After putting on his coat and shoes, he closed the door and set off. Within a few minutes he reached a massive field where a group of enslaved men and women was arriving for work. By now it was a little after 6 a.m. and already hot. The field was still smoking from the evening before when a fire had been lit to burn off the unwanted vegetation, leaving the sugar canes easier to access. The burning left a sweet molasses fragrance hanging in the air.

With a stroke of a curved blade called a billhook, the labourers hacked down the charred canes, quickly slicing off the tops and leaves and adding the trimmed stalks to the piles at the end of each row. To one side hovered the drivers, themselves also of African descent, but with whips in hand, constantly urging the labourers to work harder with yells of 'Move on!' and 'Hurry up!' This was the first time that John had seen enslaved people at work.

As the minutes progressed, he observed that the women and men ranged from their late teens to their mid-twenties and were exceptionally fit. This, he would learn, was what was known as the First Gang. When they reached their late twenties, and after a decade in the fields, they would be transferred to the Second Gang, whose tasks were less arduous. If they were lucky enough to reach their forties, they would join the Third Gang, who tended the children, looked after the animals and weeded the fields. Some of the women had babies on their backs. Nobody stopped, not even for a sip of water.

As he continued his walk, John came across four enslaved men on their way to the fields. He introduced himself and explained that he intended to preach that evening. One of those he spoke to was called Gringo. In his diary, John recorded the man's excitement. 'We're very glad to see you, master,' Gringo said. 'Very glad.' The men promised to attend chapel and to spread the word.

John spent the rest of the day cleaning the church, opening the windows and removing dead leaves and cobwebs. Laying out the prayer books. Polishing the candlesticks and adding new candles. Around 7 p.m., a man walked in and, without needing to be asked, set about lighting the candles. When John asked who he was, the man explained that his name was Peter and that he had been sexton when the previous missionary had led the congregation. Then, realising the time, he excused himself and rang the bell for service. A few minutes later, people started arriving. They came in small groups of twos and threes. Men, women and children. By 7.30, when it was time to close the doors, the hall was two-thirds full. John was amazed. Sitting quietly in front of him in the narrow wooden pews were more than four hundred people.

He wasn't sure where to look, and tried to hide his shaking hands. This would be the first time he would give a service without assistance from another minister. Luckily, he could fall back on his training. John would follow the order for evening prayer that he had learned back in Gosport: a short welcome, followed by the general confession for the whole congregation, a psalm sung loudly (he had a rich baritone) and the Lord's Prayer. For the reading, he had chosen a passage from Romans that celebrated the martyrdom of Jesus. 'But God demonstrates his own love for us in this,' he proclaimed from the pulpit. 'While we were still sinners, Christ died for us.'

As the service unfolded, he gained confidence. And with his nerves receding, there was space to reflect on what was taking place in front of him. There was much to consider. How familiar were they with the teachings? Indeed, how many of them could read? Though several held the prayer book in their hands, few appeared to be following along as the service progressed. 'Perhaps they came from curiosity,' he later noted in his journal, 'but I pray that the word spoken may be blessed to their souls.'

Over the next weeks and months, John spent most of his time at Le Resouvenir getting to know the people on the estate. Once in a while, he and Jane were able to visit Georgetown to replenish supplies, visit the doctor and catch up on the news. It had been hard to adjust to the surroundings. Much was new to them. The food and the weather. Life on the estate. The culture of the colonists. And most troubling of all, how the planters treated the enslaved people.

Early on Monday morning, 10 August 1818, the missionary was at his desk, writing his journal. The sun would soon rise; he could see a hint of pink in the sky through the window in his office. It was a moment of calm following the previous day's schedule. It had been hectic. First, Bible studies with the children, then a service in the morning for more than two hundred people, followed by a meeting with the deacons. After lunch, another service, including more than ten baptisms, then a visit to a sick congregant. John Smith was exhausted.

In the next-door room, he heard his wife preparing breakfast. Holding the pages down with one hand, John noted the previous evening's thunderstorm, which had made the house tremble and the glasses in the kitchen clatter. He was just comparing it to God's 'fiery arrows' when he was interrupted by a fierce repetitive thwacking noise. He knew exactly what it was: the sound of leather hitting human skin. A plantation manager or one of his assistants was flogging an enslaved man or woman. In the year since he had arrived in the colony, the missionary had become familiar with this sickening sound. So familiar that he could conjure the image in his mind. A White man flicking the whip back and forth. A Black man or woman leaning against a tree, a wagon, a fence post, being struck again and again and again.

The missionary's nib hung in mid-air as he counted each strike. Five, six, seven, eight … The punishment continued with awful regularity, every three seconds another crack, another scream of pain. Twenty … thirty … How long could it go on? More than five minutes had passed, and still it continued. And then eventually, thankfully, silence.

'Did you count those lashes?' Jane called from the adjoining room.

'Yes,' he responded.

'How many did you reckon?' she asked.

He made it to be a hundred and forty-one, he told her.

Her count was almost the same. 'I reckoned a hundred and forty,' she said, appalled. This entire episode was recorded by John in his journal.

The missionary abhorred slavery. It disgusted him. He was furious with Van der Haas, who ran the estate with such cruelty. He hailed the day when enslavers would be imbued with the beliefs of Christianity and enslaved men and women would enjoy their birthright – freedom. He knew a few colonists who treated those enslaved as though they had common feelings, but sadly these were the exception that proved the rule. He returned his quill to the paper. 'Ah! The men who spend the Sabbath evening over the bottle & glass; divert themselves with cards, & backgammon, are haunted with hideous dreams, & fearful forebodings during the hours of their slumber,' he wrote, adding, 'Then they rise to vent their arbitrary malice & authority – it may be upon the innocent.'

He put down his pen and closed the journal. There was a lot to do that day. He had to speak with the plantation owner about building a new chapel to house his growing congregation. He had to write to the Missionary Society back in London to update them on progress. He must ride to town to collect provisions. And when he returned, he would deliver the evening's service. If the last few days were anything to go by, there would be plenty of baptisms, at least ten, perhaps even twenty. He found each and every one of these powerfully moving. The urge to join the congregation, the need for a higher power, the hunger for deliverance from earthly woes. He prayed that his efforts would make a difference.

In his diary, he later noted, 'I could not help thinking that the time is not far distant when the Lord will make it manifest by some signal judgment, that he hath heard the cry of the oppressed.'

*H*aving spoken with several people descended from those enslaved, I now want to speak with those descended from slaveholders. What is the legacy of slavery for them?

Through a genealogy website, I track down Graham Van Cooten, who now lives in Perth, Australia. He is the great-grandson of Hendrick Van Cooten, who had a plantation in Demerara close to Success. And he 'owned' two hundred slaves. Graham tells me that his ancestor 'did a fairly good job'. Yes, he purchased and sold human beings, but he also supported the Missionary Society, which campaigned for the abolition of slavery. 'I have given a lot of thought to the way people have acted in historical times,' he says. 'It's very difficult to know how I would have reacted if I had been there myself. It seems to be very difficult not to get caught up in the culture of a time.' When I ask him about the legacy of slavery, he quickly says that any wealth amassed by Van Cooten has long gone. 'We can't turn the clock back,' he declares. 'It would be almost impossible to remedy the situation lost in history.' But, he then adds, descendants should 'find out the facts of the matter and make sure we learn from our mistakes and create a better world'.

I chat with my friend Dylan over a cup of tea. When I explain that I am researching the history of British slavery, he says that his three-times great-grandfather made a fortune buying and selling sugar from Jamaica. I ask how he feels about this legacy, what it means today, and he becomes defensive. 'It's got nothing to do with me,' he says. 'The money was all gone by the time I was born.' But what about the advantages handed down? I ask. What about acknowledging the past? He doesn't see this as his problem. I'm a little startled how quickly he becomes angry. I don't want this to affect our friendship, so I change the subject.

Next I speak with the four-times great-granddaughter of Governor John Murray (she wished to remain anonymous). 'Until recently,

I had no idea that John Murray owned slaves,' she says. 'When I found out I was horrified. At first I didn't want to know. But you can't change what happened in the past.' She then adds. 'Now that I know, I'm not sure what to do with it.'

I also speak with Tom De Wolf, whose ancestors 'owned' hundreds of enslaved men and women in the USA. Tom co-manages Coming to the Table, an organisation that brings together descendants of enslavers and descendants of the enslaved. He tells me that a lot of people come up to him and say, 'I'm sure glad I'm not you,' to which he replies, 'Didn't your family wear cotton, smoke tobacco, put sugar in their coffee?' Does he think that focusing too much on those with a clear connection to slavery lets others off the hook? 'Yes,' he says. 'Whether your family was from Germany, Britain, Brazil or North America, if you were non-African, you benefited from slavery.' Then he adds, 'The people of Europe created enslavement and racism, so it's on them to undo that racism.'

CHAPTER 3

Cheveley, August 1821

On Saturday 18 August 1821, John Castelfranc Cheveley stepped off the *Sir John Cameron* and onto the streets of Georgetown, Demerara. He was twenty-six years old and had travelled across the Atlantic to find work. It was as simple as that. Unemployment was rife back in England, and he was desperate to find a way to make a living. He had no dependents to speak of, no wife or children. All he needed was a steady job and a quiet place to call home.

He was now standing outside of Kingston Stelling, a wharf located in the north-western section of the small town. After asking directions to his lodgings and having arranged for his bags to be sent on, Cheveley set off. He was a plain-looking man, with a large head, jutting jaw and thick brown hair parted to one side. And while he was shorter than most and walked with bowed legs, he was not a man to attract attention to himself. Instead he preferred to disappear into the crowd.

He walked along Water Street, which ran parallel to the riverfront, through the busy business district, past the warehouse workers and market stallholders setting up for the day. The route was entirely flat, the streets organised in a grid pattern and therefore easy to navigate. Occasionally he had to cross a wooden bridge that spanned a canal or wait for a horse and cart to pass, but he was in no rush and he appreciated the chance to stretch his legs after the many weeks being cooped up on the ship.

After twenty minutes, he came to a shabby two-storey wooden building located at lot number 34. Further ahead, he could see the fort that overlooked the entrance to the Demerara River, and to his right, a few hundred yards away and overlooking the ocean, a large white wooden-sided building known as Camp House, which was where the governor lived.

Cheveley rapped on the door of number 34. A few moments later, it opened, and for the first time he saw his new boss, William Pattinson, a short, rotund man with a receding hairline and a dishevelled appearance, as if he had slept in his clothes after a hard night's drinking, which might well have been the case. They met in the front hall, off which lay a parlour and dining room. There was a chamber on the first floor, his host explained, and two more on the second, which was where Cheveley would be sleeping. After a brief conversation about his six-week voyage, Pattinson told Cheveley he would be running the general store, which was located underneath the house, and then, without regard for the newcomer's exhaustion or need to adjust to his new surroundings, proceeded to show him downstairs.

The general store occupied the entire basement, fronted by two large doors that opened onto the street. From the rafters hung iron pots, baking pans, tea kettles and other culinary items. Stacked in one corner were rolls of material – osnaburg, Irish linen, gingham and calico. In another corner lay a pile of sugar strainers, copper ladles and tin scales. An array of cutlasses and silk umbrellas stood next to bundles of hoes, shovels, trowels and other field tools. There were bins brimming with hammers, saws and other sundries useful for equipping a working estate, along with crates filled with tallow candles, gunpowder and indigo blue, and quart jugs of copal varnish. It was organised chaos, cramped, ill-lit and depressing.

As they returned upstairs, Pattinson explained that in return for his labour, Cheveley would be provided accommodation, food and a limited payment sufficient to cover his personal needs. This first meeting had not been particularly warm. Indeed, Cheveley later recalled in his memoirs that his new boss had received him with the deportment of a man 'who had been expecting something superior!'

As a child, Cheveley's life had been close to idyllic. He was the second eldest of eight children, and his parents, Richard and Mary, loved him dearly. He grew up in the small, peaceful village of Messing, in Essex, England, where his father, a kind, affectionate man who was often in a hurry, ran a smallholding leased from an affluent landlord. His mother, an amiable, easy-tempered and placid woman, was a home-maker. They were not rich, but they wanted for little. They were supported by a team of staff, including a wet nurse, cook, housemaid, manservant, charwoman and ploughman. In all, there were more than ten employees working at the farm. John's favourite was Old Lazell, the weekly gardener, who told him stories from his time in the army during the French Revolutionary War.

Cheveley was self-taught, having never attended school. Yet he had helped his younger siblings learn how to read and write, along with Latin and arithmetic. In the afternoons, he and his elder brother George liked to play in the brook that ran behind their house. There they built small stone dams and caught sticklebacks. If the weather was foul, he spent the time reading. One of his favourite books was *Robinson Crusoe* by Daniel Defoe. Another was *The Knowledge of Nature*, which sported pictures of seasonal activities. Indeed, his mother encouraged him to love nature. Never disturb a bird's nest, she told him, for to do so would be cruel.

His childhood had not been without hardship. For his stammer, he was bullied by Horatio Cocks, the son of the county magistrate, and if he broke the household rules, he received beatings from the cook. Cheveley was a sensitive boy, with many fears. He was scared of the sweep coming down the chimney with his soot bag to take away naughty boys. He was scared of the rooster that shrieked like a demonic woman in the farmyard. Worst of all was a feeling experienced when half asleep. 'A sensation came over me of vastness of distance and yet of horrible immensity in proximity something so steady and quiet in its approach,' he later recalled. It happened so often that he had a name for it: 'the Hard and the Soft'.

Cheveley's childhood idyll had ended in 1815 when he was nineteen years old. Two things happened. First, following Britain's defeat of Napoleon at the Battle of Waterloo, the army's demand for grain declined, leading to a collapse in prices. He had suspected something was wrong when his father began collecting the mail from the postman away from the house. Rumours started in the village that bills were not being paid. His parents looked increasingly anxious. Then the second hammer dropped. One day his father looked at their field of wheat and saw that it was covered with powdery yellow mildew. The harvest had failed. He said to his son, 'This will finish me.'

Their lives were quickly turned upside down. Within weeks, the family were forced to abandon their lease, leave the farm and move into a friend's house. The elder children were told they must find jobs away from home. For John Cheveley and his brother George, that meant securing a position on a trading ship. John Cheveley's first effort took him to India. Within a year he was back, but before long his father said they could not afford to take care of him. This time he sought a more long-term commission.

Through a family friend he was put in touch with the Reverend Thomas Driffield, who lived in Prescot in the north of England and was said to have good contacts with the Liverpool cotton and sugar merchants. So it turned out to be. It was via Driffield that Cheveley heard of a clerkship that had become available in a general store located in Georgetown, Demerara. The business was owned by two brothers, John and William Pattinson. Cheveley travelled north to meet John Pattinson in Liverpool. The position would be for three years, he was told, and would start immediately. 'I did not hesitate,' he later recalled. 'I considered it my duty to go.' Though he did not wish to leave his family, he 'felt a comforting and happy assurance that the Lord's hand was in it'.

As it turned out, Driffield was also on 'most friendly terms' with John Gladstone, head of Gladstone, Grant & Wilson and 'the leading Liverpool merchant and richest family in Liverpool'. In addition to wishing Cheveley good fortune for his exploits in Demerara, Gladstone also gave him a letter of introduction. This would be most valuable for entry into colonial society, he was told, a group that was often hard to break into for newcomers.

So it was that in early June 1821, Cheveley had boarded the *Sir John Cameron* with his sea chest and bedding. As they left the Liverpool docks, his thoughts turned to his family, which made him feel 'mawkish and miserable'. The twenty-six-year-old burst into tears. He would miss England, and he feared for his future. He had sensed that he had been 'thrown on the world'.

It was still dark outside when, on his first morning in Georgetown, Cheveley was woken by a loud boom. When he looked at his timepiece he saw that it was 5.30 a.m.. It had not been a good night's sleep having been kept awake by mosquitoes. He had read about these tiny beasts, about a quarter of an inch long with fine white markings on their legs – the *Aedes aegypti* – particularly the females, who were responsible for the blood-sucking. And he knew that they carried the dreaded yellow fever. To deal with the pests, he had risen in the early hours and put his clothes back on: trousers, shirt, socks and even boots. Though the effect was sweltering, at least the items provided some defence against the tiny assailants.

Walking downstairs and trying not to scratch the bites, he found his employer already up and asked about the sonorous alarm. It was 'The Gunfire', he was told, and it was the custom here to rely on this to commence the day. The signal for the day's end came at the second firing of the cannon at six in the evening. Over toast and

43

jam, Pattinson explained that one of Cheveley's first duties would be to report in with the colonial militia. Given his employment as clerk for a general store, he would enlist with the Rifle Corps, which was for merchants and their staff. The service was mandatory and entailed weekly drilling on the city's parade ground, starting every Sunday at 3 p.m. Failure to report within three months of arrival in the colony resulted in a fine. A repeat offence could lead to imprisonment. Nobody in England had told him that he would be required to serve in the militia.

After breakfast, Cheveley was told to distribute the weekly allowance to the people who worked at the house. Pattinson called them 'house servants'; they were in fact enslaved. Cheveley's boss took him to the back door and pointed to a large hut on the other side of the small yard, then he handed him a small ivory whistle. This was to be used, he said, any time he wished to announce his arrival. Cheveley walked outside and greeted the small group that had already assembled. He would not be using the whistle. There were five of them: Sam and Loveless, who were eleven and fourteen, Peter the cook, Corwallis, who tended the horses, and a washerwoman whose name he didn't catch. Instead of wages, he gave them salted fish and bunches of green plantains, which they would grind into a mealy bread called *foo foo*.

Back inside, Pattinson proclaimed it was time for church. It was a long walk through the scorch of mid-morning to the other end of town. When they arrived, they joined a mass of folk, all well dressed in coats and frocks and fine hats. Most came by foot, some by carriage. St George's was a plain-looking church, made of wood, with a small steeple. Inside, colonists and their families were grouped downstairs whilst men and women of African heritage and those of mixed-race were forced upstairs in the stifling balcony. Cheveley later described this division as 'hypocritical', given that many of the White men downstairs lived and slept with the Black women who were segregated upstairs.

That afternoon, Pattinson took Cheveley to watch the drill practice at the parade ground that was located a few blocks from the riverfront. There he saw the 21st Fusiliers march up and down the dusty grounds in the boiling early-afternoon heat. Pattison reminded the newcomer that he must soon register with the militia. Unimpressed by the pomp and idle chatter of his fellow observers – the months-old news from Britain, which ships were due in, the likely weather over the next few days – especially on the Sabbath, Cheveley excused himself and returned home.

That evening, the two men dined outside with one of Pattinson's business acquaintances along with a couple of ship captains. It was a rich, rowdy occasion, lubricated by champagne, followed by copious amounts of claret and Madeira. Their faces were illuminated by spermaceti candles placed along the table and in the windowsills. Afterwards, the men drank brandy and smoked cigars. By the evening's end, Cheveley had had enough. He was desperate to retire to his hot, cramped room, to read his Bible, to commune with God. But that was not to be. Good manners compelled him to remain with these blowhards, to listen to their 'folly and ribaldry'. He longed to be back home in Essex, but he knew that now he was here, he would have to make the best of it.

The following morning, Monday, and somewhat plagued by a headache, Cheveley made his way downstairs to the store and met his co-workers for the first time. There was a youth called Sutton, who was meant to help with stocking and deliveries but who, Cheveley would soon learn, was more absent than not. There was a free man called John Harris, who was in charge of clerical duties but who had so lost his way with the book-keeping that his time was entirely occupied with undoing previous mistakes. As to his boss, Mr Pattinson, he was out most of the time 'dunning', his name for hunting down clients and pressuring them to pay overdue bills. This left the store to Cheveley.

It was a busy morning. There were two boats in the harbour that required attention. The *Sir John Cameron* needed discharging, and the *Ann* had sent over a list of urgently needed provisions. Cheveley set himself to the task. He answered the enquiries that came to the store as best he could, and then, during the quieter moments, made himself familiar with the inventory.

Later, with his day's work complete, he set off to present his introductory letter. Again it was a long, hot walk, up Main Street, right on Robb Street and back along Water Street into town. Finally he came to the house he was looking for. Next to its front door was a brass plaque with the legend 'Messrs McDonald, Edmonstone & Co'. With the help of more than a hundred enslaved men and women, this company harvested timber in Demerara's interior and then sold the finished lumber to estates throughout the colony.

Inside, Cheveley met the company's co-owner, Robert Edmonstone, a twenty-nine-year-old Scotsman he later described as 'gentlemanly'. The timber merchant formally welcomed the newcomer to the colony. But he did not offer a cup of tea. Nor was there wisdom imparted on how best to get along so far away from home. Edmonstone seemed wholly uninterested in this latest addition to the lower ranks of colonial society. Just another recently arrived store clerk. To close the meeting, and with as little enthusiasm as was possible, he said that he hoped to see his visitor 'occasionally, whenever he came that way'.

With little more to say, Cheveley handed over the envelope and departed. This was the letter he had obtained in Liverpool from the gentleman who provided mortgages and other support to Robert Edmonstone and was the biggest owner of sugar estates in Demerara: a certain Mr John Gladstone.

*I have a call with one of my elderly cousins – let's call him Peter –
who is typical of many of the White British people I speak with.*

*He tells me that he has 'great difficulty' accepting that he has any
responsibility for what happened two hundred years ago.*

*'I can't see why I should pay for what my great-grandfather did,'
he says. 'There are many families who made money from slavery,' he
continues, and 'anyway, they weren't aware that it was wrong at the
time. We shouldn't apply today's values to two hundred years ago.'*

*When I point out that slavery was one of the most highly discussed
topics of the nineteenth century, and that just because others were
at fault too doesn't make it any better, Peter moves on to the next
argument.*

*'We should focus on problems today,' he tells me. Slavery is 'not
high on my list of concerns'. What about poverty, he asks, or climate
change or gender inequality? To this I suggest that focusing on one
does not preclude the others.*

The call ends with Peter saying, 'Let's just agree to disagree.'

*The conversation leaves me feeling unsettled. Unsure. It feels
presumptuous talking about Britain's role in slavery two hundred
years ago when I can't even seem to get my own family's history
straight.*

So what about more recent examples of racism in my family?

*In the 1920s, my family ran the Trocadero in central London.
Every week they put on a cabaret, including famous acts of the day.
One of these was a dance troupe who put on blackface. The use of
blackface in entertainment goes back to the minstrel shows of the
1830s in the USA, where White performers coated their skin with
shoe polish or burnt cork, and mimicked enslaved people on the
plantations. According to the Smithsonian's National Museum of
African American History and Culture (NMAAHC), the first minstrel
shows portrayed Black people as 'lazy, ignorant, superstitious,*

hypersexual, and prone to thievery and cowardice'. The use of blackface invokes a racist and painful history.

Here's another example. In addition to the tobacco business, my mother's family also ran the catering company J Lyons. It invested heavily in marketing. One of their campaigns for cocoa used racist caricatures of Africans in their outdoor billboard materials.

And then there's this. My grandfather Sam Salmon was a friend of Enoch Powell. In April 1968, Powell gave his infamous 'Rivers of Blood' speech, in which he called for the deportation of Black people from Britain. In the bitter aftermath of this speech, Powell toured the country shoring up his support. At one public meeting, Powell said 'some of my friends are Jewish', presumably suggesting that he could not be racist if he had Jewish friends. At which point, my grandfather stood up in a gesture of solidarity.

Writing about all this makes me feel deeply uncomfortable. There's also shame.

CHAPTER 4

Gladstone, March 1823

Though he had never visited the colony, John Gladstone owned seven plantations in Demerara, including Wales, Waller's Delight, Covenden, Hampton Court, Vreedenhoop and Vreedestein. The seventh was called Success. The profits from these estates were such that by his mid-fifties, Gladstone was able to live in a magnificent home, host sensationally extravagant parties for his friends and send his sons to what he considered to be the Empire's finest school, Eton College.

The Gladstone family lived at Seaforth House, a large mansion set in more than a hundred acres on the coast just north of Liverpool, England. Through the large-paned windows in the living room, John Gladstone could watch the ships sail out of the Mersey towards the Caribbean. The beach was a short walk away, and here he and his children rode horses along the sandy shore. In addition to the ornamental beds filled with colourful flowers, the expansive garden boasted gooseberries, grapes, cherries and strawberries. Despite the frequent rain and occasional gales, it was a stunning place to live. Yet for all its beauty, Seaforth was not the property for which Gladstone hankered. He and his wife were both from Scotland and wished to return to their homeland in glory. Indeed, they had named their house in honour of his wife's clan chief, Lord Seaforth. Gladstone's ambition, therefore, was to acquire a large estate north of the border. To achieve this, he would have to amass an even greater fortune.

By the spring of 1823, however, he was deeply concerned that he would be unable to fulfil his dream. From his friends in the House of Commons he had heard rumblings that a significant number of politicians planned to push through legislation that would upend the working practices that had long been traditional on the sugar plantations in the Caribbean. These troublemakers called this the 'amelioration of the slave conditions'. To Gladstone, it was commercial interference. He believed that if the legislation was enacted, it would be the first step towards full abolition and the end of slavery. And if this came to pass, it would dramatically impact the way sugar plantations could be operated, almost certainly resulting in significantly lower profits. What worried him most was that they might have the numbers to pass the legislation in the next session of Parliament.

Gladstone, however, was not without options. A tremendously powerful man, with connections throughout the highest levels of society, he planned to protect his and his family's interests. First, though, he must get the measure of the problem.

John Gladstone had many accolades to his name.

Born in 1764 to Thomas and Nelly Gladstones in Leith, Scotland, he was the eldest son of sixteen children. His was a middle-class family with few savings in the bank and no great ancestors to boast of. In 1787, he changed his name from Gladstones to Gladstone, as it sounded better to those with whom he conducted business. By the age of twenty-five, he had made his first fortune, importing grain and tobacco into Britain. In his thirties, he built on this auspicious start by investing in Liverpool real estate, shipping insurance and shipowning. This then was his first achievement: as one of Britain's up-and-coming entrepreneurs.

Once he had accumulated significant wealth, Gladstone became involved in wider society. He managed the electoral campaigns for various politicians. He won election himself as a Tory MP in Lancaster and then Woodstock in Oxfordshire. He funded and organised the building of churches and schools, such as Trinity College in Glenalmond. Later, he would become a director of the Royal Bank of Scotland and finance railways, canals and other infrastructure projects. For all these efforts and more, he would later be awarded a baronetcy by prime minister Sir Robert Peel on behalf of Queen Victoria. This was his second great success: as a man of public service.

According to his entry in the *Oxford Dictionary of National Biography*, Gladstone was 'very tall, big-boned and gangly with big feet and hands'. He was also described as a 'demanding and bitter' man. His first wife, Jane, died without having children. His second wife, Anne, gave birth to six, the fifth being William Ewart Gladstone. After his death, this would be John Gladstone's third claim to fame: father to the four-time prime minister.

Less well known was that John Gladstone was also one of Britain's largest slaveholders. He first invested in the Caribbean in 1803, acquiring the Belmont plantation in Demerara. Later, in 1812, he acquired a one-half interest in the Success plantation, which at the time included 160 enslaved people. Four years later, he bought his partner out and became the sole owner of Success. While he was an absentee landlord, he was very much involved in the day-to-day management of operations. Through his managers, agents and overseers, he transformed the estates from coffee-growing to sugar production, making them increasingly profitable. According to the records maintained by the Empire's administrators, the number of enslaved women, men and children registered in his name across all his plantations rose to more than two thousand. Some of those who were born on a colonial estate were named after the person who 'owned' them as property.

Which was why Quamina's son Jack, who was born on Success plantation, was called 'Jack Gladstone'.

*

In early 1823, concerned about the anti-slavery legislation percolating in Parliament, John Gladstone wrote to Frederick Cort, his agent in Georgetown. The son of a well-known but bankrupt Hampshire ironmaster, Cort lived full-time in Demerara managing the affairs of a select group of landlords. In his letter, Gladstone asked Cort about the conditions of the enslaved people working on his plantations. He would use this information to combat any misstatements made in Parliament or the press. Six weeks later, the reply came back via packet ship. Cort said that it was rarely necessary to punish the enslaved people and that they were generally happy and contented. He added that they were so well taken care of that they were able to dress up to go to chapel, with the men wearing nankeen trousers and the women attired in muslin frocks and sporting blue silk handkerchiefs.

Gladstone also heard from the manager of his Vreedenhoop plantation on the west bank of the Demerara River, where 356 enslaved people lived and laboured. This man had previously supervised other coffee and sugar plantations in Demerara and was considered an experienced and reliable overseer. In his letter to Gladstone, the manager wrote that he was anxious that missionaries in the colony were making life more difficult for the planters. The enslaved people's minds were being 'inflamed by the ambiguous preaching, and religious sentences, selected from various books, and explained in language strongly calculated to impress them that their condition ought to be better', and that 'their masters were their enemies, inasmuch as they deprived them of supposed rights'.

On balance, the two reports were reassuring, Gladstone believed. If Cort was correct and those working on his plantations were well treated, then he need not worry they would be susceptible to the missionaries' entreaties. Nevertheless, he did worry about the wider impact these churchmen might have on the colony. He would have to speak to his allies in the Foreign Office about reining them in, for the sake of the other planters, for the sake of his own investments. Perhaps there was a way to limit the amount of time the enslaved people could spend at church meetings? This was not about restricting religious instruction, he told himself; it was about the prevention of political meddling and interference with legitimate commerce.

*W*hen it comes to the question of whether we in Britain should spend time and energy looking into our role in slavery, I've heard many people say the following: 'If we start going back in history, where do we draw the line?'

I see a good example of this argument in a column written by Rod Liddle and published in The Times:

> Should we not compile a database of all those who connived in the persecution and murder of Catholics under Elizabeth I? ... Or a list of families descended from those who collaborated in the expulsion of 3,000 Jews from England in 1290 ... Should we not identify those distant relatives of legislators who prevented women getting the vote until 1928, and working-class men a decade earlier? Note too the executions for homosexuality until the early 19th century: where is the list naming the hangmen and judges and mass of ordinary people who wholly supported such, uh, vigorous punishment?

Some call this form of argument 'whataboutism'. The idea being that even though a specific crime results in real harm, we should not acknowledge it given the abundance of other crimes. This of course is nonsense. For if true, it would be hard for the justice system to function.

It also fails to acknowledge that Britain transported around 2.8 million captive Africans into the Caribbean, resulting in the untimely death of hundreds of thousands of men, women and children, which is of an order of magnitude many times greater than the other crimes mentioned by the whataboutists.

CHAPTER 5

Jack, April 1823

Jack had never been in serious trouble. He had always done what he was told, kept his head down, kept the manager, overseers and drivers happy. Then one day he was going about his business in the cooper shed when John Stewart, the Success estate manager, walked up to him and started berating him. He accused Jack of having sex with Gracy, an enslaved woman who worked in his house, and said she was now 'ruined'. She now would hardly 'do anything' for him, the manager continued, so he would have to send her out to the field, even though she was not accustomed to such work. Stewart rebuked Jack for 'the impropriety of their connections', and said he needed to be taught a lesson.

Without being given a chance to argue his case, Jack was marched to the yard in front of the slave houses where the stocks were located. Gracy was there already, held captive, eyes downcast and resigned. Stewart pushed Jack to the ground. If he resisted, Jack knew his fate would be worse: thirty lashes at least, a time in chains and perhaps even a trip to the colony jail. So he complied. His wrists and ankles were locked in the stocks. When Stewart asked if he had learned his lesson, Jack said he had. He would not repeat his offence. Gracy said the same. And that, hopefully, would be the end of the matter. But it wasn't.

A few weeks later, Stewart called Quamina in to see him. The manager reported that he had received a letter from Lachlan Cumming, the owner of Chateau Margo, the estate immediately to the east of Success, who had complained that Jack had 'cohabited' with at least two other women on his plantation, causing much disruption and distress. If Stewart had expected regret from Quamina, then he was to be disappointed. Instead, Jack's father defended his son and, in Stewart's view, acted 'hastily' towards him. In response, Stewart also confined Quamina – who was even less accustomed to being punished than his son – to the stocks.

The next time he attended chapel, Jack found himself publicly humiliated. Sitting on one of the wooden pews, he listened to John Smith chastise him for his 'horrid' behaviour. Apparently Stewart had sent the missionary a long letter detailing his complaints. Clearly the parson did not approve of extramarital sex, let alone adultery. None of this sat well with Jack. Being judged for his private acts, being placed in the stocks, Gracy and his father being similarly punished, being written about behind his back, being reprimanded by the parson … Why did these Europeans get to tell him how to act? He was sick of the daily humiliations. The constant reminders that he was not in control of his life. He was fed up with being enslaved.

According to the law that governed the British colony of Demerara, inherited from their Dutch predecessors, an enslaved person could complain about ill-treatment to what was known as the fiscal. Demerara and the adjacent colony of Berbice were the only British colonies to have such a position. Appointed by the governor, the fiscal received a significant salary and was part investigative magistrate and part judge. In Demerara, the fiscal's name was Victor Amadius Heyliger, a fifty-three-year-old of Dutch ancestry who had been born in the colony and had a reputation for swift and brutal justice. Heyliger had wide discretion to collect evidence, force both enslaved and colonist to testify before him, and render judgement.

The problem, as Jack knew full well, was that few if any of the complaints were upheld. Sure, the most sadistic overseers were told to temper their violence. There was the case of the manager who placed an enslaved man in a coffin and nailed down its lid even though the man was not dead. The fiscal told the manager that such treatment was unsuitable, and then let him go without punishment. In another case, an overseer had starved the enslaved people on his estate and all the fiscal did was tell him to provide adequate food. Again, no penalty was given out. In a third situation, an owner had repeatedly raped teenage girls on his plantation, causing the death of at least one. This man was told to restrain himself and once again faced no further consequence.

The truth was that those who ran Success were encouraged to use violence to maintain control so sugar production would be maximised. Indeed, Demerara was known as one of the most violent colonies in the British Caribbean. Why was this? The colony had only recently been brought into the British Empire and was therefore considered by the colonists to need 'civilising' compared to places with longer histories of British rule such as Jamaica or Bermuda. This perceived need for violence was amplified by the fact that the White population was greatly outnumbered by the Black population. As a result, the colonists believed they had to use extreme measures of control to defend their interests. Furthermore, as almost half the colony's enslaved people had been born in Africa – like Jack's grandmother – they remembered life as free men and women, leading the overseers to believe they required more force to manage them. Finally, the planters' ferocity was accelerated by greed. For sugar was being produced in Demerara and its adjacent colony of Berbice at a higher rate than anywhere else in the Caribbean. This drove up profits and attracted characters who arrived from Britain desperate to make a quick fortune, no matter the human cost.

As such, violence and abuse was an everyday occurrence on the Success plantation. And Jack was sick of it. He wanted it to end and he planned to do something about it. There were various options open to him. He could ask to be sold to another estate, but there was no guarantee this would offer improved circumstances, nor was there any way to persuade the manager to make the transaction. He could refuse to work, but this would inevitably result in punishment. Either he would be placed in the stocks or sent to the colonial jail in Georgetown. Or he could flee the plantation. Head south away from the coast, towards the forested interior, where he might if he was lucky find an encampment of former enslaved people, known as 'maroons'.

There were various problems with running away. First, he was unfamiliar with the land to the south of the plantations, and might easily become lost and die of starvation. Second, he knew what happened to runaways. Advertisements for his capture would be placed in the local papers. He would be chased by men seeking a reward, with the aid of bloodhounds and perhaps even indigenous people who were expert trackers. Then, if he was captured, he would be severely punished, including a lengthy whipping with the cat-o'-nine-tails, an example made to others. Third, and perhaps most importantly, fleeing the plantation would not help those left behind: his father, his friends, the others who suffered the daily tribulations of life on the estate.

There was another, more dramatic option. It offered more possibilities, but it also held far more risk. Revolt. He was not the first to consider such a plan.

Though few of them could read or write, the enslaved people of Demerara carefully monitored the region's political happenings. They picked up information from the roustabouts, deckhands and warehouse labourers milling around the docks. They exchanged the news while they collected their managers' and overseers' goods at the market stalls and stores. They swapped gossip and rumours in the kitchens and boiling houses. They quietly whispered the latest updates in the fields as they picked the sugar or as they washed their clothes in the river. Most exciting of all was news of a rebellion.

Perhaps the most famous modern slave revolt of all was the one that took place on the island of Saint-Domingue. There, in 1804, following more than a decade of insurrection, the enslaved people had overwhelmed the French authorities, repelled a British effort at invasion, and announced the formation of a new country called Haiti. For most of its duration, the revolt was led by the former enslaved man Toussaint Louverture, until his capture by the French. This was the first successful slave uprising since the Spartacus revolt against the Roman Republic in 73 BC. News of the Haiti Revolution was quickly shared in Demerara.

One of the key sources for regional and world news was the newspapers that were delivered by ship to Georgetown. These were often weeks old, but the stories they covered were widely circulated. Typical of the kind of article that was well read was the one published by *The Times* on 28 January 1804. On its front page was an editorial that warned of the potential impact of the Haiti Revolution on the nearby British colonies. 'For our part we have been uniformly of opinion that a Black Empire was an evil less to be dreaded in that island than French ascendancy,' the paper said, adding that 'The only apprehension to be entertained then is that the new State become sufficiently powerful to annoy its neighbours and may afford an example too encouraging to the Negroes in our plantations.'

Jack was eight years old when Haiti declared its independence. He was too young at the time to understand more than the simplest details, but as he grew up, he digested what had happened more fully. How the enslaved people had thrown off their shackles and taken control of their plantations. How they had beaten two of the world's most advanced military powers: France and Britain. How it had taken considerable bravery and patience. He also knew the colonists were terrified of slave uprisings. Particularly when more than five thousand colonists were murdered after independence was declared in Haiti. This became known as the Horrors of St Domingo.

As he moved into his teenage years, Jack heard about other insurrections. In January 1811, for instance, around a hundred enslaved men marched from sugar plantations on the German Coast in Louisiana toward the city of New Orleans. More than forty of them were killed in battle; about the same number were hunted down, tried and executed soon after. Then, five years later in April 1816, an African-born man named Bussa led an uprising of more than four hundred people against the enslavers in the British colony of Barbados. Bussa died in battle and the revolt was put down, but news of the rebellion spread rapidly around the Caribbean.

To Jack and anyone else paying attention, these uprisings demonstrated a number of crucial lessons. That overthrowing slavery was possible. That it required careful planning and coordination. That physical force was almost certainly necessary. And that such action was not without risk.

*A*s I have continued my research, it's become clear that there are very few contemporary pictures of the enslaved people in Demerara. I can't find any portraits of Jack Gladstone or any of the other enslaved abolitionists. The only images I have seen are either romanticised portrayals of the sugar plantations or generalised sketches of the uprising.

There are, however, plenty of paintings and photographs of John Gladstone. In the Scottish National Portrait Gallery alone, there are seventeen pictures of the enslaver and politician. There are another seven portrayals of John Gladstone listed at the National Portrait Gallery in London. These comprise oil paintings, miniatures, busts and photographs.

In other archives, I have found pictures of the four other Johns: John Smith, John Cheveley, John Murray and John Wray. And of course, there are plenty of paintings of Sir Walter Raleigh, the first European to 'discover' Guiana, as well as King George IV, the colony's sovereign. But nothing of Jack Gladstone. What is the impact of this pictorial lacuna? For me, at least, seeing a visual portrayal of a person helps me understand them. I find it easier to engage in their story. To imagine their life, their challenges, their situation. To relate.

There are several contemporary portraits of Black abolitionist leaders. We have portraits of Toussaint Louverture, leader of the Haiti Revolution, and Harriet Tubman 'curator' of the Underground Railroad in the USA. The American anti-slavery campaigner Frederick Douglass was one of the most photographed men of the nineteenth century. Whilst the artist Thomas Gainsborough painted the British abolitionist Ignatius Sancho in rich oil colours.

I can see three choices. First, include the Demerara pictures that are available. This, historically, has been the typical approach. The problem of course being that this inevitably skews the sympathy towards those who are represented: i.e. the White people. Second is *to include no images at all. This would provide a level playing field but, to me at least, would be a missed opportunity. The third option is to commission new artwork. Is this even possible? After some brief research, I learn that other people have already done this.*

In the New York Public library, for instance, there is a pencil and ink drawing of Nat Turner who led a revolt of the enslaved people in Southampton County, Virginia in 1833. This picture was imagined almost a century later by African-American artist Lorenzo Harris. Similarly, almost two hundred years after Denmark Vesey led a rebellion in Charleston, South Carolina, African-American artist Ed Dwight created a seven-foot bronze sculpture of the abolitionist which now stands in the city's Hampton Park. The key, it seems to me, is for the artist to be connected to the story and to base the picture, as far as possible, on historical records.

I reach out to Juanita Cox who, along with her husband Rod West-maas, convenes a diaspora organisation in London called Guyana Speaks. She likes the commissioning idea and calls it 'hugely important'. She writes that 'artwork has the power to correct history by humanising people who have been unjustly marginalised and made faceless'. A few days later, she announces a call for artwork on social media, sharing what physical information we have for Jack Gladstone. Shortly after, Juanita puts me in contact with Errol Brewster, a Guyanese artist living in Florida, USA. He says that he would be interested in imagining what Jack Gladstone looked like based on the available archival records. He will get to work right away.

Several weeks later, the illustration arrives in my inbox. It's stunning.

For the first time, I see him. Strong, charismatic, handsome, intense. And with that, my connection with Jack and his associates deepens.

That afternoon I take a look at the other illustrations I have collected so far and I'm struck that they are all of men. There are no portraits of female colonists. No pictures of enslaved women. Nothing for Jane Smith. I contact Juanita again and we discuss how we might commission some more portraits.

CHAPTER 6

John Smith, May 1823

By the spring of 1823, John and Jane Smith had been living in Demerara for six years. The Bethel Chapel congregation had grown to more than a thousand people and the pews on Sundays were regularly filled by four hundred women, men and children. A strong leadership team had been built, including several deacons who helped with the services. Meanwhile, John had also successfully raised funds and forwarded this money to the Missionary Society back in London. In one year, this amounted to £100, a not inconsiderable sum. John was pleased with their progress. 'The Lord has been equally gracious to me & my dear partner as individuals,' he wrote in his journal. 'In conversing with many of the members [of the congregation] I felt much pleasure and am thankful to discern a spirit of love & zeal among them.'

As for Jane, her experience in Demerara these six years had been mixed. On the positive side, she had embraced the missionary work. She was responsible for providing religious instruction to the women and girls who attended Bethel Chapel. Each Sunday, at 11 a.m. for the children and 12 noon for the adults, she taught Bible stories, prayers and hymns. One of those who Jane became close to was Mary Chisholm, the freewoman who lived at Success. When John was away, Jane gave the sermon to the main congregation, and she had also taken on various administrative tasks, including applying for licences from the governor's office and purchasing supplies in Georgetown.

On the negative side, Jane had struggled more than her husband to adapt to Demerara's conditions. The hot climate, the strange food, the unfamiliar insects, the potent fevers. During those first few years, Jane's health had deteriorated. Indeed, John made fourteen references in his journal to his wife's sickness. 'Mrs S very ill & low spirited', he wrote in one entry. 'Mrs S was ill in bed', in another. 'Doctor called to see Mrs S', said a third. At one point, he wrote that 'my wife had been declining in health for 18 or 20 months, that she was scarcely able to keep about, lying down almost the half of her time.' By May 1823, however, Jane's health had improved. With the help of a local doctor, John recorded that she was 'now as well as ever she can expect to be in so hot a country.'

In those early years, both John and Jane had also felt homesick. Demerara was, after all, the first time they had lived away from England. To stay connected, they maintained a regular correspondence with those back home. This included Jane's mother – with whom she was very close – John's mother, and the directors of the London Missionary Society (they had added 'London' to their name in 1818). It took more than a month for their letters to make their way via packet ship to England and another month for their return. John recalled that sometimes just hearing from those they loved, even if the contents were neutral, 'made an unhappy impression on the mind'. At other times, when the news was bad, the impact could be devastating. Such was the case when Jane learned of her mother's death. 'It was a keen affliction to Mrs S whose love to her mother always seemed to me to be beyond all reasonable bounds,' recorded John. 'It appears she died in a truly Christian frame, placing all her hopes on the atonement of Christ. Blessed be God for such a death in our family.'

John was not the only representative of the London Missionary Society in Demerara. There was also Richard Elliot, who ran the Ebenezer Chapel and lived with his wife Elizabeth on the other side of the Demerara River. The relationship between the two couples was not, however, without its problems. John thought his colleague did not pay his congregants sufficient attention. But that was not the only issue. 'Last Monday, I & Mrs S went on a visit to Mr & Mrs Elliot on the West Coast,' he wrote in his journal. 'The frequent violent quarrels between Mr & Mrs E annoyed me very much, & almost make me resolve to break off all communication with them. They are an unhappy couple. Mrs E seems chiefly in fault. She makes everybody about her miserable, and is a scandal to religion.' At one point, Elizabeth Elliot complained that Jane did not treat her with proper respect. 'Mrs Elliot's passion is like the eruption of a burning mountain,' John continued. 'It must have its course, and woe to anything that stands in the way of the lava of her tongue.' Despite such misgivings, he continued to work with his colleague. They led services at each other's chapels and continued to socialise. Far away from home, the solace of their shared mission trumped personal animosity.

In better news, as far as John was concerned, the plantation manager Van der Haas was let go from Le Resouvenir. 'This circumstance occasioned no small joy amongst the Negroes,' John wrote in his journal, noting that Van der Haas was 'discharged for his cruelty' to the enslaved men and women. In his place, the estate owner appointed John Hamilton, a man who immediately showed more compassion to those working on the plantation. For instance, when Jan Swartz was brought back after running away, instead of using the stocks or the whip, Hamilton asked John to reprove the man. Similarly, when Alec Hill stole some coffee, the manager again asked the missionary to admonish him. 'I exhorted them to think of their ways, to seek the mercy of God,' John recalled. 'They said they would. May God enable them to do so.' Indeed, as he noted in his journal, he and Jane grew so fond of the new manager that they often invited him over for dinner.

As the members of Bethel Chapel became more comfortable with John Smith, they increasingly confided in him. In general, the parson felt great sympathy towards the enslaved people. He wanted to support them as much as he could, but he was also keenly aware of his precarious role as a missionary. After all, if he was seen to become political, his position would be in jeopardy and his primary assignment, to attend to the souls of his congregants, would be put in doubt. 'I wish the Negroes would say nothing to me concerning their troubles which arise from the severe usage of the managers,' he once wrote in his journal, 'as it is not my business to interfere in such concerns, and only obliges me to treat such conduct with apparent indifference, and behave with coolness to those who relate it.' He added, 'I observe in the slaves a spirit of forever murmuring and dissatisfaction; nor should I wonder if it were to break out into open rebellion. However, I hope it may not.'

Since his arrival in the colony, John Smith had kept an eye on Success, the neighbouring estate to the east. In contrast to the relatively benign conditions in force on Le Resouvenir, where persuasion was now used more than the whip, the plantation next door was run with extreme brutality. John had dined with one of the overseers who worked at Success. 'He complains of Mr Stewart's conduct toward the Negroes,' he recorded in his journal, 'says that he [Stewart] often gives them 100 lashes. That the Negroes work excessively hard, & have but little to eat.' He noted that since his arrival in Demerara, from a total of 330 enslaved people who lived at Success, more than 27 had died. The main explanation for the high mortality rate was that Stewart and his overseers made the men and women work night and day in the cane fields and boiling house. And the reason for this, according to John Smith, was 'to accomplish the orders of the proprietors'. The missionary knew that the man who owned Success was the British politician John Gladstone.

John Smith was deeply troubled by many of the estate owners. Most of all he disliked Dr Michael M'Turk. M'Turk owned and lived at Felicity, the next-door estate, where over two hundred enslaved men and women laboured in the fields and a dozen or so worked as domestic servants. M'Turk was the local burgher captain; as such, he was in charge of the district, much like a magistrate. His estate also served as the regional military post, containing a small arsenal filled with rifles and ammunition. More importantly, he sat on the Court of Policy, Demerara's local government, giving him access to the governor and the latest intelligence. Originally from New Cumnock in Scotland, and a graduate of the School of Medicine at the University of Glasgow, M'Turk had lived in Demerara since 1811 and was now in his mid-thirties. He distrusted the missionaries, and feared their effect on the enslaved people.

In one of his journal entries, John Smith recounted the following incident involving M'Turk. The missionary was on his way back from Georgetown when he noticed a boy named Sancho holding on to the rear of his chaise. He knew Sancho worked on Dr M'Turk's estate. When the parson asked why he had not recently seen Sancho at church, the boy said that his master would not let him attend and that when another of M'Turk's enslaved men had gone to chapel he had been severely whipped. When John suggested that maybe Sancho could find someone on his estate to teach him about Christianity, the boy said, 'The Doctor doesn't like us to know God: one time he heard me say "God knows" and he said, "O, you know God, do you?" and he made me eat the soap he was washing with, and gave another boy a horse spur, and made him spur me because I knew God.'

Things came to a head with M'Turk on Christmas Eve. The parson found several congregants waiting to see him outside the chapel. They said their managers had told them not to come to chapel any more. The order had come from the fiscal. 'Be easy,' John told them, 'I do not believe the order was from the fiscal.' He said he would try to find out what had happened. He then went over to see Hamilton, who told him that the order had actually come from their neighbour, M'Turk. Apparently he had declared that smallpox might be 'latent' on the estate. Most irritatingly of all, the only place where access was restricted was the Bethel Chapel. John knew of no case of the dreaded disease in the area, let alone inside the church, and took this for what it was: a deliberate lie.

John was still at Hamilton's house when their interfering neighbour arrived on horseback. Still angered by what he had just found out, the parson told M'Turk that he was acting 'very incorrectly', that he 'had no authority' for what he was doing and that he, the missionary, had permission from the fiscal to preach to whom and when he pleased. When M'Turk asked to see a copy of this permission, John backtracked and said he would use his influence to 'bring the Negroes of the neighbourhood to the chapel and preach to them in defiance of all the authority you possess'. When he added that he intended to provide religious instruction to his congregants, M'Turk sneered. Matters only became uglier from there. M'Turk said John would be 'extremely sorry' if he was 'driven to alternative means to prevent him'. Again the missionary said that he would persist. This time M'Turk said he would 'repel any such meetings'. And then he rode away. Later, he would say that the missionary had 'attacked' him using words. It was, he said, 'rather a violent manner'.

The following morning, Christmas Day, the pews lay empty. In a journal entry John chronicled that 'I have felt my mind distressed all day that the people were prevented from coming to the House of God.' He laid the blame on M'Turk and called the man's conduct 'unaccountable'. In another passage he said of M'Turk, 'It is surprising what a malignant enmity that man has to the cause of religion. If such a burgher officer be not a disgrace and a curse to the Polity with which he is connected, I am much mistaken.'

Even after the smallpox ban was lifted, John noticed a dramatic fall in those attending chapel. Quamina and the other deacons told him that several local managers were forbidding attendance on Sunday, and if their orders were disobeyed, the churchgoers were either whipped or confined to the stocks all day. Determined to find out what was going on, John rode out to the nearby plantations and asked the managers why his pews were empty. They were only happy to explain. One told him with a sly smile that the boiling house must be cleaned on Sundays. This would take several men four or five hours. Another overseer said that if sugar was boiled on Saturday then this must be packed into hogsheads the following day. A third explained that Sunday was the day that enslaved people were given their weekly allowance, which often meant a seven- or eight-mile trek to the market to collect plantains and other provisions. John knew these explanations to be spurious; the operations of the sugar plantations had not suddenly changed. Apparently the local estate managers had made a collective decision to curtail his mission.

Over the next few days, he told anyone willing to listen that scores of enslaved people had been stopped from attending his chapel on Sundays and that this was in contravention of the colonial law, which said they were allowed one day of rest each week. It was not long before the fiscal, Victor Amadius Heyliger, heard about the missionary's concerns and demanded that he provide evidence against any individual planter who made the enslaved people work on Sundays. John declined the request. 'The ruling men here, are vexed that such a notorious fact should be made so public,' he wrote in his diary. 'It seems a strange thing to require me to come forward and prove what nobody in the Colony denies.' While he wished to prevent what he called 'future abuses of the Sabbath', he did not want to be seen as a troublemaker and be relocated like his predecessor.

In addition to the declining attendance at chapel, John noticed what he began to think of as espionage operations. On a number of occasions he spotted unfamiliar White men lurking near the chapel before service, or peeking through the windows during prayers. Some even had the nerve to sit in the pews, typically towards the back, keeping track of what was said and by whom.

When John asked Quamina what these people were up to, he was told they were worried that the missionary was corrupting the slave population. During one evening service, while he was preaching from Ephesians, John observed a colonist sitting in a remote part of the chapel. 'I suppose he was a kind of spy, who thought probably as there were no other White persons present (a circumstance which seldom occurs) to catch at some expression which he might make use of in order to impeach my veracity,' he noted in his diary. 'But blessed be God I am animated by a nobler motive, than to teach what they call here "the principles of revolt". I wish and pray and hope and labour to train the souls of the Negroes for heaven. These men who look upon missionaries as dangerous characters, are themselves generally influenced by sordid principles, and so they measure us by their own rule.'

John was determined to outlast his adversaries. He would keep his head down and attend to the needs of his congregants. Unfortunately for the parson, the attacks against his mission would soon find a larger audience.

Though Demerara had a population of only five thousand colonists and free men and women, it was served by two newspapers. The *Demerara Royal Gazette* was the official organ of the British colony, a four-page periodical that was published three times a week, on Tuesday, Thursday and Saturday evenings. It tended to be more restrained, carrying official pronouncements and news from Europe. The other paper was the *Guiana Chronicle*, also four pages in length and printed each Monday, Wednesday and Friday; it belonged to Alexander Stevenson, a plantation owner and slaveholder. Both of these papers were reliant on the income generated from notices and advertisements, from auctioneers (who 'sold' enslaved people to plantation owners), shipowners (who typically also owned plantations) and merchants (who sold items to plantations). As such, both of the newspapers were consistently pro-slavery. It was an approach supported by Governor Murray, who argued that under Dutch law, he was powerless to curtail the press. Of course, he also owned plantations worked by enslaved people.

Throughout early 1823, the planters' antagonism towards John Smith was reflected in multiple stories that appeared in these two periodicals. In one issue, the *Demerara Royal Gazette* assailed the missionary for calling his congregants 'brethren', for, they argued, that elevated the enslaved people to the same level as the White folks, which was not acceptable. Next the *Gazette* accused him of forcing his members to attend service even though they had smallpox. Of course, this was not true. Then the *Guiana Chronicle* went after him. They called him 'cunning', 'pernicious' and 'capricious', and added an attack on missionaries in general:

The influence they possess on the minds of the Negroes is more widely ramified than is imagined, or would be readily believed. It is no longer proper to say they are insignificant. In the common acceptation of the word, they are truly so; but, from their calling and canting, they have acquired a degree of importance in this colony not attainable otherwise. Let them be looked after now more strictly than ever, and we pledge ourselves to do for them in proper colours, whenever we may be furnished with the authentic particulars of any immoral or illegal wanderings from the path of their duty.

When the *Guiana Chronicle* ran a piece saying the parson was charging his members a 'tax', he felt obliged to respond. 'Mr Editor, it cannot have escaped your reflection that the busy tongue of slander often places a man's conduct in so unfavourable a light that his silence may be construed into a consciousness of guilt,' he wrote. 'That there are persons sufficiently base to invent and propagate the foulest calumnies to gratify a malicious propensity, and that others are weak enough to believe them, however incredible or absurd, are facts which almost every one's experience abundantly confirms.' He explained that the reports were 'a gross falsehood' and that the only money he received was voluntary contributions that he sent back to London, 'as will appear to anyone who will take the trouble of referring to the annual Reports'.

On 23 May 1823, John Smith was again visited by Michael M'Turk. This time his neighbour had a letter from Governor Murray, which he took great pleasure in handing to the missionary. During their first meeting, the governor had said that he was opposed to the education of enslaved people. Now, six years later, perhaps thinking of the enslaved women and men he personally 'owned', and possibly also following pressure from M'Turk, Murray went further. His letter directed that from this day forward, all enslaved people must obtain a written pass from their plantation managers or overseers every time they came to chapel. John was shocked by this curbing of his congregants' religious freedom, as was his wife, Jane. She later wrote, 'This was a rare boon to many of the planters, but a great mortification to their slaves, and a great impediment in the way of their instruction.'

John harboured secret hopes that things would soon change in the colony. As yet, however, there was no suggestion of reform. Neither was there sign of insurrection.

*I*f we are to explore our history of slavery, the first step must surely be to ensure the facts are right. That the story is correct. The history, however, is not always straightforward.

As an example, let's look at John Smith.

Those who write about the missionary remember him as a good man and martyr. In 1848, for instance, Edwin Angel Wallbridge wrote a book entitled The Demerara Martyr. In 1923, David Chamberlin wrote Smith of Demerara: Martyr-Teacher of the Slaves. Then in 1976 came Cecil Northcott's book about Smith, Slavery's Martyr.

In Georgetown, a church was built in his name, called the Smith Memorial Congregational. Unlike the traditional east–west orientation, this building was aligned north–south, in memory of Smith's opposition to slavery. At its entrance stands a six-foot-high block of sandstone upon which is etched the words 'Rev. John Smith: He championed the cause of the Negro slaves to read and championed them against the brutality of the whites whose hatred he thus attracted.'

But from my research, I know that the legacy of John Smith is more complicated.

A close read of his journal entries reveals his racial prejudice. In one passage, for instance, he describes some near-naked women washing their clothes in a ditch and says that 'They resemble the "Ourang-Outang".' At another point he writes, 'I believe there are but few of the Negroes who think it much of a sin to rob a white man.'

To be fair, the vast majority of his entries show sympathy for the enslaved women and men he encounters and a strong desire to end the system of slavery. But that does not mean we should overlook his racism.

Indeed, it was common for those who opposed slavery at this time to be racist. As Ibram X. Kendi notes in his seminal book

Stamped From the Beginning, *'most of the leading Enlightenment intellectuals were producers of racist ideas and abolitionist thought'. As an example, Kendi looked at Thomas Jefferson who publicly avowed antislavery positions and penned the famous line from the Declaration of Independence that 'All men are created equal', whilst also personally 'owning' more than 600 enslaved people and writing about Black people's intellectual inferiority. To describe such contradictions, Kendi called Jefferson 'the nation's most famous antislavery anti-abolitionist'.*

Here's another journal entry that reveals an unattractive side to John Smith. On 15 April 1821, one of his congregants told him that she had been sexually assaulted by the estate manager. Smith's response was to blame the victim. He criticised the woman for 'not making complaint' and for 'staying in the house afterwards.' Adding that if she did not 'renounce her beastly connection' with the man, he would exclude her from his chapel.

By today's standards, John Smith might be judged as 'flawed'. Certainly he was more complex than many who have written his history have portrayed him. At the time he was alive, however, he was considered to be liberal, even radical.

CHAPTER 7

Cheveley, May 1823

By the spring of 1823, John Cheveley had had enough of Demerara. He didn't enjoy managing the general store. He disliked the fact the business was losing money. He loathed his boss. And he disapproved of the way the colony was run. Most of all, he missed his family back in England.

When he had first met John Pattinson in Liverpool, he had been struck by the man's business savvy and common sense, and had hoped these would be attributes also possessed by his brother in Demerara. Sadly, maddeningly, this turned out not to be the case. At first he had remained blissfully unaware of what was going on with the business. He received the goods sent by John from England, and sold them in Georgetown. He had little to do with William Pattinson and his efforts to send commodities back to England. Gradually, though, and through a careful examination of the company books, he became aware of what he called William Pattinson's 'flimsy ideas' and 'mischief'.

One of the flimsy ideas he uncovered involved purchasing a vessel that ran between Demerara and Martinique. The plan was to sell pine boards and other lumber to the French colony and bring back liqueurs and wines, but without paying duties, which were high on both sides. In essence, this was an illegal smuggling operation. In addition to not being caught, the problem was selling the goods, which Pattinson often failed to do. As Cheveley remembered it, instead of the much-hoped-for profit, the effort was rewarded with feelings of 'distrust, chicanery, bad feeling and threatened litigation'.

Another scheme Cheveley discovered involved a large load of timber that had arrived from New Brunswick. William Pattinson purchased the entire cargo with the intention of quickly selling it on for a profit. He then sold it to one George Rainey, not because he offered a good price, but because he belonged to one of the colony's well-known trading houses. To Pattinson, prestige was more important than profit. The decision resulted in a large loss for the company. Such experiences, and many more, made Cheveley realise that his boss was a bad businessman, and reminded him of his father's financial troubles, which had been the very cause of his journey to Demerara in the first place.

The general store was not the only reason for Cheveley's distress. After two years of observing how things were done in Demerara, he had become sickened by the general attitude of the colonists towards people of African descent. People like his own boss, who treated the enslaved people who worked at his house with disdain, or Robert Edmonstone, the timber merchant, who professed high culture, but 'owned' more than a hundred enslaved men and women. Cheveley wrote that since arriving in Demerara, he had become 'aware of the prejudices of the West India whites against the slightest taint of Negro blood, be it ever so imperceptible or remote, that consigned well-educated estimable men to ignominy and contempt'.

His best friend in Demerara was thirty-six-year-old Ben Hopkinson, whose family owned Bachelor's Adventure and Cove, two cotton estates on the east coast. Having completed his education at Cambridge University, Hopkinson planned to remain in the colony for three years. His aim was to increase yields by using the latest scientific techniques and to improve the treatment of the enslaved men and women attached to his estates. He would put aside the whip and hoped to encourage productivity by deploying training and respect. Yet despite all his well-intentioned plans, he would never be admitted into White society. This was because while his father was from Hertfordshire, his mother, Johanna, was a woman of mixed-race from Tobago, and Hopkinson had a 'somewhat dark' appearance.

William Pattinson's attitude towards people of colour particularly offended Cheveley. One day a free man came into the store and started looking around. He picked up seemingly random items and then put them down again, making a lot of noise in the process. Pattinson instructed Cheveley to 'turn him out', which the clerk attempted, but the man resisted. 'Knock him down,' said one passer-by. Another said, 'Break the rascal's head.' It was at this point that Pattinson rushed out wielding a metal bar and struck the man in the head. The man ran off up the street with blood streaming down his face, roaring with rage. Later Cheveley learned that he belonged to the King's Black Regiment. Pattinson was lucky not to be fined by the militia.

Cheveley also disapproved of young British men taking up with what he called a 'West Indian Wife'. Often these men already had wives and children back in England. According to Cheveley, the infidelity was 'detrimental to their moral character', while it encumbered them with large families, whom if they did not disregard, they found a heavy tax on their means of subsistence and a heavy burden on their consciences'. Often the colonists purchased these women at the Vendue, and they then, as one English writer noted, 'embrace all the duties of a wife, except presiding at the table'. If they had children, these were sometimes manumised (released from slavery), but more typically they were not. A rare few were sent to England to be educated; most remained in the colony receiving little or no recognition from their European fathers.

The latest to tread this path was Cheveley's boss, William Pattinson, who had shacked up with a young woman named Susan Morris. For Cheveley, there was one advantage to this relationship: it meant that Pattinson had vacated his bedroom on the first floor. Thinking this might be an improvement, he moved into Pattinson's quarters. If he had imagined it would improve his sleep, he was wrong. He had just fallen asleep the first night when he heard the sound of little footsteps on the stairs. The noise came closer and closer. Then the scampering of furry feet was all about him. He looked down and saw a sea of rats. If they had remained on the floor, he would probably have been fine. But they didn't. Instead, the 'ruffians', as he called them, 'began their nightly raids'. They scuttled up the bedpost, up the side of the mattress and, to his horror, across the mosquito netting, and then, 'jump, jump, jump' onto the floor. He leapt out of bed, grabbed his cutlass and started attacking the rodents wherever he could find them. Off ran the rats. He climbed back into bed, but within a few minutes they were back. Sleep now being impossible, he went upstairs and returned to his former bedroom in the attic.

All in all, it had been a wretched time. Cheveley was two years into his three-year contract. With twelve months to go, he was counting the days before he could return home.

In May 1823, Cheveley received a letter from John Pattinson in England. He had long been worried about the way his brother was running things in Demerara, he said, and hoped that Cheveley could bring some rigour and common sense to the enterprise. Would he join them as a partner? The new company would be called 'Pattinson, Cheveley & Co.'.

Cheveley was unsure. If he agreed to the partnership, he would not be able to return home in twelve months as planned, and worse, would he not be taking on a business that was sinking under its liabilities? John Pattinson, however, was a wily businessman. Anticipating Cheveley's reluctance, he made an offer he could not refuse. If he agreed to become a partner, they would make his brother George captain of one of their ships. And if it would help further, Cheveley's younger brother Henry could also be hired on as first mate. This had been a smart calculation; if Cheveley had a weak spot, it was his family. 'How did I feel?' he later wrote. 'Anything but pleasant.' He disliked Demerara, its climate, its people, its society. But despite his misgivings, he signed on to the deal.

Although he now had new responsibilities as a business partner, Cheveley was no longer able to avoid the call of the military. It is not clear how he evaded the authorities for this long. After all, it had been more than two years since his arrival in the colony. But having received orders directly from the adjutant general, he reluctantly enlisted. The following Sunday afternoon, he arrived at the parade ground and reported for duty. There was nothing about the militia that he liked. He found the uniform tight and uncomfortable, the rifle foreign and heavy. He did not know how to close-march or walk in lock step, nor did he wish to learn. Yet he had no choice.

He was terrible at drilling and his comrades complained that he trod on their heels. At the end of the session, the sergeant called him over and told him that he would need additional practice. He was to report first thing each morning at the offices of the *Guiana Chronicle*, where the sergeant worked. This was the same paper that railed against John Smith and his efforts to introduce religion to the enslaved people. The same rag that published frequent diatribes against William Wilberforce and the other anti-slavery campaigners back in England.

So it was that outside the offices of the colony's most conservative media outlet, Cheveley was taught the basics of military training: how to follow commands, how to march, how to operate a rifle. Within a couple of weeks, he had mastered the necessary skills and became a fully fledged member of His Majesty's militia. He just prayed that he would never have to use those skills. That he would never see action.

*A*s I have continued my research, I have repeatedly asked myself: why don't I know about this history? One of the reasons, I think, is that the history has been curated to favour those in power.

Let's take the history of Demerara.

When John and Jane Smith arrived in Demerara, only a handful of books had been written about the colony. One of the few that might have been available to them was Henry Bolingbroke's A Voyage to the Demerary, *written in 1807. About the enslaved people Bolingbroke wrote: 'The transfer of such wretches from Africa to America is a real service,' and that 'their treatment is improved by the removal'. He then added that by being shipped to Demerara, 'these people have become more humanised, more enlightened, their minds undergo a new formation'. Turns out Bolingbroke was not unbiased. For six years, he was in charge of slave auctions in the colony.*

Here's another instance of how skewed history becomes accepted. In 1888, James Rodway wrote The History of British Guiana. *In his book, Rodway described the enslaved people as a 'working animal'. He also called them 'half-savages', and 'children' who were under the care of the planters, who were like 'fathers'. Yet as recently as the year 2000, the* New York Times *called Rodway an 'outstanding chronicler of Georgetown's history'.*

Now, let's look at the Demerara uprising.

The first book to be written about this history was by Joshua Bryant, an English artist who lived in Demerara from 1809 till 1830. It was called Account of an Insurrection of the Negro Slaves in the Colony of Demerara *and published in 1824. For more than a century, this book was considered the definitive account of the uprising, with many quoting directly from its text and reprinting its illustrations. Yet Bryant supported the system of British slavery, blamed Smith for the insurrection and celebrated the efforts of the militia.*

When I looked a little deeper, at least part of the reason for this bias became clear. As was common at the time, Bryant advertised his book ahead of publication to underwrite its cost. A list of those who paid for copies is included at the back, and includes John Murray, the governor; John Croal and Lieutenant Colonel Leahy, who led the counter-insurgency; Michael M'Turk, the burgher captain; along with various other plantation managers and members of the militia.

That is not to say that no other books have been written about the uprising. There are plenty. Several were published by missionary groups and featured John Smith. Yet none of the accounts placed the enslaved men and women at the core of the narrative.

The most recent effort was written by Brazilian academic Emilia Viotti da Costa and is called Crowns of Glory, Tears of Blood. *Some consider this to be the new definitive account. But it too places John Smith at the centre of the narrative, and gives scant space to the enslaved point of view. Indeed, it does not mention Quamina till page 104 and Jack until page 172, whereas John Smith is mentioned four times by the end of the introduction.*

Part of the problem for anyone trying to write a more complete history is the imbalance in the records. John Smith wrote a diary, Cheveley left a memoir, and various biographies have been written about Gladstone and his family. A few accounts of British slavery were written by men and women enslaved by Britain – notably Olaudah Equiano, who was enslaved in Barbados and published his memoir in 1879; and Mary Prince, who was born in Bermuda and wrote a book about her life in 1831 – but none from Demerara in the 1820s.

But the situation is not hopeless. Unlike many slavery-related histories, we do have sources for Jack and his associates. These come from the court testimonies and complaints made to authorities. Typically, these were oral statements written down by colonists, which historians say can be relied upon as authentic. This is helpful, although they should be treated with some scepticism.

All this makes me think about how my being White affects the way I interpret the source material. How my growing up in Britain impacts how I read the histories of this period. What some call my 'positionality'. My family did not suffer enslavement. We did not experience the intensity of Black suffering. I am reminded again how much I have to learn. That I must be cautious, treat this history, with all its nuances and complications, with delicacy.

CHAPTER 8

Gladstone, May 1823

On 15 May, John Gladstone sat on one of the green leather benches situated towards the back of the House of Commons. Though he had been member of Parliament for Woodstock for six years, he liked to keep his name out of the newspapers. As such, his attendance was infrequent, but today's issue held tremendous personal and business interest for him, so he had made the effort to travel down from Liverpool.

In front of him stood the thirty-seven-year-old Thomas Fowell Buxton, social reformer, Quaker and sometime brewer. Gladstone felt little connection to this man. Top of the list of reasons to dislike him was his obsession with bringing about the end of slavery. Ever since Parliament had outlawed the Atlantic slave trade in 1807, the drumbeat for total abolition had grown louder. For while it was now illegal to transport enslaved people from Africa to the Americas, it remained lawful to 'buy' and 'sell' human beings within the British colonies. If an enslaved woman gave birth in Jamaica, Barbados or Demerara, the child still became the 'property' of the slaveholder. And while there were regulations limiting the punishment of enslaved people, a slaveholder and his agent or manager were allowed to whip, beat or otherwise physically assault enslaved men and women without fear of criminal retribution.

Today, Buxton had the audacity to bring a resolution to this venerable place that condemned the state of slavery as 'repugnant to the principles of the British constitution and of the Christian religion', and called for its gradual abolition 'throughout the British colonies'. He started by feigning pity for owners of Caribbean plantations such as Gladstone. 'I consider them as eminently unfortunate,' he proclaimed, calling slavery 'the worst, perhaps the only capital stain, on British policy'. To bolster his argument, Buxton presented a petition to the House that had been signed by thousands of people, calling for the abolition of slavery.

The use of petitions to effect change was a long tradition for the anti-slavery movement. Starting in 1788, a few months after the formation of the Society for Effecting the Abolition of the Slave Trade, campaigners had made extensive use of the tactic. Orators such as William Wilberforce, Olaudah Equiano and Thomas Clarkson gave speeches at church and village halls, at the end of which the audience were encouraged to sign a petition calling for the abolition of slavery. City and regional committees were set up to gather more names and addresses. In the 1792 campaign alone, more than 390,000 signatures had been collected. Following the British abolition of the slave trade in 1807, however, and with the exception of a short-term effort to encourage the French to follow suit in 1814, the petition campaign had dwindled.

Like many of his colleagues, Gladstone was fully against talking about emancipation, particularly in such a public space as the House of Commons. First, and most pressing, any discussion about freeing those enslaved, even if it came to nothing, would raise their hopes and inexorably increase the chances of insurrection in the Caribbean. Second, nobody had yet suggested a way in which the plantations could be managed without slave labour. The good denizens of England, Scotland, Wales and beyond were addicted to their sugar, cacao, cotton, tobacco and coffee. Who was going to produce such necessary commodities if the enslaved people were emancipated? Third, and most importantly as far as he was concerned, the enslaved men and women were an asset. It had cost an enormous amount of money to purchase the plantations in Demerara, whose value mostly comprised the enslaved. If abolition was enacted in Parliament, Gladstone and his like would be rendered bankrupt overnight. This had to be avoided at all costs.

Buxton's speech was followed by others including William Wilberforce, the grandee of the abolitionist movement, who unsurprisingly supported the resolution, as well as many who were against. Typical of these last was the businessman and slaveholder Alexander Baring, who stated that 'as far as the physical sufferings of the Negro go, they have been much over-stated', and that 'the condition of the slaves is undoubtedly, in many respects, superior to that of most of the European peasantry. They are well clothed, well fed, and, I believe, generally treated with justice and kindness.' He added, somewhat apocalyptically, that if the Black population did gain their freedom then 'we must bid adieu to our colonial system. The colonies would be of no further value to Great Britain.'

Nobody really believed that Buxton's resolution would be passed that day. It was too rash, too brazenly abolitionist, too insensitive to the feelings of the slaveholders. The man was clearly trying to impress his anti-slavery supporters, who would read about the proceedings in the next day's newspapers. But there was a general feeling in the House that something must be done to curtail the most obvious abuses in the Caribbean.

At one point during the debate, in a quiet corner away from prying ears, a cabinet member approached Buxton and said that if he withdrew his resolution, the government would back an amendment calling for the 'gradual amelioration of the condition of the slaves in His Majesty's colonies'. As part of this hastily arranged compromise, the cabinet member agreed to promptly write to all the colonies alerting them to Parliament's increasing concerns about slavery. The deal was done. So it was that on 28 May 1823, much to the dismay of Gladstone and his allies, Lord Bathurst, the colonial secretary, sent a dispatch by ship to Demerara.

When it arrived in Georgetown in early July, Bathurst's letter was carried straight to Governor John Murray, who, upon reading its contents, immediately grasped its importance. A few days later, he convened the Court of Policy – the local government council – and read out the missive. The fiscal Victor Amadius Heyliger was present, as was Michael M'Turk and Charles Wray, the chief justice of Demerara. When they heard the contents of the letter, they were shocked. The first page was a copy of the resolution that had passed in the House of Commons, including this statement: 'This House looks forward to the progressive improvement in the character of the slave population, such as may prepare them for a participation in those civil rights and privileges which are engaged by other classes of His Majesty's subjects.' To those assembled, this sounded very much as though the politicians in Britain were anticipating the emancipation of the Empire's enslaved people.

Next Murray read out Bathurst's own words. The colonial secretary informed them of the king's 'command' to immediately adopt certain resolutions that would ameliorate the working conditions of those enslaved. In particular, the new laws would prohibit the flogging of female slaves, end the driving of enslaved people by the sound of the whip, and discontinue the practice of working on Sundays. Bathurst, however, left the governor some leeway. He said that the prohibitions should be seen to come from the Court of Policy, not from London, so he would leave it up to the local council to decide how and when to implement the policy, though it should take effect as soon as possible.

Aware that these changes would have an enormous impact in Demerara, John Murray adjourned the discussion to a future meeting. The Court of Policy met again on 21 July, but once again the governor postponed the debate, saying he wanted the full council to discuss this vital issue, which was not possible at the time as the fiscal was away on business.

If the governor thought he could bury the news from London and hope it would just go away, he was wrong. For despite the confidential and extremely sensitive nature of the letter, its contents were soon circulating amongst the people who worked in government. One of those to become aware of the momentous dispatch from London was a free Black man named Daniel.

I go for a walk with my friend Joan. I tell her that I'm looking into Britain's involvement with slavery. She asks if I'm trying to feel guilty. Do I want to feel shame?

That doesn't seem right to me and makes me a little annoyed. The need to learn about this history is not driven by a need to feel remorse, I tell her (perhaps a little sanctimoniously) but a desire to find the truth. A need to acknowledge what has happened. Unless we understand what has gone before, it's hard to agree on anything going forward.

I speak to my friend Yasmeen Akhtar, co-founder of TrustLab, a consultancy that provides diversity and inclusion training for organisations. We talk about the negative reactions I'm getting from some of my friends when I tell them I am exploring the legacy of British slavery.

She suggests I read White Fragility by Robin DiAngelo. I do and I find it very helpful. The book explains how some people who identify as White can get defensive when they are challenged about racism. So defensive that people of colour, who become afraid of their response, stop challenging them.

And I wonder, as a White person, how my own defensiveness affects my understanding. Of my family's legacy of slavery. Of Britain's legacy of slavery. Of today's racial injustice and equity.

'Rejection of inner conflict can hold us back from action,' Yasmeen says. 'Until you really regret something you are not committed to transforming. It can feel difficult. It can feel uncomfortable. But it's worth the effort.'

To learn more about how other people might have dealt with their difficult family legacies, I decide to speak to a descendant of a Nazi war criminal.

To be clear, I don't believe there is an equivalence between what enslaved people suffered at the hands of Britain and what

Jews endured in Nazi Germany. These are two separate historical tragedies, and to draw out similarities and differences, or worst of all to judge which crime is the greater, would be a mistake.

But I sense that there may be some lessons to be learned.

Over the last few years, I have frequently visited Germany. And when people find out that my Jewish grandparents were forced to flee the country in the 1930s, there is often a moment as they digest this information, a pause, followed by an expression of sorrow and then an apology. This has always felt appropriate. Never mawkish or cloying or self-aggrandising. I've appreciated the sentiment of solidarity. I would have felt anxious if they had failed to acknowledge the crimes of the past; I would have felt unseen.

I make contact with German author and journalist Alexandra Senfft. She tells me that her grandfather was Hanns Ludin, the Nazi who ran Slovakia and oversaw the deportation of more than 70,000 Jews to the death camps. When she learned about this history, she says she felt 'a sense of deep sadness, of mourning and of anger'. But her family was extremely resistant to discussing her grandfather's Nazi past.

Over time, she realised that if she did not talk about it, she felt like an accomplice. An accomplice to the original crimes? I ask. 'No,' she says, 'an accomplice to the silence. To the cover-up. I'm not responsible for what my grandfather did, but I am responsible for facing up to it. For finding the courage to look at the frightening issues.'

But why discuss this in public, I ask; why not keep it within the family? 'It's crucial to go public to break the silence, to encourage others to speak up and thus to change society,' she says. Then adds, 'This is a political act, not a personal act.'

Later that day, I speak with one of my cousins and tell her that I am researching our family's legacy of slavery. She says I need to be very careful. Over the years, some people have focused on Jewish slave ownership as a way to fuel anti-Semitism. I fully understand this fear, especially given the rise of anti-Semitism in recent years.

I search online and quickly find that the subject of Jewish links with slavery has been extensively studied and that historians have found no evidence that Jews were more responsible than anyone else for slavery.

It's possible, though I admit challenging, to hold two things at the same time: my family has been persecuted for being Jewish and, also, my Jewish family benefited from slavery.

CHAPTER 9

Jack, July 1823

On Sunday 27 July, Jack went into town to speak with his friend Daniel, who worked as a junior secretary for the governor. He would miss the morning service at Bethel Chapel, but that was okay. He didn't always go, and as far as he was concerned, this trip was more important. For weeks now he had heard rumours that the big men in London had taken a decision that would change all their lives dramatically. Just the possibility was overwhelming.

He had known Daniel since they'd been boys. They were what he called 'church brothers', though Daniel now attended a Methodist church in Georgetown, where he lived and worked. A few years earlier, Daniel had been manumised, the legal process through which an enslaved person secured their freedom. Most likely, this happened after the death of his former 'owner'. Manumission was a rare occurrence in Demerara. In fact, the rarest in the Caribbean. In 1820, for instance, only two in every ten thousand enslaved people were manumised in Demerara. The rate was five times higher in Jamaica, twenty times higher in the Bahamas and thirty times higher in Trinidad. Manumission was uncommon in Demerara partly because the colony's sugar business had become one of the most productive in the Caribbean, increasing the 'price' of enslaved people, as a result of which the plantation owners were increasingly reluctant to give up their highly valued 'assets'. This made Daniel's freedom even more unusual.

According to both Jack and Daniel's later court testimony, it was around nine in the morning when Jack arrived at Camp House, the governor's residence, one of the largest buildings in Georgetown.

He found Daniel working in a small room upstairs. Though Daniel considered himself to be a devout Christian, he often had to work on the Sabbath. His supervisor gave him more work than could be delivered during the normal work week and to let him down would mean risking his job, something he would hate to do. It was a good position, well paid and secure, and best of all, he had never seen his manager carry a whip.

After exchanging greetings, Jack asked Daniel what news he had. He knew that his friend was in the habit of reading the newspapers that were shipped from London and New York, and sometimes, when he was sure nobody was looking, also the official correspondence that crossed the governor's desk. Daniel asked Jack what he was after. 'I have something very particular I wish to see you about,' Jack said. He had heard that the enslaved people were all to be freed, and he wished to know if it was true.

Daniel became immediately afraid. The building was full of people, and if anyone heard them speaking like this, not only would he lose his job, he would be severely beaten. Rather than replying directly, he spoke in code. He recalled that the third chapter of the second book of Timothy contained the words 'ever learning, and never able to arrive at the knowledge of the truth'. What he did not have to say, because he knew that Jack was as learned in the Bible as he was himself, was that seven verses further on, Timothy declared, 'But as for you, continue in what you have learned and have become convinced of, because you know those from whom you learned it.' Jack understood this to mean that the rumours he had heard were true. He was equally careful in his reply to Daniel, saying that in chapel the previous Sunday their text had been from Romans, Chapter 8: 'All things working together for good for those who love God.' It was a call to collective action.

Daniel's statement was the final confirmation Jack was looking for. He had already heard that an overseer from New Orange Nassau plantation had said they were to be freed, that all the great men in

London had agreed to it but not the colonists in Demerara. Even more persuasively, a week before meeting Daniel, Jack had spoken with Susannah, the enslaved woman who worked as housekeeper for John Hamilton at Le Resouvenir. According to Susannah, Hamilton had said that he too had heard that the enslaved people were to receive their freedom. His declaration came with a caveat, however: that liberty would not come easily. It would only be won if the enslaved people 'went by force about it', and that it would take a 'positive promise' from the governor. Jack had asked Susannah what Hamilton meant by force; did he mean take up arms? She said no, not fight, but they should seize the plantation owners' weapons and then drive all the buckras into town. Hamilton had added one more thing. He didn't care either way; he only asked that if a revolt was to take place, they give him sufficient warning so that he could prepare his affairs.

That was seven days ago. Now, with Daniel's coded but unambiguous assurance, Jack was certain that a directive had arrived from London to give the enslaved people of Demerara their liberty. The question was, would the colony's White elite follow through on the directive, or would force be required to encourage them to take the necessary steps to ensure that slavery was abolished? Before parting, Daniel told his friend that he had heard that several people had lost their lives during a slave revolt in Barbados. 'I told him to beware,' he later recalled.

Back home, Jack discussed his plan with Quamina. Where once his father might have cautioned restraint, fearing the heavy hand of the enslavers, he now supported his son's strategy. For Quamina's view of the colonists had recently changed. A few months ago, the estate manager, Stewart, had sent him away to work by the seaside even though his wife Peggy was extremely ill. This meant that Quamina could not see Peggy from six in the morning till seven at night. He had asked repeatedly for his work to be moved closer to home, but his requests were denied. As a result, he was absent when Peggy died. They had been together for almost twenty years. His grief was exacerbated not only by the fact that he could not be with her at the end, but also by the bitter reminder that his routine was controlled by the plantation manager. He was fifty-two years old, and after a lifetime of servitude, he was ready to challenge the system.

Once the decision had been made, father and son discussed how to go about it. Key to the success of an uprising, they agreed, would be careful planning and organisation.

Over the next few weeks, Jack launched himself into the preparations. First came intelligence. He had already confirmed with his friend Daniel that orders had been sent out from London to set them free and that the governor was refusing to implement these instructions. By making careful enquiries amongst colonists he came into contact with – managers, shopkeepers and dock workers – he learned that they were unprepared for an uprising. There was no unusual military activity in Georgetown. The reservists had not been called into the militia. There were no reinforcements on their way to the colony. In his view, Demerara was vulnerable and ripe for revolt.

Next came the question of tactics. If they were to persuade the governor to implement the instructions from London, how best to do this? Should they march into Georgetown and demand a meeting? They would be vulnerable in the capital; better to remain in the countryside, whose terrain they were more familiar with. Should they take over an estate and hold hostages? It would be difficult to build a large force taking this approach; smarter to remain in the open. And how about violence? Many of the enslaved men and women would want to mete out revenge against the buckras. Jack fully understood the motivation, and it would be difficult to stop them. Yet he remembered what Daniel had said about Barbados. How that uprising had led to a draconian response from the colonists. Quamina agreed. As far as was possible, it would be better to avoid violence against the planters.

Instead, the best tactic would be a decentralised uprising made up of overwhelming numbers. This would be a good way to counter the colonists' chief advantage: a small but well-trained and well-equipped military force. An insurrection could only work if they had large numbers of women and men on their side. The trick would be to start the uprising at the same time across the entire colony. That way it would be difficult to suppress. If it was taking place in multiple locations, to which hotspot would the governor deploy his militia? In addition, they needed to seize the planters' muskets, pistols and cutlasses before they could be used against them.

There was one more thing. They must neutralise the district burgher captains, particularly the dreaded Michael M'Turk, who would try to disrupt their plans. As to when to start, Jack thought the best time would be at the end of the day, when the workers were still in groups and about to set off home. A Monday might be best. They would be less tired after a full day's rest on the Sabbath, and many would have attended church the day before, providing an opportunity to organise and share any last-minute information. Launching in the evening would also give them more time to consolidate their position overnight before word got back to Georgetown.

Most important of all was recruitment. To reach as many people as possible, Jack realised he needed a cadre of highly motivated, highly persuasive men and women who would travel from one estate to the next picking up conscripts. Luckily, through his work as head cooper, he had travelled extensively up and down the East Coast and had developed a wide circle of friends. Similarly, Quamina had built up an extensive list of contacts through his position as deacon to Bethel Chapel, whose congregation now exceeded two thousand people. Such a wide social network was rare amongst enslaved people, as few were permitted to travel between plantations.

So it was that Jack set about creating a command structure. With himself as leader and his father in support, he built a small team of lieutenants whose job it was to spread the message and recruit. There was Goodluck, who used to live with Jack, and Peter, who had rung the bell on the day of the parson's arrival. From further afield, Jack convinced Telemachus, Joseph and Timney from Bachelor's Adventure, along with Paris from Good Hope, Sandy from Nonpareil, Seaton from Van Cooten's estate, Attilla from Plaisance, and Bristol and Manuel from Chateau Margo.

Over the next few days and weeks, these lieutenants fanned out across the colony, reaching out to trusted friends and family members on scores of other estates. In the plantations of Essequibo. Along the banks of the Demerara River. Over to the far west next to the Mahaica River. In Georgetown. They were careful where they had the conversations; to be caught inciting would not only undermine their cause but would lead to terrible punishment. In quiet conversations in the fields, or behind the slave house, or on the road, and always out of earshot of the drivers and overseers, the instigators probed to see if the listener was discontent, and if so, if they were willing to take part in an uprising. When concerns were raised – why not wait for the governor to implement the instructions from London? Was it not too dangerous? Who else was involved? – they calmly gave answers conveying confidence and urgency. And always, the instruction was given to keep the plans secret. For if the uprising was to be successful, it must be a surprise.

With word already out that the governor was refusing to grant them freedom, and with anxiety high given the fast-approaching harvest and the inevitable increase in the use of the whip, it proved remarkably easy to attract support to the insurrection. As the campaign to enlist continued, reports on numbers were passed back to Jack at Success. They had fifty signed up, then a hundred, then three hundred, then even more. If they waited, they would be able to build up larger numbers, but to wait too long might result in fatigue, apathy and a loss of momentum. Jack knew that time was running out. They must soon fix a date to start the uprising.

What word best describes Jack and his associates – protestors, demonstrators, revolutionaries, rebels, insurrectionists? Such terms are vexed, each with different meanings depending on context and point of view.

'Protesters' and 'demonstrators' fail to capture the radical nature of the effort.

'Revolutionaries' sounds hyperbolic for what happened in Demerara. Suitable for those who took part in the Haiti Revolution, as it resulted in the overthrow of the existing order, but not for Jack and his associates.

Looking at the historical records, I see that Governor John Murray and the other colonists typically used the word 'rebels' to describe the enslaved men and women who started organising for their freedom in the summer of 1823, but I can't see examples of Jack using it.

The more I think about it, the more the word 'rebel' doesn't feel right to me. It has negative connotations. Echoes of someone who is 'not one of us', on the outside, disobedient to a ruler who has right on their side. Such distancing seems inappropriate, unhelpful, unnecessary.

True, the word 'rebel' does have some positive modern associations – the 'Rebel Alliance' in Star Wars, *for instance, or James Dean in the film* Rebel Without A Cause – *but at best its meaning is ambiguous.*

And 'insurrectionist', like 'rebel', strikes me as pejorative. So what word to use?

Dr James Dawkins, who researches the history of slavery at the University of Nottingham, gives me two further suggestions. The first is 'freedom fighter'. Apparently this has gained currency amongst academics in the Caribbean. I like this phrase, with its focus on the objective: freedom. But to me, as someone who grew up in Britain in the twentieth century, 'freedom fighter' also conjures up something more militaristic, reminding me of Fidel Castro and his comrades in Cuba, the mujahideen in Afghanistan, the Viet Cong in Vietnam.

It is Dawkins' second option, however, that really surprises me. He suggests that I could describe Jack and his associates as 'abolitionists'. I have always associated abolitionists with politicians and activists in England, the USA and other slaveholding countries.

I pull my Oxford English Dictionary *(circa 1979) from the shelf and look up 'abolitionist', and find this definition: 'Applied specially, and probably originally, to persons seeking the abolition of negro slavery.' When I check out 'abolition', it says: 'The act of abolishing or putting an end to; the fact of being abolished or done away with; annulling, destruction or annihilation.' Clearly Jack and his associates were trying to put an end to slavery in Demerara.*

In my mind, I conduct a thought experiment, comparing the following sentences: 'British militia shot two hundred rebels' and 'British militia shot two hundred abolitionists'. The difference is startling. I am far more sympathetic to the second sentence than the first. I acknowledge that I am writing this from the perspective of a White man who grew up in Britain, but I am struck by the dramatic differences in my responses. To put it bluntly, while I am a little afraid of the rebels, I want the abolitionists to succeed.

I hesitate for a moment, not wanting to conflate the anti-slavery campaigners in Britain with the enslaved men and women in Demerara. I certainly don't want to confuse the history. There were, after all, obvious differences. Not the least of which, one group was free and the other was not.

But there were also many things shared. They both wanted to abolish slavery. They both were looking for policy changes that would bring this about. And they were both aware of each other. There are also examples of those formerly enslaved who were widely regarded as 'abolitionists', including Frederick Douglass, Olaudah Equiano and Mary Prince.

I search my manuscript and find more than fifty instances of 'rebels'. I replace each with 'enslaved abolitionists' or simply 'abolitionists'. This feels like an important change.

CHAPTER 10

John Smith, August 1823

It was early Sunday morning, 10 August 1823, and John Smith was in the chapel preparing the day's first service. He stopped for a moment, out of breath and sweaty. This was happening more and more often. Simple tasks such as climbing the steps to the bell tower or laying out the prayer books on the pews had become challenging.

For some time now he had been feeling poorly. He was beset by wheezing and tormented by painful and exhausting coughing fits. There was a fixed pain in one part of his chest, and when he looked in the mirror, he saw that his eyes had a pearly quality. After much complaint, Jane had at last persuaded him to visit a doctor in Georgetown, but the physician had just told him he had pulmonary disease. It was almost certainly consumption, the doctor said, and recommended that John avoid damp weather, which was hardly helpful given that Demerara had two rainy seasons. He and Jane had discussed taking a sabbatical, maybe a trip back to England to see their families, but any such plans had been put off until things calmed down, hopefully later that year. For now, he needed a moment's rest. He sat down in a pew. Which was when he saw Jack and Quamina enter the chapel.

After the usual greetings, Jack said they had an urgent matter to discuss. Many of their friends and family were talking about a letter that had come from London giving the enslaved people their freedom; did the parson know anything about this? John said that he had also heard about the letter, but he cautioned them to be patient.

Something good would come of it, he said, but they needed to wait two or three weeks to find out what was going on. He thought the governor would probably announce something soon, most likely in Georgetown.

The following morning, a Monday, the missionary was visited by Stewart, the manager of Success, and Frederick Cort, Gladstone's agent. Cort said that his object in calling was to enquire what was the parson's opinion about the 'state of the Negroes' mind in reference to the rumour among them that they are to be free'. John said that he was aware that such a rumour prevailed, but that he knew nothing about the state of mind of those who worked on the plantations.

Through his contacts in Georgetown, Cort knew that on Thursday the week before, the Court of Policy had finally agreed to implement Lord Bathurst's instructions, including the prohibition of whipping enslaved women. Indeed, his boss, John Gladstone, along with more than fifteen other Demerara plantation owners, had written to the governor encouraging the implementation of these changes in the hope of delaying the adoption of more extreme, as he saw it, abolitionist measures. As yet, however, the governor had still failed to announce these changes to the public. Cort told John Smith that the colonial government was acting 'very imprudently in withholding the necessary information from the slaves, whose minds must, in the nature of things, be greatly agitated'. To this, the missionary agreed. After his visitors had left, he took out his diary and wrote the following: 'The rigors of Negro slavery I believe can never be mitigated. The system must be abolished.'

A week later, at around 4 p.m. on Sunday 17 August, John closed the door of the chapel and walked the few steps to his house. The afternoon service had just finished and he was looking forward to going home. He was in a lot of pain; his side throbbed terribly. He had told Jane that he would visit the doctor again the following morning, and would take the chaise as he didn't fancy riding on horseback. Inside, he found his wife speaking to Bristol, one of his deacons. They were talking about taking care of a little girl. When John overheard that the girl had measles, he objected, saying that others might catch it, and she could only stay with them when fully recovered. It was then that he saw Quamina, Seaton from Van Cooten's estate and some others enter the room. This was not unusual, as the Smiths were relaxed about people coming and going through the house. 'How are you, master?' said Quamina amiably. 'How are you, missus?'

John went to fetch a glass of wine, and when he returned, he picked up on what Quamina and the others were saying; something about 'new law' and 'manager'. This prompted him to rebuke them for speaking of such things. Quamina said, 'O, it is nothing in particular, sir, we were only saying it would be good to send our managers to town to fetch up the new law.' This irritated the parson more. He said they were fools to say such things and should not speak to their managers about it; after all, they were not politicians. Instead, as he had said before, they should wait patiently and see what the governor decided. Quamina then said, 'Very well, sir, we will not say anything about it, for we should be sorry to vex the king and the people at home.'

John watched as Quamina and his companions set off down the narrow path called the Middle Walk. He noticed that they were moving towards a gathering of Black men and women about a hundred yards away. At the centre of the group was an unmistakable figure. The tall, charismatic man who sometimes read Bible stories to the children at the chapel: Jack Gladstone.

As Quamina and the others arrived, they found the group engaged in an urgent discussion. Around Jack was gathered a tight ring of key leaders, including Goodluck, Peter, Telemachus, Paris, Sandy, Seaton, Manuel, Taddy, Smart, Donderdag and Primo. Jack was explaining that they would have to use force to take over the estates but that they should try and avoid hurting the plantation managers and owners.

According to Primo's later testimony, it was at this point that Quamina said that his son was being too hasty. 'Wait till this month is gone', he suggested, urging patience. 'You are an old man', Jack replied, clearly annoyed. 'The thing the people have got, you won't let them have.' Now Sandy jumped in. Jack's plan made him nervous, he said. Some enslaved people had tried the same thing in Barbados and it had failed badly. A lot of people had ended up killed; many others received terrible lashings. He suggested an alternative idea. 'Every man upon his own estate let us put down our tools', he said, 'and when the driver sees nobody going to work they will tell the manager to let us go to town and ask for one day besides Sunday to rest.' But the others were unconvinced by this argument. Some shook their head, others muttered their disagreement. Finally Paris said, 'If we lay down our tools what will become of us? They will shoot both the men and women like fools.' The solution, he suggested, was to put the White folks in the stocks and to take their weapons. Everyone agreed.

There was one last question to answer: when? Should they go now or wait till they could attract more people? Again there was a heated discussion. If they had more time, perhaps the governor would change his mind. And if not, it would allow them to attract even more people to their effort. But Jack said no, there was no more reason to wait. It had been more than six weeks since the letter giving them their freedom had arrived from London, and without a little pressure, the governor was clearly not going to bring about the reforms. He instructed them to rouse as many people as possible to join their cause. That night, Peter would go back to Essequibo and let people know they were ready. Taddy would go to town and raise as many folks as he could there. Goodluck would inform all the plantations between here and Georgetown. Someone else would alert the estates to the west, as far as Mahaica Creek. Jack was just handing out the last assignments when he saw an overseer approach on horseback. He made a small gesture and the enslaved abolitionists quickly dispersed.

'Well, are you ready?' asked Goodluck as they walked away. Jack said he was. He then paused and added, 'Do you think that we are to live all the days of our lives this way, and have people cutting our skins, to know that there is something good for us and not taking it?' Goodluck replied, 'No, before I will live to have my skin torn up, I will sooner die.' Jack nodded his agreement. They had no choice but to act.

The uprising would start at 5 p.m. the following day.

PART 2

UPRISING

You may write me down in history
With your bitter, twisted lies
You may trod me in the very dirt
But still, like dust, I'll rise.

Maya Angelou

She is a region in Guiana, all gold and bounty.

Falstaff, *Merry Wives of Windsor*

CHAPTER 11

Jack, August 1823

A little after 4 p.m. on Monday 18 August, Jack and his father were in the cooper's shed at Success, working on some barrels that needed to be completed for the next shipment. So far, everything had gone according to plan. More than twenty plantations had said that they would join the cause. The weather was cooperating too; it could sometimes rain hard in August, but it looked to be fine. Most of all, their plans hadn't seemed to have leaked.

They were both surprised, therefore, when in through the shed door walked Stewart the estate manager and his burly overseer Murchieson. Stewart roughly grabbed Quamina, while Murchieson tied Jack's hands behind his back with a rope. Then Stewart told Murchieson to take Jack to Michael M'Turk. Quamina was left in the shed; clearly they were not worried about the old man starting any trouble.

It was not far from Success to M'Turk's house. A short walk to the edge of the estate, through Le Resouvenir, past the missionary's house and chapel, and then into Felicity. Murchieson tugged on the rope as he led the way, though there was no need. Jack knew where he was going. As he walked away from Success, he must have wondered how the manager had found out about their plans.

A few minutes into their journey, they came to two men and a woman walking alongside a canal pulling a punt full of canes. Recognising them, Jack smiled at his captor and said politely that he would 'prefer to go no further'. One of the boatmen stepped towards them, withdrew a knife and reached out to cut him free, but

Murchieson tried to stop him. In the ensuing struggle, the boatman slashed Murchieson on the shoulder. His shirt now soaked in blood, Murchieson scampered away and jumped into the canal. The boatman ran after him. 'No,' Jack shouted, 'let him go!' As Murchieson climbed out of the other side of the waterway and ran back towards Success, the boatman looked at Jack, aware of the significance of what had just happened. He had injured one of their bosses. Punishment would certainly be harsh. Jack hurried back home.

When he arrived back at Success, he moved rapidly to take control. He walked up to the bell that hung near the slave houses and rang it loudly. This was the sign that the uprising had started, and soon forty men and women gathered around him. With the sun disappearing from the sky, Jack said they must act quickly. First they needed to secure the estate manager and his overseer. The search was led by Richard, Bethney and Jessamine, who lived at Success and knew the plantation well. It didn't take them long to find their quarry.

Murchieson was hiding in one of the farm sheds. He was swiftly overpowered and placed in the stocks. They found Stewart standing in front of his house. As they approached, he told them to stop what they were doing and threatened severe punishment if they didn't leave him alone. 'No, no,' said Richard, 'we must have you.' He then grabbed the manager's feet while somebody else took hold of his coat collar. They pulled him down the steps, away from the house, and dumped him on the dusty yard in front of the sick house. Stick in hand, Richard walked up to him and was about to strike when Jack intervened. He held his hands over the manager's head to prevent him from being hit, and then, after he felt it was safe, told Stewart to go back to his house. The others would be less enraged, he said, if he was out of sight. If it hadn't been for Jack, the manager would later recall, the 'mob' would have killed him.

With Stewart locked in his house and Murchieson shackled in the stocks, Jack led Richard, Bethney and the others to the plantation storehouse. To their good fortune, it was unlocked. Inside, they found a stack of weapons: several muskets, a small supply of ammunition and a cutlass, which Jack took for himself. The enslaved abolitionists had taken their first estate.

Leaving behind a handful of people to guard the colonists, the gang now headed eastwards towards the next-door plantation, Chateau Margo. As they marched, they heard the sound of drums beating in the distance, lifting their spirits. It was a sign that the uprising had started on other estates. After the near disaster of Jack's capture in the cooper's shed and subsequent rescue by the canal, they had regained momentum. The excitement of collective action filled the night air. It was dark now, but the waxing moon cast enough light to help them see their way.

A few minutes later, they arrived at Chateau Margo. There Jack once again instructed that the estate's managers be rounded up and put in the stocks. Finding the bosses was surprisingly straightforward; there were few places to hide on the estate. Soon the stocks were full and the posse, now sixty strong, was again on its way. Moving eastwards, away from Georgetown and the British militia, the enslaved abolitionists continued on to the next three plantations: La Bonne Intention, Beeter Verwagting and Triumph. At the entrance to each, the party was met by those ready to join the uprising. Some had already gained control of their estate. Others requested assistance, and Jack dispatched a few of his followers to secure the plantations.

As they entered the next estate, Mon Repos, three shots were fired. At the time, Louie – an enslaved driver who worked on the estate – was hiding under the estate manager's house. In his later testimony, he recalled Jack being alarmed by the shooting. 'You must not fire any more guns,' Jack ordered, 'you will hurt white people, which you must not do.'

By 1 a.m., they had reached the plantation known as Paradise. 'Barson, where is Barson?' one of them called out. Barson, who worked as a domestic servant and who had been part of the meeting on the Middle Walk the previous day, revealed himself. He took them to the main dwelling house and opened the front door; others came in through the back. Once again they broke into the store and took away guns, powder and various swords. Someone put a double-barrelled gun into Barson's hands and the entire group moved off again. Few remained behind, as it was felt they were stronger if they stuck together. As they headed east along the public road, the party was kept company by a chorus of raised voices, beating drums and ringing bells.

Around 2 a.m., they came to Porter's Hope, the sugar estate half a mile east of Paradise. There they found the estate manager, Samuel Shepherd, standing on his front porch. In his hand, pointed towards them, was a wooden-butted fowling piece. Though this gun was better suited to shooting ducks than providing defence against home invasion, it could nevertheless kill a man if used with skill.

The gang was now hundreds strong. A handful had guns of their own; most carried sticks or small knives. Out of the multitude, a woman stepped forward with a musket on her shoulder. She told the manager that her name was Amba and that she was from the nearby Enterprise plantation. They were taking over his estate, she declared. Two of her associates then approached Shepherd and tried to take his weapon. To their surprise, the manager attacked them with tremendous agility, striking both men in the face with the butt of his gun. They both fell back.

'You allow one buckra man to knock down so many of you,' Amba mocked her comrades. 'Take his gun,' she commanded. Others came forward and this time successfully took hold of Mr Shepherd. They did not kill him. Instead, they placed him in the plantation's stocks. Once the estate was secure, the group continued on their journey east.

*

It was around 4 a.m. when they came to Nabaclis, a sugar plantation located ten miles up the coast from Success. It was a long day's ride from the capital, its culture and its military. Remote. The abolitionists now had control of more than twenty estates, though it was hard to know what was happening further east. They had been going for more than ten hours, but Jack had no intention of slowing down. Soon the militia would be upon them. This was no time to stop.

As they approached the manager's house, Jack saw a man open the door and fire his gun towards them. Nobody was hit. A small group rushed forward, grabbed the man and hustled him towards the stocks. Above them, on the first floor, the shutters were thrown open and in the dim moonlight a figure appeared. 'Look at the lady at the window,' someone shouted. 'Fire at her.' The woman let out a shriek of pain and withdrew, but a few seconds later she returned to the window. If she had been injured, clearly it was not life-threatening. Raising her hands as a sign of submission, she called down that they should be calm. In return, she was fired upon again. Jack called out to stop the shooting and instructed four men from the estate to secure the building. Their names were Calib, Sandy, Rodney and Joseph.

Calib led the way, a pistol in hand. They entered the house and were immediately fired upon by a man they recognised as Tucker, the estate overseer. Someone shot back, Tucker was hit and fell to the ground, no longer a threat. After a quick search, they found nobody else on the ground floor, so they headed upstairs, moving slowly, alert for attack. They checked a number of rooms, all empty. There was one room remaining; the door was locked. They forced it open, and inside they found the woman. They knew her at once. It was Mary Walrand, the wife of the plantation owner, Francis Walrand. She was clearly surprised to see the gun; she looked scared. Trying to reassure her, Sandy said that he knew her to be a good woman, that she took care of the sick people who lived on the estate and that she should not worry. Slightly calmer now, she asked what they wanted. Calib said their freedom had come from England and they were taking it.

Mary turned back to Sandy. 'Well then,' she demanded, 'tell me what they have done with Mr Walrand.'

'He's not hurt, madam,' Sandy said. 'He's only in the stocks.'

Clearly relieved that her husband was still alive, Mary replied, 'Then I must go there too.'

Calib said, 'Oh no, you must be guarded in the house.' He and Sandy then left, leaving behind Rodney and Joseph to watch Mary.

A short while later, it began to grow light outside, revealing there to be more than a hundred people milling about the yard. Some were pulling furniture out of the house. Others were drinking wine, clearly having found the kitchen. Still more were lounging about, making the most of not having to go to the fields that day. Joseph and Rodney decided it was better to have all the colonists in one place. They escorted Mary out of the bedroom and down the stairs. On the way, they passed the lifeless body of Tucker, the overseer.

Rodney encouraged Mary forward, out of the house, across the yard and into the sick house. There they found her husband, Francis, who had been released from the stocks. He appeared tired but unhurt. Also there was another of the estate's bosses, a Mr Forbes, who appeared more seriously injured. 'What a scene is this for you, madam!' declared Forbes as she entered the room. She offered to tend to his wounds, but he responded, 'No, I would rather die. This is now no country for a poor man to get his living in.' He then added, 'I wish Wilberforce was here in this room, just to look on me; for we may thank him for all that has happened, that the same might be dealt to him by some hand.'

Mary looked at her captors and again asked what they were trying to achieve.

'We want our freedom,' Rodney repeated, adding that the 'king had sent it out and the owners would not give it.'

This was not true, she protested, and demanded, 'Who told you so?'

'He preached it every Sunday,' Rodney replied. 'Parson Smith.'

*T*o find out more about the country, its people, landscape and history, I fly to Guyana.

On the plane, I do some reading. Guyana won its independence from Britain in 1966. Today it has a population of around 750,000 people. The largest ethnic group is Indo-Guyanese, with 40 per cent. These are mostly descended from the indentured labourers brought to the country from India after the abolition of slavery. The next largest is the Afro-Guyanese at 30 per cent. These are mostly descended from the enslaved people. Those of mixed heritage make up 20 per cent. The Indigenous peoples are around 10 per cent, whilst the Chinese and White population comprises less than 1 per cent of the total.

Getting off the plane in Georgetown, I'm hit by a wall of warm heat. Outside the airport there are a few men with signs proclaiming whom they're waiting for. I can't see my name. I call Chris, the driver who was recommended by some friends in London. A second later, I see a man in front of me raise a phone to his ear. On his shoulder perches a large green parrot. We laugh and greet each other. 'This is Peekaboo', he says, pointing at his parrot, and then walks me to his car, a beaten-up silver Toyota Camry.

The roads are busy. Trucks, buses, taxis, mopeds. We pass a casino, a nursery school, a house previously owned by a drug lord (now in jail), a cemetery, a small power station, a cow walking by itself along the side of the road. After thirty minutes or so we are into Georgetown proper: the old horse-racing track, a billboard advertising Magnums, the high court, the marketplace, various hotels under construction, and a sign that reads 'I love Guyana' in front of which newly-weds take photographs.

An hour after we leave the airport, Chris drops me off at the Herdmanston Lodge, which at one time was an estate manager's house on a sugar plantation and is now a hotel. This will be my home for the next two weeks.

On my first full day in Georgetown Chris drives me to the seashore. By chance it's also the annual commemoration of the Maafa, 'great disaster' in Swahili, which remembers the Atlantic slave trade. I am invited to attend by Elsie Harry, a young Afro-Guyanese activist. When we arrive, there are thirty people already sitting on white plastic chairs under a large tent by the seashore. Gradually the space fills up with sixty people. I am the only White person there.

After a few minutes, Sister Penda takes the microphone and welcomes everyone. She explains that the event has been organised by the African Cultural and Development Association to commemorate the more than fifteen million men, women and children who were the victims of the transatlantic slave trade. Others take the stand and talk of how the Afro-Guyanese are still suffering. Guyana is blessed with many resources, including oil recently discovered off its coast, and yet is one of the poorest countries in South America. It has the highest suicide rate in the world and is beset by domestic violence against women.

Once the speeches are complete, each of those present, including me, are handed a three-foot-long Heliconia topped with bright red, orange and yellow flowers. We form a parade and walk sombrely to the water's edge. There we stretch in a line along the shore as a spiritual leader pours water from a wooden bowl onto the sand and in a high, urgent voice recalls the ancestors who came before.

As he makes these libations, three young men beat the drums hanging from their necks. Just as the tide reaches its highest point, we walk into the waves and one after another place our flowers onto the water. I think of the shackled women, men and children in the bowels of those dreadful ships, the pain and fear of the hours and days ahead of them. The first landing in Demerara, the examination and the slave auction, the brutal work on the estates, the high mortality rate, the beatings.

Later, as I drive around town, I notice that many of the roads are named after slaveholders, such as Croal Street, Peter Rose Street and Albouys Street. The enslaver Joseph Bourda is remembered in the name of a city ward, a market and a cemetery. Many of the villages just outside town still carry the names given to them when they were sugar plantations.

Here in Guyana, the legacy of slavery is very much alive.

CHAPTER 12

John Smith, August 1823

John and Jane were at home on the evening of Monday 18 August. At about 6 p.m., they heard a tap on the door. It was Guildford, an enslaved man from Dochfour estate, who handed them two letters and then sat down on the step to wait for a response.

John opened the first. It was from Jack to Jackey Reed, also from Dochfour estate. The script was neat and the language fluent; clearly someone had written it for Jack, as he couldn't write this well. The message was obscure, mentioning an 'agreement' but not what it was, and that 'it' would begin on the Thomas estate. But what were they beginning? Confused, John opened the second letter; this one was for him from Jackey. Again the contents were vague. The writer spoke of 'some actions' that were due to start at 7 p.m. that evening. If true, that would be in an hour's time.

John went to his study and hastily penned a response. In his note, he said that he had no idea what Jackey was talking about and that he hoped they were not planning anything reckless. 'Hasty, violent or concerted measures are quite contrary to the religion we profess,' he wrote, 'and I hope you will have nothing to do with them.' He placed his letter in an envelope, walked outside and handed it to Guildford, who ran off.

With the sun about to set, John suggested to Jane they go for a walk. The letters worried him. Around 6.30 p.m., they were close to the seashore when they heard loud voices from behind them and the sound of shots being fired somewhere in the plantation. They turned back. As they approached their home, they saw Hamilton standing in his doorway, waving frantically at them to come near.

Hamilton explained what had just happened. He had been in his house when he heard the estate bell ringing. A few moments later, scores of enslaved men and women had gathered in the yard. There was much cheering, shouting and raising of fists. Realising they were in danger, he and two of his overseers, Mr Gun and Mr Parker, had locked themselves in an upstairs room, each with a musket. Then, from the back of the building, he'd heard a man shouting. He looked out and saw it was Sondag and a dozen others from the estate. A few moments later, the men ran up the stairs and started banging on the door, calling on the manager to open it. When Hamilton asked what they wanted, Sondag said they had come to put him in the stocks and take away his guns. A few seconds later, they smashed through the door and rushed inside. For a moment, there had been a stand-off – three bayonets pointing towards the small mob – but the planters had been quickly overwhelmed and forced to give up their arms.

John Smith felt the need to comfort the manager. 'It is the only method you could have adopted,' he said, 'for resistance to such a multitude would have been in vain and would have exasperated them to take your lives.'

As they spoke, a crowd of men and women carrying the recently seized rifles edged towards them. Trying to calm the group, the missionary said, 'Haven't you done enough already? You have got their arms, what now do you want?' When they ignored him, he repeated the question.

One of the enslaved abolitionists spoke up. 'We want the guns and our rights,' he said, brandishing his cutlass in the missionary's face. Seeing the alarm in Jane's eyes, the man softened and said that he was not going to hurt them – he knew who they were – and begged them not to be frightened. When Jane asked why they needed more guns, the man looked at Hamilton and said that it was to 'keep the managers from cheating us'.

Realising that they were powerless to intervene, John, Jane and

Hamilton stepped back and watched as the abolitionists entered the manager's house in search of more weapons. A short time passed and the men returned outside carrying additional rifles and canisters of gunpowder. A few fired shots in the air and cried out in triumph. It was around this time that Sondag announced to his comrades, 'We will now go and hold Dr M'Turk.' The gang then marched away towards Felicity plantation. After thanking the missionary for his help, Hamilton set off to secure his horses. It was striking that unlike the other colonists, Hamilton and the Smiths were allowed to roam free. Presumably this was because they were better regarded by the enslaved women and men.

It was suddenly quiet. John and Jane quickly assessed their options. They could ready their cart and ride into town, where they could stay with one of their friends. The way, however, might be dangerous. They had no idea how far the trouble had spread, and whilst some of the insurrectionists knew them, there were plenty who did not. A second option would be to hole up at a nearby estate with another family. But this too came with uncertainties. Would they be welcome? Also, they didn't want to leave their house and chapel unprotected. 'In the next place,' Jane later remembered, 'the Negroes had no cause for complaint or quarrel against us, quite the contrary. Why then should we run away in a panic?' In the end, they agreed that they would be safest remaining in their own home. They would keep the lights off and stay indoors. They had plenty of food to keep them fed for a while. There was also Elizabeth, a teenage girl who was living with them, who could provide help. They would reassess things the next day.

Tuesday passed without incident. Le Resouvenir was oddly quiet. There was little to do. No services to organise. No sermons to give. They could not go outside for fear of attracting attention to themselves. Jane went about the house trying to keep herself busy with chores. John spent much of the day in his study, reviewing his papers. At one point, he picked up his journal and looked at the last entry he had made, written the previous day, before all the commotion had started. He recorded how he had ridden to town to see his doctor about his health. The physician had recommended cupping and blistering to relieve the pain on the left side. Best of all would be a change of air. 'The season being so far advanced he recommends a voyage to Bermuda,' John wrote, 'or if I could wait 4 or 5 months, to England, as being preferable.'

Over the past four years, almost from the very day he had arrived, John had been consistent in chronicling his time in Demerara, recording the details of his public life, the Bible verses that were read out in church, the numbers attending. He had also included more personal matters. The people he and Jane had visited. Their health concerns. He had written about the enslaved men and women and his views on how they were treated in the colony. And most privately of all, his opinions of the people he had met: the plantation owners, the fiscal, even the governor. His journal was more than an aide-memoire or a summary of daily activities. It was a full account of his time in the colony, comprising more than 60,000 words. It is odd, therefore, given that he now had time on his hands, that he did not write about the uprising, the seizure of Le Resouvenir and the other dramatic events of the previous twenty-four hours. Perhaps he was waiting to see how events unfolded.

John and Jane's solitude was disturbed just once that day, when a rider from Georgetown arrived at their home. On his side hung a bag, from which he withdrew a pamphlet. He handed it to John and then, without another word, rode off. The paper was a copy of the governor's proclamation, announced earlier that day. Apparently, Murray had declared martial law throughout the colony.

Wednesday 20 August started out very much like the day before. John and Jane remained inside, disconnected from what was going on in the nearby estates and in Georgetown. They wondered how the authorities were responding. How big had the rebellion become? Had it spread across the Demerara River and into Essequibo? How would the governor react? Would the militia be called up? Wanting to find out what was going on, Jane asked Elizabeth to see if she could find Quamina and bring him to them.

A few hours later, there was a knock on the door. It was Quamina. He was carrying a stick from which hung a bundle, as if he was on his way somewhere. They greeted him, ushered him inside and closed the door. As soon as they were seated, John told his deacon that the people had been 'foolish and wicked and mad' to revolt, but that now that they had begun, 'you must go on with it'. Throughout this meeting, which lasted no more than three minutes, Quamina said nothing, even when John asked him where he'd been and what he'd done.

After Quamina had left, John asked Jane how the deacon had come to be there, and she explained that it had been her doing. It was then that she saw Elizabeth watching from the kitchen and realised that she had been there the whole time. She hoped they had spoken too quietly for the girl to hear what had been said, but she couldn't be sure. 'If I find out that you have told anyone,' she told her, 'you will be whipped.' Once the words were out of her mouth, she realised what she had said. She was horrified. But by then it was too late.

Early the next morning, Thursday 21 August, the fourth day of the uprising, John and Jane Smith remained at their home at Le Resouvenir. The missionary had still not added to his journal. Instead, he wrote letters. The first was to James Mercer, a fellow missionary in Trinidad. He wished his friend well and provided news on the uprising. 'How all this will end I know not,' he wondered. 'I feel perfectly safe, not because we have so many soldiers patrolling about, but because I am conscious we have not wronged any one.'

Next he wrote a letter to George Burder, the secretary of the London Missionary Society back in England. 'Dear Mr Burder,' he began, 'the whole united colony of Demerara and Essequibo is now under martial law. The Negroes on this coast, at least, have seized the fire-arms belonging to several plantations.' He then went on to share his analysis of what had led to the uprising.

Ever since I have been in the colony, the slaves have been most grievously oppressed. A most immoderate quantity of work has, very generally, been exacted of them, not excepting women far advanced in pregnancy. When sick they have been commonly neglected, ill-treated, or half starved. Their punishments have been frequent and severe. Redress they have so seldom been able to obtain, that many of them have long discontinued to seek it, even when they have been notoriously wronged.

Having explained how the colonists refused to implement the new regulations sent from London, he turned to how the estate managers had prevented the enslaved women and men from attending chapel. 'On this account,' he reported, 'many of them have suffered an almost uninterrupted series of contumely and persecution.'

He was just about to start the next sentence when he heard a commotion outside. He went downstairs and opened the door, and was met by a soldier who introduced himself as Lieutenant Thomas Nurse from the 1st Battalion Demerara Militia. Nurse said that the reports of insurgent slaves were now so alarming that every colonist and free man of fighting age was required to join the militia. He had orders from his commanding officer, Captain Michael M'Turk, that John Smith must immediately report to the Felicity plantation and enlist. If he had no gun of his own, he would be supplied with one, and he would be given a position that suited his skills and circumstances. As to Mrs Smith, she could accompany him to Felicity, or, if she preferred, she could repair to Georgetown and would be given an armed escort to assure her safety.

If they were surprised by the sudden appearance of the lieutenant at their front door, and his unambiguous order, the Smiths did not show it. According to Nurse's later testimony, John Smith declared that M'Turk had no authority over him because he was a priest and his work as a missionary exempted him from military duty, adding that though he was grateful to M'Turk for his kind promise of civility towards Jane, they preferred to remain together at their home.

Frustrated by the parson's obduracy, the lieutenant asked if he had seen the governor's proclamation of martial law, which had been declared two days earlier. When John said he had, Nurse asked him to fetch it. He went upstairs and returned a few moments later with the document in hand. Lieutenant Nurse then read out the key parts of the proclamation:

> I have thought fit to issue this my Proclamation, hereby declaring, in the name of our Sovereign Lord King George the Fourth, the United Colony of Demerara and Essequibo to be, from and after the issuing of this Proclamation, under MARTIAL LAW: and I do here by enjoin all Faithful Subjects of His Majesty within this United Colony, to govern themselves accordingly, and to be aiding and assisting, to the utmost of their abilities, in restoring the peace of the country, and in protecting their fellow-subjects. And it is further our will and absolute command, that ... all persons, without distinction, capable of bearing Arms, being required immediately to enroll themselves in some Troop or Company of the George-Town Brigade of Militia.

To the soldier's not inconsiderable surprise, however, the reading left John totally unmoved. He said that the meaning had been so unclear to him that after he had first read the proclamation he had been forced to look up 'martial law' in the encyclopedia, and was still none the wiser. Struggling to maintain his composure, Nurse asked if the missionary would allow him to illuminate the nature of martial law and perhaps then he would understand it. John coolly said that he had no objection to this, and so the lieutenant explained the 'positive and absolute nature of the law' and that it was the missionary's duty to comply with the orders of Captain M'Turk, or any other officer employed by the commander-in-chief, adding that the colony's inhabitants had been called upon 'without distinction to take up arms'. Finally, he warned of the possible negative consequences of refusal to comply with M'Turk's order.

John, however, appeared indifferent to either the legal tutorial or the threats. 'I differ from you in opinion,' he said, 'and I do not intend to join any troops or company, or to do any militia duty.' He added that he would, however, be willing to contribute any service of a 'pacific nature'.

Lieutenant Nurse had been instructed that if the missionary refused to enlist, he was not to arrest him. Instead, he now asked the parson to show him where he stored his papers and manuscripts so that he could seal them for later investigation. When John asked who had ordered this extraordinary demand, Nurse replied, 'Captain M'Turk's order is my authority,' and enquired if the missionary planned to make any resistance.

'No,' said John calmly. He led the lieutenant upstairs and pointed at the desk drawer where he kept his papers, including his journal. He said that he had nothing to fear from fair and impartial examination, but one of the letters he preferred to keep to himself. It was from his friend John Wray, the previous incumbent at Bethel Chapel, stating how pleased he was that the politicians in England had agreed to ameliorate the conditions of slavery in Demerara. Lieutenant Nurse insisted all papers must be handed over, which John reluctantly agreed to, and then, using rope, the soldier proceeded to seal the desk, cautioning that this should not be tampered with.

About three quarters of an hour later, Lieutenant Nurse returned with Captain Alexander Simpson, who was also a plantation owner. They were supported by a cavalry unit. Unlike his colleague, Simpson was in no mood to argue the niceties of martial law. He castigated John Smith for daring to disobey Michael M'Turk's order. The parson once again said calmly that according to his research, he was exempt from military service. This infuriated Simpson. 'Damn your eyes, sir,' he shouted, waving his sword in the missionary's face. 'If you give me any of your logic, I'll sabre you in a minute.'

Lieutenant Nurse now ordered several soldiers to enter the house and seize the previously sealed documents, including the missionary's journal. He turned to John Smith and, in an official voice, announced that the missionary was to be removed from his house, though he was not, he added, under formal arrest. Hearing this, John understood that he had no choice. 'If I must submit,' he said, 'I will if you order me.' He did not swear, nor offer any resistance. Two of the soldiers took him by the arms, led him outside and loaded him onto the back of a cart. Jane was given the option of choosing where she wanted to go. She said that she wished to remain with her husband, wherever that might take her. The Smiths were not given the chance to bring a change of clothes or to lock the door. They were escorted westwards to Georgetown, where they would be held pending trial.

The day after the Maafa commemoration, Chris drives me out to Success. Peekaboo his parrot sits on his shoulder, from time-to-time nibbling on his ear. 'He's a boo, boo,' croons Chris, 'my baby, he loves me.'

With me is Vishani Ragobeer, a twenty-one-year-old journalist who has agreed to help me with my research. We leave Georgetown and drive along the public road that runs parallel to the ocean. In my mind, the road should be a single-lane track made of crushed shells. Today it is a four-lane highway lined with billboards advertising Ben & Jerry's and auto-part companies.

Ten minutes after leaving Georgetown, at the Rubis gas station, we turn into Success. This is where Jack and Quamina lived. What was the sandy Middle Walk is now a paved road. The estate is now a village. We drive three or four blocks. On our left is a ditch filled with water, on our right a row of one-storey concrete houses painted in bright greens, purples and oranges. We park the car and climb out. I want to see the layout of the place. To my surprise, it only takes fifteen minutes to walk from one side of Success to the other, from one side dam to the next. I'm reminded how narrow the plantations were.

At the edge of Success, we cross a drainage trench into Le Resouvenir. This is where John Smith lived, where the Bethel Chapel stood. Three large pigs sleep in the shade cast by a small metal shack, their owner in a hammock strung inside. The rusty metal husk of a punt that used to ferry sugar canes through the plantation is half sunk in the canal we walk along. Another fifteen minutes and we reach the side dam that marks the end of Le Resouvenir and the start of Felicity, the next estate. It's midday now, and brutally hot. These were the conditions in which the enslaved peopled worked in the fields.

Vishani suggests we take a break, and invites me home for lunch. It's a small, lime-coloured house on the 'line-top', the main road that cuts through the village. Sitting on the covered porch, her mother passes us chai tea along with plates of fried shrimp and 'cook-up', a mixture of rice and chicken.

Vishani says that after abolition, the enslaved people left Success. Some moved to Georgetown. Others went further away, looking for work. A few banded together and purchased land – what became known as 'the village movement'. Today, Success is inhabited almost entirely by people of Indian descent, most of whom commute to Georgetown for work. Growing up here, Vishani says, nobody told her about the 1823 uprising. And she doubts anyone in the village has heard of it.

After lunch, she suggests we visit the backlands behind Success where the sugar fields used to be. We park in front of a narrow channel of water, next to which a few bored-looking police officers lounge on white plastic chairs. As we climb out of the car, Vishani explains that a large number of squatters have moved onto the land, claiming they have nowhere else to live. For decades, she says, there has been a housing crisis along the coast. The demand for accommodation has far outstripped supply. This has resulted in periodic squatting and 'regularisation', the process of transforming squatted land into long-term development, including the provision of public water and electricity.

She is just starting to give me more details about the squatters when four men and three women approach us. 'Where are you from?' one scrawny-looking man asks. 'We are media,' says Vishani. Immediately they start talking, eager to share their stories with us. They've been there for a few months. There are a lot of them. At least a thousand. The police have fired rubber bullets at them, they tell us, and at one point the government cut a hole in the dyke and tried to flood them out. But they aren't going anywhere.

We walk further into the backlands. Around us we see the temporary structures, mostly just four thin poles covered with tarpaulins or corrugated plastic. Every few steps we are stopped *by someone who wants to tell us their story. Under one shelter we meet Laretta. She tells us that their struggle is linked to that of their ancestors who worked as enslaved men and women on this land. She needs housing for herself and her five children. She needs a place to call home. She tells me that she wants 'success'.*

CHAPTER 13

Cheveley, August 1823

John Cheveley was in bed on the night of Monday 18 August, when he heard the sound of a bugle. He knew at once that it came from the Rifle Corps, and he was being called to muster. From down in the street he heard someone yell for him to make haste; that the slaves were in revolt and he must join the militia. 'A pretty piece of business this,' he thought to himself, 'to be called out of bed at this time of night, and go, I don't know where, for the pleasant chance of having my throat cut by these same savages.'

He climbed out of bed and hurried downstairs. There he found William Pattinson still in bed, who declared himself still recovering from fever and therefore unable to join the colony's heroic defence. Cheveley was minded to also stay behind. He had visions of a bullet through his head or a knife at his throat. But then he worried that someone might accuse him of being a coward, so he returned to his chamber to dress. 'I went on buckling on my armour,' he later recalled, 'muttering and grumbling, with that pretty confused and indefinable set of ideas running through my brain, not at all unusual on such sudden emergencies.'

It was still dark outside when he arrived at the parade ground. There he found a few dozen other men gathered and ready to join the fray. Among them was thirty-four-year-old Captain John Croal, the owner of two estates on the east coast and the man who would be his commanding officer. Looking around, Cheveley recognised the men with whom he had practised drilling. All of them worked in the stores or warehouses in town. Those with businesses outside Georgetown, like his friend Ben Hopkinson or the timber merchant Robert Edmonstone, must have already assembled and left with their units.

After a short muster, they marched in formation out of Georgetown and headed east, towards the sugar plantations. Nobody knew what was going on. There had been rumours in town earlier that day that something was taking place 'up the coast', but no more than that. Those with knowledge were keeping things secret, perhaps fearing that the details might cause panic.

They marched in the moonlight along the public road that ran parallel to the seashore, unsure how far they were going or what they were heading into. To their left they could hear the waves crashing onto the beach. To their right ran a deep ditch, and beyond that, the fields of the sugar estates. Suddenly the captain called a halt. There was a dark heap on the road. He shone a light on it, revealing the dead body of an enslaved man, apparently shot. This sent a chill through the group and awakened their senses. 'Keep a good lookout,' whispered the commander, 'and don't fire without orders.' They continued, more carefully now, looking left and right, expecting attack at any moment.

Ahead they came to the entrance of Vryheids Lust estate, home to Hendrick Van Cooten, the Dutch settler. A few steps further, they arrived at the remains of a small wooden bridge. Standing nearby was an enslaved man holding a musket and bayonet. The sight was shocking to the colonists, who had never seen a Black person holding a gun before, let alone one pointed at them. Two of the militiamen rushed forward and grabbed him by the collar. He immediately protested that he was on their side. He said that 'Massa Buckra' – the big boss – had sent him out to guide them to the dwelling house, and pointed to some planks that had been laid across the trench in place of the ruined bridge. Suspicious that they were being led into a trap, the group headed warily towards the plantation, looking out for the ambush that might fall on them at any minute. It never came. Fifteen minutes later, they arrived at Van Cooten's house. After swapping news, the Dutchman invited Captain Croal and his men to set up camp in the yard. Here they rested for the night.

The next morning, Tuesday 19 August, the militiamen continued east, coming first to Brothers and then Montrose, both estates eerily deserted, the enslaved men and women apparently having either joined the insurrection up the coast or gone into hiding, waiting for normality to return. Next they arrived at Felicity, where they met with Michael M'Turk. After exchanging information, they continued east along the public road until they came to Chateau Margo. Here too it was calm. There were no enslaved people in the fields, nor were there any to be found in the slave houses or farm sheds. Deeper into the estate, they came to the main house, from which ran an elderly man, his face covered with blood. 'We found the old proprietor, Lachlan Cummings, in an awful temper,' Cheveley later wrote; the enslaved abolitionists had treated him 'rather roughly', and in the fight over a musket that Cummings was endeavouring to load, he got his nose broken, presenting 'rather a piteous spectacle'.

Whilst Cummings had been allowed to stay in his house, the estate manager had been put in the stocks, which had entertained those watching, particularly the enslaved women. According to Cummings, the women had taken it in turns to walk up to the shackled manager and slap him in the face. Cheveley concluded that this was 'administered probably with no gentle hand but by no means an excessive chastisement, considering the free use of the cart whip which he had inflicted on them'. Once Cheveley and his colleagues had released the manager from the stocks, Cummings invited them into his house to shelter from the sun. 'He must have found his newly arrived friends rather more troublesome than his recently departed foes,' Cheveley later joked, 'as being exceedingly thirsty the whole party availed themselves without scruple of his drinkables.'

Later that afternoon, with the plantation secure, Cheveley and the other militiamen set off once again along the public road. After a few minutes, they came across a small group of enslaved men sitting around a fire. They were unarmed and appeared to be cooking dinner. 'Fire upon them,' screamed Croal without warning. Once the smoke dissipated, nobody was left around the steaming pots. It was not clear how many had been hit. Further on, they heard women and children calling out from the fields, begging for mercy. Someone near Cheveley shouted out, 'Tell the men to go back to work or we'll shoot.'

On the militiamen went. Mon Repos and Good Hope. Annandale and New Orange Nassau. Friendship, Vigilance and Elizabeth Hall. It was hard, deliberate work. Liberating the planters from their captivity. Making sure the estates were clear of abolitionists. Securing the buildings. Their progress was slowed even further by the fact that several wooden bridges had been destroyed. They were forced to take timber from nearby buildings and build temporary crossings. On and on they went, clearing one estate and then the next, into Tuesday evening.

It was dark when Cheveley's company reached the forty-first plantation, a desolate-looking cotton plantation named Bachelor's Adventure. Having marched more than fifteen miles, they were exhausted. It was quiet as they entered the yard in front of the main house. Here, in an exposed corner, they found five men and three women locked in the stocks, whom they quickly released. After hearing what had happened, Captain Croal asked if they could stay the night. The militiamen desperately needed some rest. One of the estate managers pointed to a nearby slave house where they could camp out. Cheveley and his comrades trudged gratefully over to the dirt-floored barracks. Too tired to care about the quality of accommodation, they were soon asleep.

*

A few hours later, Cheveley was woken by the sun. It was now the morning of Wednesday 20 August. Dressed and rifle in hand, he walked outside to assess his surroundings. Strewn across the dusty yard in front of the slave house were the bodies of more snoring reservists. There was also a further detachment of regulars — soldiers who served full-time in the British Army — who must have arrived from Georgetown during the night. There were about a hundred of them. Cheveley kept walking. To his left was the book-keeper's small house; to his right, the house where the manager lived. What concerned him most, however, was what lay in front of him. There in the cotton field on the other side of the public road, he saw that a large group of enslaved men and women had gathered. There had to be at least a hundred of them. A few carried muskets, cutlasses and knives. The rest brandished an assortment of home-made weapons fashioned from cane poles. As the light grew stronger, more freedom fighters appeared through the haze. There were a thousand of them. Then two thousand. The crowd grew larger and larger, until there were perhaps as many as four thousand men and women.

As he watched, Cheveley was joined by his comrades. Captain Croal instructed them to quickly form into two lines and prepare for battle. Even with the reinforcements who had arrived overnight, there were fewer than two hundred militiamen. As such, they were outnumbered twenty to one. The front row went down on one knee, pointing their rifles towards the cotton field. The back row stood stiffly behind. Then, following some unheard command, the enslaved abolitionists moved forward en masse towards the soldiers. As they walked, they shouted defiantly, until finally stopping at the public road, a hundred yards short of the militia line.

'It was an awful moment of suspense,' Cheveley later wrote. 'Everyone felt that the crisis had arrived when it was decided who should be masters.'

*O*n my tenth day in Guyana, I take a trip out to see one of the country's sugar estates. We drive out of Georgetown, across the long metal bridge that spans the Demerara River, and over to what the locals call the West Bank. There we drive through several villages, including Vreendenhop, which once belonged to John Gladstone.

The Co-operative Republic of Guyana nationalised the sugar industry in 1976 under the umbrella of the Guyana Sugar Corporation, or GuySuCo. Today, there are five mega-estates in operation, each hundreds of times larger than the original plantations. Sugar is still responsible for approximately 15 per cent of the country's annual revenue and 35 per cent of all agricultural production.

After an hour, we arrive at Uitvlugt (pronounced 'Iflut'). The estate manager, who is Indo-Guyanese, is on the phone when we walk into his office. He waves at us to sit at a large table covered with charts, reports and a plate stacked high with sandwiches. On one wall is a map of the estate showing which fields are in cultivation and which lie fallow. Another wall is covered with blackboard paint, upon which is chalked lists of those employed: field workers, factory workers, truck drivers, managers, totalling more than 1,200 people. Once he is off the phone, the manager explains that it costs around 31 cents to make a pound of sugar and he can sell it for a little more than 18 cents. The chief expense is labour. Such losses have plagued the industry for decades. He says, hopefully, that they will turn things around in the next few years.

The tour of the factory is next. A loud, smoke-filled building with metal walkways suspended high above giant cogs, conveyor belts and other amply greased machinery. The equipment is ancient. The boilers that heat the sugary syrup were installed in the 1940s. The rollers and drying pans are not much younger. The thick smell of warm molasses hangs in the air.

After that, we hop into the back of a pickup truck and are taken *out to the fields. The sky is cloudless; it's very hot. We drive along a dusty track, past fields tall with sugar canes of different varieties. After ten minutes, we stop next to a task gang hard at work. It's now 1.30 p.m. There are forty men scattered around, all of Indian descent. Agile, lean, immensely strong. Most wear baseball hats, long shirts, shorts, knee-high socks and work boots. Each has a small machete in his hand, and with an efficient motion they hack the canes, remove the leaves and dump the stalks onto a pile.*

I walk around the field and ask the men about their work. 'We start at six in the morning,' Vinan tells me, 'and we stop whenever we finish.' Sometimes this is 2 p.m., he says, 'sometimes it's six in the evening'.

The next man tells me his name is Kevin. 'It's hard work,' he says, 'very hard and little money.' He says he can cut four tons of cane in one day. I ask him why they burn the field before cutting. 'To get rid of the trash,' he says, by which he means the vegetation that grows around the cane. The cane itself, though charred, remains unburned. 'And the snakes, plenty of snakes,' he adds. The one he fears most is the labaria – 'serious snake', he says. Its poison can kill a man. As we talk, he doesn't stop cutting.

I walk around a heap of canes and find another man rhythmically hacking away. I don't catch his name. I ask him how long he can keep doing this job. He says he will likely stop in his forties. It's simply too hard to continue beyond that age. Many of the men develop back and neck issues from the heavy lifting, and kidney problems from the years of dehydration.

Back in the truck, I'm told that this harvesting method is called 'cut and load' – the canes are cut and loaded onto the canal punts. Remarkably, sugar cane is still harvested the same way it was back in the 1820s. Today the task gangs receive a small amount of money for their labour, but the work remains brutal.

CHAPTER 14

Jack, August 1823

Jack Gladstone was standing a hundred yards from John Cheveley. In his hand was the cutlass he had taken from the storehouse at Success. He surveyed the situation. To his left and right stretched a sea of enslaved abolitionists, nervous, unsure of what would happen next. In front of them, on the other side of the public road, were two lines of heavily armed British soldiers.

By this point, 10 a.m. on the third day of the insurrection, the uprising had spread across thirty estates, from Le Resouvenir in the west to Lancaster in the east. A handful of plantations on the other side of the Demerara River had also joined in. At least twelve thousand people were taking part in the insurrection, and maybe as many as fifteen thousand. As such, this was the largest slave revolt to take place in a British colony. Perhaps even more remarkable, though upwards of seventy overseers, managers and owners had been placed in stocks, there had been few reported casualties. It was a testament to the careful planning and strategy developed by Jack and the other ringleaders. By any measure, the uprising had so far been a dramatic success. They controlled more than twenty miles of coast. Morale was soaring, as was belief. Perhaps they could pull this off. They could force the colonists to deliver what had been promised from London and then go back to their estates. But they had not won yet. It was clear that today would be a crucial turning point.

Jack watched as a lone figure left the British ranks and rode out towards them. He appeared young, perhaps in his thirties. In one hand, he carried a flag of truce. As he approached, thousands of abolitionists began to jeer and whistle. Jack held up his hand, commanding silence, then walked towards the colonist. It would be a parley. The man in uniform introduced himself as Captain Croal and asked Jack what it was he wanted. Jack said that they knew the British king wished to set the enslaved women and men free. They simply wanted the governor to carry out the sovereign's wishes. Croal said that they had been deceived, that it was not the king's intention that they should be free. This must have astonished Jack. He had heard the truth from his friend Daniel and so many others. Was this soldier lying to his face? Taking a moment to compose himself, he replied that it was not fair that they had to work without rest. At the very least, they wanted Saturdays to dig their gardens and Sundays to attend church. From behind him, others called out that they wanted three days off.

Croal now sat up in his saddle. He looked beyond Jack and in a loud voice addressed the throng. Their rebellion was pointless, he told them; they must lay down their arms. Hundreds of men and women yelled back that they would continue the fight. They were going to march to Georgetown and would speak directly with the governor. Croal tried again, but once more he was shouted down. Realising that there was nothing more to be gained, he turned his horse around and trotted back to the colonist lines.

An hour later, another man rode out to speak to Jack. This time it was Lieutenant Colonel John Thomas Leahy, who was in overall command of the British forces. Jack presented Leahy with a piece of paper. It had been signed by three estate managers along the coast stating that they had been well treated by the abolitionists – by Jack in particular. In return, Leahy told Jack that Governor Murray had declared martial law the previous day, and gave him a copy of the proclamation. He explained that if the abolitionists attempted to march to town, even if their intention was simply to meet with the governor, they would be arrested and most likely hanged. If they wished to negotiate, it would have to take place with him right here. 'Catch the big buckra,' a heavily armed man standing close to Jack cried out. 'Tie him up, tie him up,' shouted someone else. Another called out that perhaps they could hold him hostage. No, Jack said, they must leave the colonel alone. Seeing there was no point in continuing the discussion, Leahy said that he would give them half an hour to surrender, and if they did not, he would be forced to fire upon them. Then, not wanting to outstay his welcome, he retreated back to his men.

A tense silence hung between the two lines. The militia kept their rifles trained on their targets across the public road. The abolitionists held their ground. Thirty minutes came and went. Nothing happened. And then Leahy called the order: 'Right face, march!' The line of soldiers headed towards the abolitionists, stopping less than fifty yards away. 'You Negroes,' the colonel shouted, 'I ask you once more, in the governor's name, will you lay down your arms and go to your work?'

Those around Jack yelled out, 'No!' and 'We fight for freedom.'

The colonel shouted, 'Fire!'

The sound of gunpowder exploding in a hundred rifles filled the air. Scores of men and women collapsed in the cotton field, screaming in pain, clutching at their wounds. Those close by tried to help, holding their fallen comrades, reaching to stop the bleeding.

Meanwhile, the militia front row reloaded while the men behind stepped forward and fired. Another hundred bullets were let loose. A handful of the freedom fighters fired back, but they had far fewer guns and little or no training. In less than fifteen minutes it was over. Hundreds of abolitionists were dead. It had been a bloodbath. Those able to escape had fled. Meanwhile, the militia kept loading and shooting, loading and shooting, loading and shooting.

Somehow Jack had avoided injury. His cutlass was useless in the firefight. As soon as he heard the command to shoot, he had turned and run into the cotton fields. He headed west, jumping over a ditch and into Elizabeth Hall. Then crossing Enterprise, Nonpareil and Coldingen. On and on he ran. If he gave himself up, he knew there would be only one outcome. Execution. So he continued towards Georgetown, retracing the route they had taken in the previous days – Strathspey, Vigilance, Friendship, New Orange Nassau, La Reconnaissance. But this time he avoided the public road, and the British soldiers, instead pushing his way through the fields that hugged the shoreline.

As the morning air heated up, he must have wondered about the next steps. How to build on all they had achieved: the thousands who had taken part, the discipline, the camaraderie, the hope. And how to respond to the overwhelming military force of the British militia. Surely, given that the enslaved people outnumbered the Europeans thirty to one, there must be a way to defeat them.

He needed to find his father, Quamina. To discuss what to do now. To devise their next plan of attack. To regroup. He needed to get back to Success.

I am very aware that I am not the first person to explore this history. That I owe an enormous debt to those who have gone before. Particularly those from Guyana.

I have been told by various people that it is not uncommon for researchers from Europe to make use of research and analysis carried out by West Indians without acknowledging their sources. This is, they say, another aspect of the legacy of slavery.

So while I'm in Georgetown, I reach out to various historians, political scientists and sociologists.

I first speak with Winston McGowan, a pre-eminent historian who for decades has written about the Demerara insurrection. In a half-hour conversation, he generously shares his insights. Winston tells me that the 1823 uprising was a critical moment in Guyana's history and that it had a huge impact on the anti-slavery movement in the UK.

I then have a Zoom conversation with Nigel Westmaas, who explains how the enslaved men and women used informal networks to communicate with each other. Nigel also encourages me to understand that the Demerara insurrection took place within the context of regional and global economic forces. That the rising costs of sugar production and marketing resulted in falling profits, and that this led many West Indian sugar traders to look for alternative ways of making money.

I also take part in a panel discussion with David Hinds from Arizona University and Dwayne Benjamin from the University of Guyana. Dwayne says that the 1823 uprising was not a 'success' because it did not immediately lead to the emancipation of the enslaved people. David replies that if you see the achievement of freedom as a process rather than a destination, you can definitely argue that 1823 had a significant impact on the abolition of slavery. And that therefore it was a 'success'.

I also speak to Cecilia McAlmont, historian at the University of Guyana. Sitting on upturned tree stumps in front of her house, and surrounded by orange and purple blossoming bushes, we discuss the 1823 uprising. Cecilia knows this period perhaps better than anyone I've met. 'We are doing very badly telling our young people about our history,' she tells me. 'Teaching them what they owe their ancestors, the contributions they made. As a descendant of some of these people, I give them credit for not being much more ...'

She pauses a moment, and takes a breath as she appears to remember the brutal conditions endured by her enslaved fore-parents. She then commends their 'passive resistance' and adds, 'It could have been more bloody than it was.'

CHAPTER 15

Cheveley, August 1823

'Well done, Rifles!' Colonel Leahy proclaimed when it was over. The militiamen now stood along the public road at ease, cleaning out their guns and swapping stories about what had just happened. The shooting had lasted less than a quarter of an hour.

As far as Cheveley was concerned, 'there was surely no great cause for glory over a victory so easily obtained'. In the end, he had fired only once, because his rifle had failed. Captain Croal rode up to find out why he had not shot more. Cheveley showed him his gun, and the officer appeared satisfied. As they marched away from Bachelor's Adventure, they passed the bodies of more than two hundred men and women. Not a single soldier had been injured, with the exception of a trumpeter who had rendered himself unconscious by drinking too much rum and had been set upon by the abolitionists. 'Whatever my abhorrence of slavery,' Cheveley later recalled, 'I felt I was justified in defending my own life and those of others in peril.'

Over the next few days, Cheveley and his fellow reservists continued east, away from Georgetown, going from one plantation to the next, rooting out any last remnants of the uprising. They had been joined by a number of regulars and were under the command of Colonel Leahy. As they progressed along the coast, they discovered scores of bedraggled colonists awaiting rescue. Some were holed up in their houses; others were hiding in remote sheds or field houses. There were even a few found cowering in their privies. It was dull, exhausting work. The insurrection was over, but the militia felt they were being followed, out there in the tall grass, just beyond the range of their guns. They could never quite relax. Sleep was impossible. They continued on under the burning sun, tormented by fatigue and thirst.

On one occasion, Colonel Leahy saw an abolitionist in a field close by and ordered Cheveley to go after him. As he drew near, Cheveley took a shot and missed. When he pulled the trigger a second time, nothing happened. There was clearly something wrong with his gun. He hammered away at the flint but it made no difference. After it was clear that the enslaved man had disappeared, Leahy asked Cheveley, in front of everyone, whether he had intentionally chosen not to shoot the man. Cheveley protested his innocence, but his commander appeared not to believe him and walked away. The unit resumed their march. After taking a moment to pull himself together, Cheveley ran to join them on the public road.

On they went. One estate, and then another. Beehive and then Greenfield. Orange Nassau and then Grove, followed by Unity. Finally they arrived at Lancaster. It was twenty-two hard miles from Georgetown, the sixty-fifth estate along the north coast and the last before the Mahaica River crossing. Here they found two wounded overseers, one of whom had been shot three times near the wrist. The doctor with the militia unit, who was a bit of a wag, announced that the only solution was to amputate, and proceeded to walk around the buildings looking for a suitable carving implement. When he returned, he admitted his prank and quickly removed the shot from the man's arm. Everyone laughed; it was a moment of genuine *esprit de corps*.

Cheveley was glad of the humour. Over the past few hours, his comrades-in-arms had looked at him strangely. Like he was an outsider. He had heard them calling him a 'saint', not to his face, but quietly, to each other, away from him. He knew what this meant. They thought he was like one of those missionaries who were sympathetic to the slaves. He would keep his head down and try and stay out of trouble. Hopefully this campaign would soon be over and he could return to the peace and quiet of the general store.

Once the Lancaster estate was secured, Leahy turned his men around and they started the long trek back towards Georgetown. After crossing sixteen plantations, they came to Cove, which was owned by Cheveley's friend Ben Hopkinson. When asked if there were any enslaved people still on the plantation, Hopkinson led them to one of the estate's buildings. Inside they found a handful of men hiding out, including Dablin, the head driver. Colonel Leahy declared that he was immediately convening a court martial, and set about interrogating Dablin. He was just getting started when he saw a tall mixed-race man leaving the back of the house. Once again he chose Cheveley to go after the runaway.

When Cheveley caught up with him, the man was trembling in fear. 'Oh massa,' he said, 'are you going to kill me? I am innocent.'

Having determined that the man's name was Alick, Cheveley tried to calm him, saying, 'Suppose you are innocent, you'll come to no harm. You tell the truth, that's all.' Reluctantly the man accompanied him back to the house.

As they approached, they found Colonel Leahy and the others standing in the yard. One of them held Dablin, whose hands were now tied behind his back. The trial was apparently over. It had lasted only a few minutes. 'Bring that fellow to the front,' commanded Leahy, pointing at Dablin. There was silence as the prisoner was pushed forward. 'Now, you rascal,' Leahy said, 'what have you to say for yourself?' Dablin vigorously protested his innocence, betraying no sense of guilt or fear. Cheveley recalled that he was 'much moved by the man's appeal'.

At this point, Hopkinson stepped forward and said, 'Colonel Leahy, I must beg to intercede for this man. I have always found him a most faithful servant; I cannot believe he is guilty. Let me entreat you to give his case further consideration.'

This angered the colonel. 'Who are you, mister? Go back to mind your own business. I am sent to punish these fellows and by God they shall receive their deserts.' Then, looking at two regulars standing nearby, he said, 'Tie that fellow up.'

The soldiers took Dablin over to a coconut tree that stood in front of the house, pushed him to the ground in a sitting position and looped a rope around his body and then round the trunk of the tree. Throughout, Dablin protested that he'd done nothing wrong, over and over. Hopkinson tried again. 'Colonel Leahy, I will stake my life upon that man's innocence. Let me beg you, sir, not to be so precipitate. I entreat you to spare him till his case can be more fully investigated.'

This did little to please the colonel. 'I'll tell you what it is, sir, it's of no use your talking to me. You're acting from interested motives and by God if you talk to me any longer I'll put you under arms and send you down to the governor. If you are afraid of losing your Negroes I am not coming up here to be humbugged by you and have all this trouble for nothing. Let alone to do my duty, and you may all sleep quiet in your beds for years to come, but if I am to be interfered with, you'll all have your throats cut before you're twelve months older.' Leahy now turned to the prisoner. 'Pray to God, Daddy!' he said. 'Pray to God.' Then he gave the command to one of the regulars standing nearby, 'Shoot him.' The soldier fired his gun. Dablin moaned and collapsed; several men and women nearby screamed. Cheveley later recalled that he felt 'amazed' and 'bewildered'. This was the first time he had witnessed an execution.

But they were not finished. For Alick, who Cheveley was still holding on to and who had witnessed the killing of Dablin, was then called forward. 'Now what have you to say for yourself?' demanded Leahy.

'Mr Buckra Massa, I'm innocent, truly,' said Alick.

This seemed to enrage the colonel, who shouted, 'You lie, you rascal, haven't we the clearest evidence that you were one of the ringleaders.' Alick repeated that he had nothing to do with the rebellion. 'You scoundrel,' screamed the colonel, now furious, 'do you persist in telling me such lies? Do you know you'll be in hell in five minutes?' He then instructed Cheveley to tie the prisoner to a nearby tree, Alick protesting his innocence all the while.

Not knowing what else to do, Cheveley quickly encouraged Alick to ask Jesus Christ for mercy, and then stepped away. The colonel gave the command, again to one of the regulars, and Alick was shot in the head. It had all happened so fast. Cheveley was sick with guilt, for leading the captive back to the colonel, for doing nothing while he underwent the thinnest of trials, for tying him up for his execution. From there, however, the 'mission of death', as he later called it, only grew worse.

At the next estate, Nabaclis – where Mary Walrand and her husband had been held captive just days earlier – the troop met a large group of enslaved men, all of whom immediately surrendered. Twelve of them were deemed ringleaders, and, after a brief investigation, were taken outside and shot by the regulars. The bodies were laid out on the grass and the troop moved on to the next plantation. They spent the night in a cramped cotton shed at Coldingen, and the following morning Leahy split off with his regulars to continue his grisly suppression efforts. Cheveley's unit of reservists was tasked with stopping off at each estate to pick up the already arrested ringleaders and escort them back to Georgetown.

Within a short time, they had a long line of abolitionists chained together in a coffle, including two of the key figures, Prince and Telemachus. Late in the afternoon, about five miles from Georgetown, the group halted for a water break. Seeing an opportunity, Prince slipped off his chains and made a dash for it. As he was the nearest person, Cheveley ran after him. He was followed by another militiaman, who shouted, 'Fire, Cheveley.' Cheveley lifted his rifle, took aim and missed. Another gun went off and

Prince was hit. They left his body in the long grass. Back with the others, Cheveley was mocked for yet another failed effort. 'Who let him run away?' someone called. 'Why, Cheveley,' came the reply, to much derision.

On Saturday 23 August, they arrived back in Georgetown with the prisoners in tow. The streets were full of people, who cheered them as they marched by, welcoming them back as heroes. Some called out, 'Brave Rifles.' Others cried, 'Pity!' when they saw the state of the militiamen. Many shouted insults at the prisoners. It had been five days since Cheveley had first set off. He had marched more than fifty miles, cleared more than a dozen plantations and taken part in numerous skirmishes. He was exhausted, filthy and ready for it all to be over. After depositing the abolitionists in the colonial jail, he headed home for a wash.

Two days later, however, he was called out again, this time to La Bonne Intention plantation, ten miles east of Georgetown and two estates beyond Success. As he walked up to the main buildings, he saw fifteen enslaved men lined up along a ditch, awaiting execution. There had been no trial, no evidence taken, no witnesses called. Across from those sentenced to death stood a line of reservists. Up till now, executions had been carried out by regulars, soldiers with some experience with their rifles. Not now. Some of the reservists, Cheveley later remembered, showed 'the greatest repugnance' at the task in front of them. Others 'flatly declared they would not be executioners'. Their commanding officer stepped up and reminded them that the colony was under martial law and failure to obey orders was punishable by death. This seemed to change their minds.

The order was given and the guns fired. Being amateurs, their aim was poor. 'It was a fearful sight,' wrote Cheveley. 'Some few were killed outright but many were struck by balls in parts that were not immediately vital, and were long dying.' Soon Cheveley and the others were marching off the plantation. He turned to see one of those shot lift his head and chest from the ground and call out for help.

After several hours, they arrived at Beeter Verwagting, which happened to be run by another friend of Cheveley's, Baron Grovesting. Seeing his friend look pale and horrified, the baron brought him some coffee and bread, but Cheveley did not have the stomach for it. A few minutes later, it was time to execute another group of hastily seized enslaved people who were believed to have taken part in the rebellion. Once more, as far as he could determine, there had been no trial; certainly not one of any substance. Again the execution went badly. One of those struck, a mixed-race man who worked on the plantation, was shot in the bowels. 'I can't be dead,' he cried holding his writhing innards. 'Oh God, I can't be dead.'

Two men were ordered to shoot him again. They fired their muskets. Still the man lived, and called out again, until their commander, Lieutenant Owen Kerman, walked up, placed his rifle against his head and pulled the trigger. 'Horror upon horror, it misfired,' Cheveley remembered. Someone else ran up and this time successfully put the enslaved man out of his misery. Those remaining were forced to decapitate the bodies with their knives. They were then told to sharpen the ends of cane poles and place the heads on top, and then stick these at the entrance to the plantation as a warning to anyone who was considering participation in a revolt or insurrection.

Cheveley wrote that these last few days had been 'odious and painful and sickening'.

As soon as he was back in Georgetown, Cheveley went in search of his boss. Finding him at the store, he told Pattinson that he was desperate to leave the colony. The state of the business continued to be perilous, he said, and a visit to England would hopefully sort that out. He would meet with Pattinson's brother, John, and together they would come up with a plan. But more than this, the suppression of the uprising had been horrific and he needed some time away. Watching the executions of the enslaved people had left him deeply traumatised. It was worse than any childhood nightmare.

Seeing the dreadful state of his former employee now business partner, and perhaps thinking it would be of some commercial advantage to have him be one of the first to reach England with news of the insurrection, Pattinson said that he would help Cheveley leave the colony. To do this, he had to secure a letter of passage from the governor. Cheveley was not sure how it was accomplished – after all, the commander-in-chief had plenty else on his mind at this time – but a few hours later, the letter arrived.

Before leaving, he had one more thing to do. He hurried over to the barracks and tracked down Lieutenant Rainey, one of his superior officers. After explaining his plans, Cheveley begged permission to leave. Not only did the officer give his blessing, but he said he wished he could go home himself, and asked that he be remembered to his friends back in Scotland. They shook hands and Cheveley ran down to the docks and boarded the *Glenbervie*. Twenty-four hours after returning to Georgetown, Militiaman Cheveley was headed for Glasgow.

'It was a great relief,' he later wrote, 'to be freed from the business turmoil of the last two years and the tumult of the last two weeks.'

*W*hile I'm in Guyana, I visit Bachelor's Adventure. I'm taken around by Ras Blackman, a social worker and community historian who grew up in the village. He shows me the area between the public road and the coast that used to be a cotton field. This was where the enslaved abolitionists stood and were shot down by the militia. Today it's a swathe of brownish scrubland surrounded by a few single-storey houses made of concrete blocks.

Next to the public road stands an obelisk monument commemorating this key moment in their uprising. It's five feet tall, painted white, has '1823' emblazoned at its tip and is surrounded by a low black metal fence.

Each year, Ras meets with others to remember the massacre at Bachelor's Adventure and the bravery of the abolitionists who took part in the insurrection.

I am truly shocked by the brutality and scale of the British militia's response to the uprising. More than two hundred abolitionists were killed during the battle at Bachelor's Adventure. Between five hundred and a thousand people were killed in total during and after the insurrection. Maybe more. This is more than the official number killed in the 1919 Amritsar massacre (when the British Indian Army opened fire on a crowd of unarmed civilians), but I've never heard of the 'Demerara Massacre' or equivalent.

Growing up, I learned about slavery in the USA. I saw the movies. Read the books. But few if any of us – and here I'm talking about my White friends, acquaintances, family – speak about British slavery in the Caribbean. Its scale. Its horrors. Why is this?

An answer, at least in part, is given in a few lines from one of Ras Blackman's poems 'Sugar Cane', which he recites to me from memory. Here are a few lines:

Kings they brought from African lands
To work as slave in their back lands
Producing sugar under their plans
Black queens they whipped on the plantations
To strengthen their hold on colonization
While we see a massa enjoy their destruction.

So why do so few White people talk about slavery? Fear. Denial.
Confusion. Guilt. Ignorance. Perhaps all of the above.

CHAPTER 16

Jack, August 1823

It was dark by the time Jack arrived at Success. Rather than returning to his home, where he might be found, he hid in one of the sugar cane fields. There he waited. A few hours later, around 8 p.m., he was joined by his father, who brought a basket containing two bottles of porter beer and some bread. As he ate, Jack updated Quamina on what had taken place earlier that day at Bachelor's Adventure. The thousands of enslaved men and women who had stood bravely in the cotton field, the terrifying sound of a hundred rifles firing at once, the bodies falling all around him, and then his escape. The news must have been shocking for Quamina, who had only days before urged restraint and caution.

Once Jack had completed his report, Quamina said that he had just been to see John Smith at his house. The missionary had told him that 'now that you have begun, you must go on with it'. Surrender would almost certainly result in arrest and execution. Their best option was to hide, regroup and reassess. It was now the father's turn to urge action. The British militia would surely soon arrive at Success looking for those who had taken part in the insurrection. Despite Jack's exhaustion, they had to leave immediately. They had to hide in the bush.

After gathering a few belongings, Jack and Quamina set off. With them went eighteen women and men from local estates, including Cudjo, Quabino, Sammy, and Primo, the latter having been present at the Middle Walk meeting the day before the uprising. In addition to Jack's cutlass, they had two guns. They also carried two copies of the Bible, a hymnal and several hammocks. The party headed due south, away from the coast, past the windmill and boiling house and along the dusty track that took them towards the back of the estate. There was nobody at work; the fields had been deserted since the start of the uprising. After an hour's trek, they came to the Crown Dam, the raised embankment that marked the rear of the estate. They were now about three miles from the public road and the estate manager's house.

Having climbed over the Crown Dam, they entered a meadow of razor grass, whose edges were sharp enough to slice the skin. The ground was swampy, cooling their feet. Next came a wall of thick vegetation made up of black sage, white knotweed and other thorny plants. A few hundred yards further on, they reached a bank of tall ité palms, more than forty feet high and casting dark shadows on the undergrowth beneath. This was the bush. A short distance in, they found a dry spot that was well concealed. Here they stopped and made camp.

In many ways, it might have made sense for the fugitives to keep going south, through the bush and into the wilderness beyond. Yet even though the remoteness of the interior would have provided additional cover, the strangeness of those lands was also a problem for the runaways, who had spent their lives on the sugar and cotton estates along the Atlantic coast. They also were not ready to give up on the uprising. If they were going to keep in touch with their friends and families, they would have to remain close to the plantations. For now, at least, they would remain here in the bush.

As the days progressed, Jack and his companions developed a routine. They travelled by day, agile and light. At night, they used large leaves and branches to conceal their hides. They only cooked when it was dark, not wanting the smoke to give their position away. Luckily, the weather was their ally. For the most part it was dry and, under the thick canopy, not too hot. If they had spent May or June in the bush, when it often rained every day and the water flooded the few dry spots, it would have been far more difficult to survive out there for any length of time.

Thirst was not a problem, given the abundant supply of fresh water. The alleviation of hunger took some effort, but there was plenty of food available. Wild rabbits, deer and iguana could be caught with little effort, while a variety of fish swam in the creeks and waterways, including hassar, houri and patwa. In addition, the centre of the ité palm was edible and in their trunks could be found tacoma worms, whose heads were broken off and then roasted on the fire like marshmallows. Life in the bush, however, was not easy. At night, the fugitives were tormented by mosquitoes and other insects. They were also dealing with the consequences of the uprising. Many had lost close family and friends; several had sustained injuries during the fight. As the days progressed, it became harder to maintain morale.

It was around the seventh day of their exile that Primo, according to his later testimony, declared that he had had enough; he was ready to return to his plantation. Apparently Quamina reacted angrily to this. Primo was being foolish, he said; the planters would never allow them to simply go back to the sugar fields. At best they would receive hundreds of lashes; at worst they would swing from the gallows. Think of all the sacrifice, he shouted; if they gave up now, what would it all mean? Surely they were entitled to their freedom? Primo shot back that he wasn't sure any more; he didn't believe they could win their liberty. The colonists were too strong, too powerful. Quamina insisted they could win. If Primo wanted to leave, he was free to go, but he, Quamina, would remain in the bush, and no buckra would take him alive. After a few minutes' more discussion, Primo agreed to stay with the group.

But the tension remained. A few nights later, they had another heated argument. This time it was about where to camp. Quamina said he wanted to hide around Mahaica Creek on the other side of Lancaster plantation. There was plenty of cover there, he said, and it was close enough to the estates to keep in touch with their friends. Joseph said he knew of a good spot that was located further away and suggested they head there. Nobody would find it, he said; they would be safe. Others had different ideas, but Jack agreed with his father. Best to remain where they were familiar with the landscape. With Jack's support, the decision was made. They would stay close to the plantations.

On 30 August 1823, a public notice was placed in the *Demerara Royal Gazette*. Under the headline 'ONE THOUSAND GUILDERS!', the announcement declared that a reward was available to any person who apprehended 'Quamina and Jack, of Plantation Success, two noted ringleaders of the rebellion'. The notice described Jack as '6 feet 2 inches, about 25 years of age, handsome, well made, rather an European nose, good white teeth'. The runaways, the advertisement continued, 'are accompanied by eight other Negroes, together with ten women'.

The following day, 31 August, Governor Murray sent a letter to Lord Bathurst, secretary of state for war and the colonies, in London. He had been providing periodic updates on the uprising since its start two weeks earlier.

My Lord,
The peaceable aspect which affairs had assumed here, when I last had the honour to report to your Lordship (26th August) has, I am happy to acquaint your Lordship, not been materially interrupted since an evil spirit does, however, still manifest itself: there are about a hundred Negroes still unaccounted for, and about the same number of arms. The two principal leaders belong to Plantation Success, Quamina Gladstone and his son Jack, who have escaped into the woods with a small party of men, and eight or ten women. They are pursued by a party of militia, under Captain M'Turk, 2nd battalion Demerara

militia, and sixty Indians. Major St Gravesande, with a party of the same battalion, and the Mahaiconi Indians, have also moved up the Mahaica Creek to intercept them. I have instituted a commission to collect facts relative to the revolt, that your Lordship may be furnished with every authentic information on the subject. The Commissioners are not to embody any opinion. I have the honour to be, my Lord, Your Lordship's most obedient humble servant,

John Murray

Over the next few days, scores of people contacted the governor's office with sightings of Jack and his band of fugitives. Each lead was followed up and suspected conspirators were dragged in for questioning, but so far nothing solid had resulted. On 4 September, Murray again wrote to Bathurst in London. 'The parties detached into the woods have returned, after having ascertained that the rebels had previously moved outwards.' They had so far failed to track down the renegades. After a few days' rest, he would send Captain M'Turk and his men back out. Hopefully they would be luckier next time.

On 6 September, after two weeks in the bush, Jack left his comrades and visited Chateau Margo, the estate immediately to the east of Success. It might have been to collect information. Or maybe he wished to gather supplies. Whatever his reason, he was inside one of the slave houses when, a little after midday, he heard a commotion outside. It was the unmistakable sound of stamping hooves and the clatter of muskets being drawn, followed by a loud voice of authority issuing an ultimatum that he either surrender himself or the building would be stormed. Somebody must have given him away.

He had few good alternatives. He could rush through the door and make a run for it, but the odds of survival were slim. He could make a stand, but it was unlikely the colonists would easily give up their siege. He waited for five minutes, then ten, then twenty. His pursuers, how many he did not know, remained outside. Minutes passed into hours. Finally, around 3 p.m., an order was given to enter. Realising he had no choice, Jack pushed open the door. Immediately, three militiamen grabbed him and yanked him out. After the darkness inside, the light was dazzling. There were a lot of them. A few dozen militia, at least forty indigenous people and two men on horseback. One he didn't know; the other, the man in charge, he instantly recognised. It was Michael M'Turk, the burgher captain from Felicity.

As Jack stood outside, M'Turk sent more men in to search for other abolitionists. A few moments later, they came out holding a woman. She had been hiding in the rafters, they said. Concluding that she was Jack's girlfriend and had nothing to do with the uprising, they let her walk away. Half an hour later, after a further exploration of the building confirmed that there was nobody else inside, M'Turk said it was time to call it a day. Jack's arms were placed in irons and a rope was tied around his neck. He would be escorted to Georgetown, where he would be deposited in the colonial jail.

The colonial jail was a two-storey wooden building located on Camp Street, three blocks from the Demerara River and a few steps from the guardhouse. Traditionally it was home to two types of criminals. The first comprised petty thieves, prostitutes, debtors and a handful of murderers and violent assailants. The second and much larger group was made up of enslaved people adjudged in some way delinquent. This included runaways, people who re-peatedly refused to work, and those caught out on the street after 8 p.m. without a pass.

Jack was placed in one of the cells. It was a damp and windowless stone-walled room that measured ten feet by twelve. There was no bed or blanket. Nor was there a chamber pot. Defecation was done in a squalid corner. He was not alone. For now there was a third population residing in the prison: those who had taken part in the uprising. There were over fifty abolitionists being held there, including some of the ringleaders, such as Telemachus, Paris, Sandy, Manuel, Joseph and Seaton. It was from his cellmates that Jack would have learned what had happened while he had been hiding in the bush.

Two weeks earlier, on 26 August, the governor had opened a court martial. The first to be tried were Natt from Enterprise plantation and Louis from Plaisance. There was no lawyer to advise them. The only person available to them was the timber merchant Robert Edmonstone, who served as an interpreter. The proceedings had lasted only a few hours and the two accused had been found guilty of taking part in a rebellion and sentenced to death. At 5 p.m. that very day, they had been marched through town to the parade grounds. First came the advance guard, then eight enslaved people carrying two wooden coffins. Next were the prisoners, then the garrison chaplain and the members of the court. At the rear was a military band, which played a dead march, along with a detachment from the 1st Battalion Demerara Militia.

Once they reached the parade grounds, Natt and Louis were walked up to the freshly erected gallows whilst the militia formed a square around them. Their sentence was read out to them, and then, without further ado, a cord was pulled, the drop-board sprang open and their bodies fell through. Their deaths were announced by the firing of a single rifle.

The following day, two more abolitionists were marched out to the parade ground: Murphy of Foulis and Harry of Good Hope. With a rope around his neck, Murphy proclaimed his innocence and begged for his life. According to one observer, 'he was so little resigned to his fate that the executioner was peremptorily ordered to do his duty without delay'. The next day, 28 August, four more were hanged. There was some mistake with the rigging – the rope was too long – so that three of these hit the ground. Two appeared senseless, but one sat up and seemed to have survived, until a minute later he fell over. A doctor declared him dead shortly after.

Eleven days after arriving in prison, Jack heard terrible news. Michael M'Turk had gone out on the hunt again, this time supported by Lieutenant Nurse and a band of indigenous trackers. Around 4 p.m., they discovered one of the abolitionists hiding near the Crown Dam at the back of Chateau Margo. M'Turk told him that he would spare his life if he took him to the others. He agreed, and led them deeper into the bush. It was then that they saw movement. According to M'Turk, they called out to the fugitive to stop, but when he didn't, one of the indigenous men raised his rifle and fired. M'Turk approached the body to check for a pulse. There was none. He turned it over. It was Quamina. With dusk upon them, the party headed back to Felicity.

Early the next day, M'Turk set off on horseback towards Success, pulling Quamina's body behind him. At the entrance to the plantation, a large crowd awaited, including all the enslaved men, women and children from the neighbouring estates. At the centre of the gathering was a wooden gibbet, which had been built overnight. Two of the militiamen grabbed a metal chain, wrapped it around Quamina's body and hoisted it onto the scaffold.

The following morning, 18 September, less than twenty-four hours after hearing of his father's gruesome lynching, Jack was told that he was required to appear before the court martial.

PART 3

THE TRIAL

Oh those white people have small hearts who can only feel for themselves.

Mary Prince

British historians write almost as if Britain had introduced Negro slavery solely for the satisfaction of abolishing it.

Eric Williams

CHAPTER 17

Jack, September 1823

Given that the first police force in the British Empire would not be established until 1829, and the first Director of Public Prosecutions was not appointed until 1880, the English criminal justice system of the early nineteenth century was very different to that of its end.

In 1820s London, for instance, a suspect would be arrested by a constable, watchman or even private detective and held in prison pending trial. For serious crimes, such as murder and treason, trials took place in courts of assize, such as the Old Bailey in London, and were subject to criminal law and guided by precedent. They were overseen by representatives of His Majesty's judicial system – judges, clerks, magistrates, bailiffs – and their verdicts were typically handed down by juries, comprising property-owning men. The facts of the case were normally presented by the victim of the crime, supported by witnesses, who provided evidence under the questioning of the judge. Guilty verdicts in cases of murder, rape and treason – even lesser offences such as poaching, burglary and criminal damage – could all end in a trip to the gallows.

In previous decades, it had been unusual to see lawyers assisting defendants in court, even for murder cases. This was now changing, with the arrival of barristers who aggressively, and successfully, advocated for their clients' rights. In 1740, less than 1 per cent of defendants had counsel; this rose to 20 per cent by 1800 and then to more than 30 per cent by 1820. The success of such advocates would lead to bills being introduced to Parliament requiring that all felons be given access to counsel. Many of those supporting such legislation were also abolitionists.

For the slave insurrection trials that took place in Georgetown during the late summer and early autumn of 1823, however, few of the niceties of a London court applied. First, the governor's proclamation of martial law was still in force, so typical criminal protocols were irrelevant. The abolitionists were to be treated as enemy combatants rather than criminals and would be tried under military law. Second, the accused were enslaved people. As such, normal rules did not pertain. The testimony of an enslaved person or freed Black man or woman was not considered by the court to be as reliable as that of a European. Third, and to make matters even more complicated, Demerara was subject to the Dutch law inherited when the British took control of the colony in 1814.

It was against this confusing backdrop that, early on the morning of Thursday 18 September 1823, almost exactly a month since the start of the uprising, a jailer approached the cell where Jack Gladstone was held, unlocked the door, placed a pair of manacles on his wrists, and handed him over to two guards. He was then escorted outside and marched up Brick Dam, the oldest street in the city, towards the Demerara River. It was early, so there were few people on the streets. Those who were up and about watched as the prisoner went by. They would likely have known that he was one of the leaders of the uprising; news of that day's trial had spread widely amongst the city's residents. September weather in Demerara was typically hot and dry, and today was no exception. It was already well over eighty degrees Fahrenheit. Within a few minutes, Jack's shirt was damp with sweat.

A frequent visitor to the capital city, Jack would have known the landmarks as they walked by. The old parade ground, where the soldiers used to train. The stone-walled arsenal that guarded the army's ordnance. Right onto High Street and up to the court of justice, a large white building one hundred feet long and two and a half storeys high. This was where enslaved men and women were typically tried and sentenced. But they did not stop here. Instead they continued on, past the fire house and the marketplace, where free men and women sold their vegetables and other goods, then the butchers' shambles, where one could purchase freshly slaughtered pork, beef and mutton, until finally they arrived at their destination: a two-storey wooden structure that stood on the corner of High Street and South Street. This was Colony House.

Jack was led into the building through a side door and into a large wood-panelled room on the ground floor. He was escorted to a high-backed wooden chair at the front of the room. Next to him, behind a table, sat Victor Amadius Heyliger. Normally Heyliger worked as the colony's fiscal. Today he would be acting as judge advocate, equivalent to the role of prosecutor in a criminal court. On the other side of him was his assistant along with various civil servants, whose job it was to ensure the smooth running of the proceedings, and an interpreter who would translate for witnesses who spoke creole.

Behind Jack, the room was filled with people wishing to witness the day's proceedings. Sitting expectantly upon the wooden benches were business owners and residents from Georgetown, including Robert Edmonstone and William Pattinson; managers and overseers from plantations across the colony, such as M'Turk, Stewart and Hamilton; as well as a handful of curious visitors from overseas who happened to be in the city at the time. Also amongst the assembled were journalists from the colony's main newspapers, the *Demerara Royal Gazette* and the *Guiana Chronicle*, along with the recently founded *Colonist*. Each was eager to record the dramatic happenings for their readers unable to attend. Jack Gladstone was the only Black person in the room. He was also the only one not to be dressed in formal attire. He was still wearing the same dank clothes that he had been captured in, smeared, stained and odorous after his time hiding in the bush.

At 10 a.m. precisely, the clerk called the room to order. Everyone present stood as Lieutenant Colonel Stephen Arthur Goodman walked in. As commandant of the Georgetown Brigade of Militia, Goodman had been appointed president of the court martial. He had had a celebrated career in the British Army, having commanded the light companies of Stewart's brigade of Hill's division at the Battle of Talavera and served as deputy judge-advocate of Wellington's army in the Waterloo campaign. He had arrived in the Caribbean in 1819, and for the past two years had been the colony's vendue master. As such, the man presiding over Jack's trial was also the man in charge of the valuation, sale and transfer of enslaved people in Demerara.

Goodman now asked for the members of the court martial to be brought in. A few moments later, twelve White men took their seats to Jack's left. They were the equivalent of a jury in a criminal trial and were no more independent than the president. Eleven had been active in the suppression of the slave uprising, as either professional soldiers or reservists, and the twelfth was Charles Wray, the colony's chief justice. Wray had no military experience and only qualified to be a member of the court martial by having been gazetted into the Demerara militia just days before the trial's start. All the members of the court martial wore military uniforms, declaring not only their allegiance to the Crown but also their support of those who had so recently suppressed the uprising.

With a gesture, the president urged Victor Amadius Heyliger to begin his case. The fiscal took to his feet, turned towards the members of the court martial and read out the charges against Jack: 'For causing, exciting and promoting revolt and rebellion against the peace of our Sovereign Lord the King,' he proclaimed, 'and also for having, on or about the night of Monday the 18th of August last, been actively engaged in such revolt and rebellion; and further, for acting as a chief or leader or headman in such revolt and rebellion; and also aiding and assisting others therein.' The president told the defendant to stand, and asked how he pleaded. Jack rose as instructed and declared in a strong voice so that all could hear: 'Not guilty.'

The fiscal's first witness was Dumfries, a carpenter who, like Jack, worked on the Success plantation. After taking the oath, Dumfries said the defendant had sent him to the Rome plantation to recruit people for the uprising. Then, a few hours before the start of the revolt, he saw Jack and his father in the cooper's shop. This was when he had heard Quamina 'endeavouring to prevent him [Jack] from commencing the war'. According to the witness, Jack had said that 'the time had past already'. The implication was clear: Jack Gladstone was the decision-maker, and despite his own father's advice to desist, he had chosen to proceed with the uprising.

Having never appeared before at a trial – he had worked hard to keep out of trouble – Jack must have felt overwhelmed as he listened to all this. There was no one to help him navigate the process. Nobody to explain the protocols or suggest strategies, or to clarify the baroque legal language. After all, he was representing himself, the court having failed to assign him an advocate.

He raised his hand. Seeing this, the president dipped his head, giving him permission to speak. The defendant stood, and in a firm voice asked if he could examine the witness. He was told he could. Thinking it important to demonstrate from the very start of the trial that he had protected the colonists during the uprising, Jack asked Dumfries about his treatment of the Success estate manager. 'Did you not perceive me rescue Mr Stewart from the stocks?' he asked. The witness nodded his head in agreement. Jack paused, and then asked another question. 'And did I not take him to the dwelling house and stand guard at the front door where Richard wished to make an attack on him, and did I not prevent the attack?' Again Dumfries confirmed this was true. Jack sat down, indicating that he had no further questions. His testimony over, Dumfries was told to leave the stand.

Malcom Murchieson, the overseer of Success, was now called to give evidence. Heyliger asked him about Jack's role in the uprising. Murchieson said that Stewart had heard from M'Turk that Jack was the leader of the enslaved people and that they must arrest him. He said that they seized him in the cooper's shed and then took him away from the plantation. Jack was then rescued by some associates, during which time the witness said he was 'assaulted'.

When it was Jack's turn to cross-examine, he didn't need to be prompted by the president. He was getting into the rhythm of things now. 'At the time Dick, Windsor and Beffany and others came to release me,' he said, with growing confidence, 'did not Dick aim a blow at you with a cutlass?' The witness said that he did. 'Did I not prevent him from chopping you?' Again Murchieson said that yes, he did. 'At the time you jumped in the company canal, when Richard and others were coming after you, did I not assist you, and prevent those people from attacking you?' 'Yes, you did,' replied the witness, adding that 'it was a deep canal'. Many of those watching laughed at this last comment, releasing some of the tension in the room.

Over the rest of Thursday and into Friday, this pattern continued. More than twenty witnesses were called, first by the fiscal and then by the defendant. A statement by Jack's friend Daniel, the government clerk, was read out. Captain Croal and Lieutenant Leahy both appeared and provided evidence, as did John Stewart. There was little disagreement amongst them; the story was always the same: that Jack had been the instigator of the uprising, that he had led the abolitionists in various skirmishes, but – and this was emphasised again and again – that he had made valiant efforts to stop violence against the colonists.

As the trial progressed, one of the mysteries was revealed: how Jack's plans had been discovered by the colonists. According to various witnesses, it had started with Joe, a mixed-race domestic servant who worked at Le Reduit, an estate between Success and

Georgetown. Having heard that trouble might be starting on the east coast, and anxious that this might affect his position (which was preferable to working in a field), Joe had asked his friend Donderdag to eavesdrop on the ringleaders. A few days later, on Sunday 17 August, Donderdag had managed to take part in the discussion at the Middle Walk, and the following day had passed along what he had learned to Joe, who in turn informed the owner of Le Reduit. Immediately recognising the significance of the intelligence, this owner had ridden to town to tell the governor. Along the way, he had stopped by Michael M'Turk's house, warning him about the impending revolt. This was when M'Turk had ordered Jack's arrest.

On Friday evening, at the end of a long day in court, Jack was returned to the jail, walking back under escort the same way he had come that morning. His cellmates must have been curious, for soon they would face their own hearings. How had it gone? Who was in court? What had been said? What would happen tomorrow? After listening to people talk for more than eight hours, Jack might have preferred some time for himself. Or maybe he enjoyed unpacking the day's events, planning for what would happen the next morning. The record is not clear.

What we do know is that after dinner – which was typically a bland gruel with some stale bread – he received a surprise visitor. It was Charles Herbert, a young barrister newly arrived from London, who offered his help. Herbert said that having heard the day's evidence, it was his view that Jack's case was extremely weak and almost certain to end in the death sentence. He suggested that he help Jack compose a statement that admitted his crimes and emphasised his efforts to protect the managers and overseers from the most heinous attacks. Jack accepted the offer.

Removing his jacket, Herbert sat down at a small wooden table and took out a piece of parchment and a quill. The scant available light was provided by a flickering candle. Over the next couple of hours, the prisoner dictated his thoughts to the lawyer who wrote them down. It was slow, laborious work. Jack had much to say and the documenting of his words had to be exact. The court would not accept anything but the finest calligraphy. When they had finished the statement, it was ten pages long. Herbert said he would leave it with Jack so he could think about it overnight, and they could discuss it in the morning. On his way out, he placed the affidavit on the jailer's desk.

Early the following day, another person came to the jail. This time it was Robert Edmonstone. The same Robert Edmonstone who had so grumpily received John Cheveley's letter of introduction two years before. The same man, who had a business relationship with John Gladstone, was a slaveholder and was also an employee of the court martial. Walking into the prison, Edmonstone saw Jack's affidavit on the jailer's desk. With nobody around, he picked it up and read it over. He then added thirty lines of his own. After a short while, Charles Herbert arrived, and Edmonstone explained what he had done. Herbert was outraged, but it was too late to do anything about it. To rewrite the statement would take too long; they would simply have to make do.

Half an hour later, the court was back in session. With the fiscal having closed his case, it was now Jack's turn. The prisoner was asked what he had to say in his defence, and he requested that his statement be read to the court. As his own reading was not fluent, he asked the clerk to deliver it for him. Much was familiar to the court. Jack recounted the origins of the uprising, the rumours that the king was about to set the enslaved people free, the meeting near Bethel Chapel in which they had agreed their plans, the taking of the various plantations, the parley at Bachelor's Adventure. He also took responsibility for his part in events. 'I cannot and do not deny that I have been concerned in this rebellion,' he said, 'but I declare solemnly, that I would not have acted thus had I not been told that we were entitled to our freedom, and that it was withheld from us by our masters.'

After twenty minutes, he came to the final sentence that he and Herbert had drafted the previous night; this was meant to be the climax of his statement: 'I hope my witnesses will prove that I have spoken the truth,' and then, 'I humbly throw myself on the mercy of the Court.'

But it was not the end. For now came the lines added by Robert Edmonstone. 'I am satisfied I have had a fair trial,' Jack's statement continued. 'From the hour I was made prisoner by Dr M'Turk up to this time, I have received the most humane treatment from all the whites, nor have I had a single insulting expression from a white man, either in prison or anywhere else.' Not only was this sentence a non sequitur, the style was out of keeping with Jack's previous words. It was clearly an effort to assuage the guilt of the governor and the colonists.

Finally the statement came to John Smith's role in the uprising. According to the lines written by Edmonstone, Jack admitted that in the weeks and months before the insurrection, the missionary had encouraged a culture of dissent. 'Before this court, I solemnly avow, that many of the lessons and discourses taught, and the parts of scripture selected for us in chapel, tended to make us dissatisfied with our situation as slaves,' he declared. 'Had there been no Methodists on the east coast, there would have been no revolt.' In response to this statement, there was much muttering in the room, but although Jack's admission was damaging to John Smith, it wasn't a knockout blow. It was little more than had already been established during the previous proceedings.

Silence fell again, and people leaned forward to hear what the defendant would say next, desperate not to miss a word or phrase. 'Not only was every deacon and member of the church acquainted with it [the rebellion] before it broke out,' the statement continued, but 'Parson Smith knew the whole plan.' Again, these were lines added by Edmonstone, as was the next: 'He wanted us to wait. If he did not know what we were going to do, would he have told us to wait?' At this logic, loud gasps were heard. Here, at last, was proof of the missionary's treason, clear as day.

When asked by the court if he had written his statement, Jack said, that he had 'dictated the substance of the words' to Mr Herbert. Pointedly, he did not say that the phrases added by Robert Edmonstone were his. When Edmonstone was asked about the provenance of the last few paragraphs, he said that he had spoken with the defendant and, to bolster his case, double-checked the facts with one of the other ringleaders, adding, 'I would not have given it to Mr Herbert if Bristol had not said it was true'. Edmonstone took pains not to mention that Bristol had cut a deal with the court so that his sentence would be commuted in return for adverse testimony against the defendant.

With no more witnesses left to call, the prisoner was asked if he had any final words. 'I know that I have been guilty of this rebellion,' Jack declared to a stony-faced court, 'and that I deserve to be convicted of it; but I hope from the leniency I have shown, I hope the Court will recommend me to mercy, and speak to the Governor in my behalf.' Those seated in the court were asked to stand, and the members of the court martial left the room to make their decision. Proceedings had lasted only three and a half days.

The court was reconvened that afternoon. Jack rose to hear the verdict read out. He was told that after the court had 'most maturely and deliberately weighed and considered the evidence', it found that he was 'guilty of the charge preferred against him, and does therefore sentence him, the prisoner Jack, to suffer death, at such time and place as his Excellency the Commander-in-chief may deem fit'. The day was 22 September 1823. Jack Gladstone was 28 years old.

Under the court martial system, there was no possibility for appeal. There was, however, one hope: clemency. The governor himself did not have the power to pardon or commute sentences

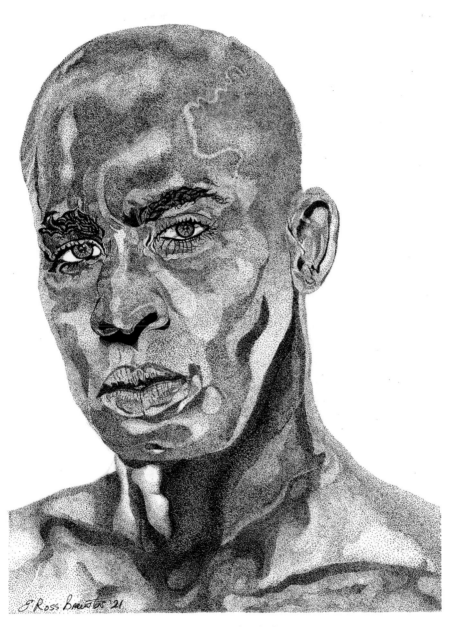

Jack Gladstone (*imagined by Errol Brewster*)

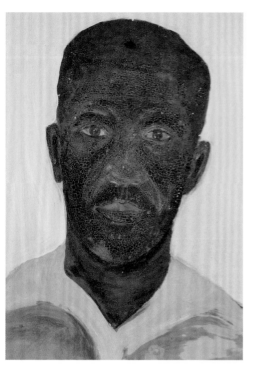

Quamina
(*imagined by unknown artist*)

Amba
(*imagined by Errol Brewster*)

Slave register for Success plantation with Jack Gladstone and Quamina's names, 181?

ABOVE Rev. John Smith

ABOVE LEFT Jane Smith (*imagined by Barrington Braithwaite*)

LEFT Rev. John Wray

BELOW Le Resouvenir plantation (L–R) John Hamilton's house, overseer's house, Bethel Chapel, missionary house

John Murray

Ellen Murray

John Cheveley

John Gladstone

FOR SALE, to an approved Purchaser—a Family of excellent

FIELD NEGROES,

viz. the mother, 36 years of age, her daughter 18, her son 15, and child 9, years old. Terms, 6, 12, and 18 months. Apply to

JAMES WATT,
Exchange Coffee House.

Notice for 'Field Negroes', *Demerara and Essequibo Royal Gazette*

RUNAWAY about nine weeks past, from the Subscriber, the negro girl, Princess, a creole of this colony, she is a tall yellow skin girl about 20 years of age, full breast, and thick lips, well known about town and country. Also the negro woman Phœbe, who has also absconded some time back; she is a tall black skin woman of the Chamba nation, likewise well known in town and country. A reward of One Joe is offered for the apprehension of either of the above slaves, and lodging them in the colony jail, or delivering them to their owner in Kingston. All persons are forbid harbouring either of the above mentioned slaves, and masters of vessels from taking them off the colony, or captains of boats crossing them over the Ferries, as the law will be put in force against all so offending.

January 6.   MARGO CUMING.

Notice for 'runaways', *Demerara and Essequibo Royal Gazette*

Militia gather in Georgetown. Guard House in front, Colony House in background

Massacre at Bachelor's Adventure

The following is copied from the Demerary Royal Gazette of the 30th August last, received yesterday morning by the sloop *Two Friends* :—
"PUBLIC NOTICE.

"Whereas QUAMINA and JACK, of Plantation *Success*, two noted Ringleaders in the Rebellion on the East coast, have to the present period eluded the search of the troops.— Notice is hereby given, that a reward of

One Thousand Guilders !

will be paid to any person or persons, who shall apprehend each or either of the aforesaid Ringleaders, and bring them alive."

We are informed that the above Runaways are accompanied by eight other Negroes, together with ten women; and that the description of the person of the Negro JACK, is as follows, viz :— height, 6 feet 2 inches; about 25 years of age; handsome, well made; rather an European nose; good white teeth; &c.

We are happy to learn, that although Martial Law still continues in force, and that Courts Martial are daily sitting in Demerary, yet the late disturbances appear to be completely suppressed, and there is every reason to believe, that tranquillity and good order will be speedily restored there.

Wanted notice for Jack and Quamina, *Berbice Royal Gazette*

Quamina hanged at Success plantation

Execution of enslaved abolitionists, Georgetown

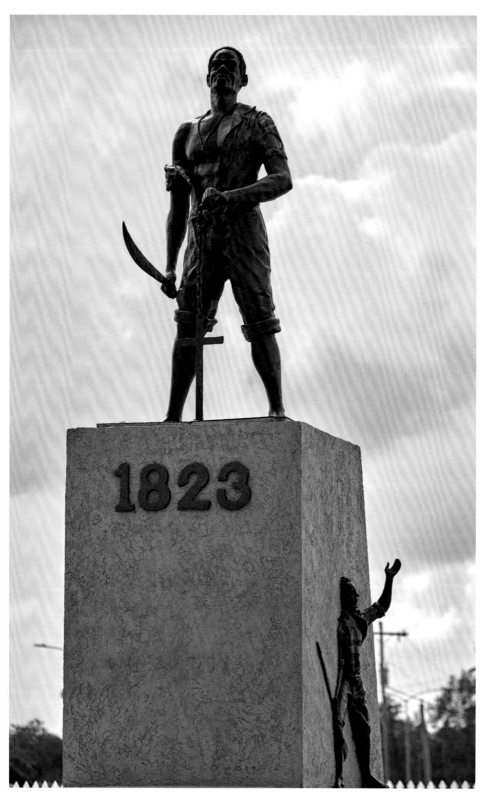

Monument to Demerara Uprising, Georgetown, Guyana, by Ivor Thom

in cases of high treason; this resided in London with the king and his administrators. So the governor wrote once more to Earl Bathurst in London, laying out the arguments for and against royal clemency. On the one hand, Jack was obviously the principal leader of the uprising. 'There is no doubt,' Murray wrote, 'of his having been in arms, and among some very desperate parties on the night of Monday the 18th of August.' On the other hand, he continued, there were political reasons to reduce his sentence. From the court testimony of both enslaved and colonist, it was clear that Jack had saved the lives of several colonists, and to reward such behaviour would be a useful sign for other would-be insurrectionists. It was also worth noting that members of Jack's family had already been punished. After all, Quamina's body was still gibbeted on the coast. 'I look upon it to be good policy in the event of a repetition of such struggles on the part of the slaves,' argued the governor, 'to show them that any benefit they bestow on the whites, even though in the act of rebellion, will not be lost sight of in awarding a punishment for their crimes.'

Such strategic thinking did not come without political peril. The Court of Policy – including Michael M'Turk, Charles Wray and the fiscal himself – had made it known to the governor that they did not support clemency for the abolitionists, particularly in the case of the man who had led the uprising and who had spent weeks evading capture. A view that was buttressed by the general feeling of the colony's plantation-owner population.

There was, however, one slaveholding family who wished to see the condemned man saved from the hangman's noose. Via his agent in Georgetown, Gladstone wrote to Governor Murray proclaiming his support for Jack. He was liked 'by us all for his good behaviour, intelligence and usefulness', Cort wrote on Gladstone's behalf, then reiterated Jack's numerous efforts to protect the colonists from harm during the rebellion. To hang him would upset too many people on the plantations, which would be bad for business. Better that he should be deported from the colony. And if he was sent away, then he, Gladstone should be compensated by the government for the loss of his 'property' as if Jack had been executed. For the Liverpool trader, it was always about the money.

Gladstone's arguments won out. Murray informed his superiors in London that he was convinced that if Jack were to remain in Demerara it would 'create a very general and a well-founded alarm on the minds of the inhabitants' and would be 'dangerous to the welfare of the colony'. Instead, he 'humbly suggested' that Jack be sent to an island that had a 'congenial' climate. There he would work in a prison system that would not 'afford him opportunities' to misconduct himself. The governor recommended that Jack be deported to Bermuda.

*E*very day in Guyana, I meet people who say that they are descendants of African people enslaved by the British. They tell me how the brutal legacy has slid down the generations, how it affects them today. I feel terrible when I hear these stories. A mixture of sadness, anger and shame.

One woman explains how after slavery was abolished in 1833, her ancestors banded together, pooled their meagre savings and purchased land to build a village. Unhappy with such uppity behaviour, the White colonists flooded the village. When one of her ancestors tried to stop the flooding, she was tracked down and hanged from a gibbet.

More than once, having heard about the horrific consequences of slavery, I find myself apologising for what Britain did, for being so ignorant about this history, for not saying anything sooner. And it leaves me wondering what exactly was my family's role with slavery.

So at night in my hotel room, I spend hours researching online databases, reading academic journals, learning what I can about the tobacco trade. Here's what I find.

My family started their tobacco business in 1843, when my four-times great-grandfather Samuel Glückstein arrived in London from Belgium. With nothing but the clothes on his back, he taught himself how to roll cigars and then sold them on the streets. Eventually he and his brother and brother-in-law formed the company Glückstein & Co. The tobacco they purchased came from the USA, almost certainly from plantations worked by enslaved women and men.

Through the 1850s and up to 1865, when slavery was abolished in the USA, Glückstein & Co. continued to purchase tobacco from American plantations worked by enslaved people. The business outgrew the family home and moved into a Soho workshop. It was profitable enough to hire an Irish servant and support more than twenty members of the family for more than two decades. This much *is clear: Glückstein & Co. gave the family money, power and prestige. And this was based on slavery.*

In 1870, the company was disbanded following a dispute between my four-times grandfather Samuel Glückstein and his partners. The family's next company was called Salmon & Gluckstein (they had dropped the umlaut from their surname). Does the fact that this new company began operations after *slavery was abolished in the USA let it off the hook?*

No. For as well as selling rolling tobacco, pipe tobacco and snuff from the USA, Salmon & Gluckstein also sold Cuban cigars. But, slavery was not abolished in Cuba until 1886. This means that in addition to selling tobacco worked by enslaved people in the US, the family business also sold cigars produced on slave plantations in Cuba.

After yet another late-night deep dive on the internet, I find an additional connection between my family and slavery. In 1902, Salmon & Gluckstein was sold to Imperial Tobacco for £400,000. In today's money that is equivalent to around £40 million. At the time, 70 per cent of Imperial Tobacco was owned by the tobacco company W. D. & H. O. Wills, whose name adorns various build-ings in Bristol, buildings the University of Bristol is currently con-templating renaming because of the company's connection with slave plantations. In other words, my family made a fortune by selling its tobacco business to a family that made at least part of its money from slavery.

The next day I walk around Georgetown blurry-eyed. What my family did was connected to the USA and Cuba and not Guyana. But to me the location is immaterial. Just like John Gladstone or Robert Edmonstone or William Pattinson, my ancestors chose financial advancement over compassion for other human beings. My family knew exactly what they were doing. In the 1840s, 1850s and 1860s, slavery was one of the most talked about topics in Britain. As good business people, they knew precisely where their tobacco came from and how it was cultivated. They could have pursued another trade or profession. They chose not to. For decades, and like so many others in Britain – insurance brokers, shipbuilders, cotton traders, dock workers, bankers – they benefited from slavery. They benefited from other people's suffering.

For this, I am very sorry.

CHAPTER 18

Gladstone, October 1823

On Monday 13 October 1823, John Gladstone was at his home in Liverpool eating his breakfast and reading the newspaper. He was deeply engaged with a story on page 3 of *The Times*. It was truly an extraordinary piece. The previous week, a young woman named Harriet Smith had been thrown off the top of a stagecoach in west London, receiving many injuries, both internal and external. She was carefully transported to her home in Hammersmith, where she lived with a cousin. There she was cared for, but despite the efforts of her relative, she grew weaker. Finally, late into the night on the Thursday, all efforts to rouse her failed. 'She was quite cold,' the article reported, 'her lips colourless and her eyes glazed, all pulsation had ceased.' Realising that her kinswoman had died, her relative washed her, dressed her and then laid her on her bed, where the body remained for two days waiting to be interred.

On Saturday afternoon, the funeral director arrived, but as he lifted the body into the coffin he had brought, he noticed something odd: the corpse felt atypically warm to the touch. 'A closer examination convinced them they were about to commit to the cold grave a living subject,' chortled the paper. A physician was called, and after conducting a series of bleedings and applying warm bricks, he confirmed Harriet to be still breathing. By the evening, the girl was looking dramatically better. Since then, the paper continued, 'She has improved not only in health but in spirits since her visit to the other world and is now likely to be long an inhabitant of this.'

When Gladstone looked to the other stories on the same page, he must have been shocked to see a far more worrying report. 'Accounts of a very alarming nature were received the previous Saturday by the Leeward Islands mail from Demerara,' he read, of 'an insurrection having broken out amongst the slaves in that colony.' The paper emphasised that the accounts were 'given in a moment of great alarm' and might be 'exaggerated'. That said, it proceeded to report what had been learned. Thousands of enslaved women and men had taken part in the uprising and then sent a message to the governor demanding emancipation. A regiment had been dispatched, and during the fighting that followed, more than three hundred abolitionists were killed, two hundred of them at Bachelor's Adventure. The article concluded that 'the utmost apprehension exists, however, amongst the merchants trading in Demerara, and the next intelligence from thence is expected with much anxiety'.

The news did indeed make Gladstone anxious. He owned seven plantations in Demerara, along with more than two thousand enslaved people. The loss of income from an insurrection would be difficult to bear; the loss of capital from the death of an enslaved man or woman – or worse, a number of them – would be calamitous.

Over the next few days, more reports began to arrive. Gladstone read that martial law had been imposed throughout the colony and that, happily, the militia had swiftly put down the uprising. They had apparently displayed great 'daring', 'bravery', and 'zeal'. Crucially, the 'Negroes had returned to their work and all was then tranquil and quiet'. He read the articles again carefully. There was no mention of Success or his other plantations; perhaps his investments would be spared after all.

Gladstone had never visited Demerara and had no intention of going there. For him, the estates and the enslaved people attached were items on a profit-and-loss account. Given the excruciating amount of time it took for correspondence to travel between

Liverpool and Georgetown and back again, however, he knew he could not micro-manage the situation. He would have to leave it to his agent to respond to matters on the ground.

Finally a letter arrived from Frederick Cort. The insurrection was indeed over and none of the Gladstone plantations had been damaged. So far so good. Then came the rest of the news. According to the agent, the plantation owners had put enormous pressure on the governor to respond vigorously to the uprising. To send a message. Hundreds of abolitionists had died. One of Gladstone's estates, Success, had been at the centre of it all and at least ten of what he considered to be his slaves had been killed by the king's militia. Gladstone decided he would later petition the authorities to compensate him for his losses. For now, he would concentrate on the politics.

What really worried him was how people in Britain would react to the news. The planters had clearly overreacted. Seeking revenge against the Demerara abolitionists and imposing overly harsh measures would likely upset people here, particularly members of Parliament. The British abolitionists like William Wilberforce and Thomas Clarkson had already stirred up the do-gooders and the chattering classes. The last thing that was needed was a public outcry about a campaign of retribution carried out by a frenzied mob of colonists. That would be bad for business. Gladstone was still in the middle of his search for the perfect estate in Scotland; it was not the time to be losing money.

But he was a realist. If the damaging reports coming in from Demerara were corroborated, there would likely be an inquiry, even a debate in Parliament. He would have to work hard to mould public opinion in the run-up to any major decision.

In the days and weeks following the story breaking in *The Times*, more details of the Demerara uprising arrived in Britain. Numerous newspapers published copies of Governor John

Murray's proclamations in full, along with letters written by various Georgetown colonists and articles that had appeared a few weeks earlier in the Demerara press. The number of dead or missing enslaved people kept growing. It was now believed to be at least five hundred, whilst a hundred and fifty others were in prison. Meanwhile, two or three militiamen had been injured, and a handful of 'stragglers' had been killed.

On 25 October, another long article was published in *The Times*. This one, Gladstone was pleased to see, described the Demerara insurrection as 'evil'. It reported that those taking part had a 'mischievous design' and that 'some incendiaries (amongst them whites)' had spread false news about emancipation. In another article, the paper wrote that it had been the missionaries who had made 'efforts to cause disaffection amongst the slaves'.

The coverage of the Demerara uprising worried missionaries of all stripes. The Wesleyan Methodist Society, for instance, took out an advertisement in *The Times*, proclaiming that their ministers were not amongst those arrested in the colony. They added that their members were trained to not become involved in local politics and to abide by the teachings of the Bible, in particular Colossians, Chapter 3: 'Slaves, obey your earthly masters in everything. and do it, not only when their eye is on you and to curry their favour, but with sincerity of heart and reverence for the Lord.'

The London Missionary Society followed suit. They confirmed that two of their members – John Smith and Richard Elliot – were under arrest but they were awaiting further information. Like the Wesleyans, they stressed that their missionaries were given clear instructions to stay out of local politics and they begged readers to keep an open mind until more evidence arrived in Britain.

The role of the Church in the Caribbean was well known to Gladstone. He was familiar with the missionaries and their efforts to educate the enslaved men and women who worked on the plantations. Yet as a regular churchgoer himself, he was also aware that not all Christians were abolitionists. The Church of England, for one, was deeply enmeshed with slavery. Almost a hundred of its clergymen were registered as slaveholders. The Church also received significant funds from philanthropists, such as Gladstone himself, who had made their money from slavery. These contributions were used to build churches and schools and the benefactors received wide coverage in the press for their good works. Gladstone knew that such largesse was much appreciated by the general population and that, along with the significant number of jobs that were dependent on the importation of sugar, cotton, coffee and other commodities, there was widespread support for Britain to continue operating its plantations in the Caribbean.

Throughout the autumn of 1823, therefore, and despite the efforts of the missionaries and British abolitionists to the contrary, the reports published in the British papers were almost entirely favourable towards the Demerara colonists. Public opinion remained with John Gladstone and the other traders, many of whom were based in Liverpool.

By the 1820s, Liverpool had become Britain's second busiest trading port after London. Acting as a western gateway, it handled more than 30 per cent of the country's imports and exports. Over the past century, shipping in Liverpool's port had grown from 14,600 tons in 1709 to 450,000 tons in 1800, rising to more than 1 million tons by 1820. At any one time, more than seven hundred vessels (ships, barges and other flat-bottom boats) were operating in the port. Key goods included cotton, tobacco, timber, rum, salt and cocoa. The port was particularly dominant in sugar, which came almost entirely from the Caribbean. Which is why the city was also host to the West Indian Trading Association, whose president was none other than John Gladstone.

Gladstone was not the only Liverpudlian to notice the stories arriving from Demerara. Another was James Cropper, an American-born merchant who managed cotton trades between England and India. Cropper was an avowed opponent of slavery, and realising that the Demerara uprising presented an opportunity to raise awareness of the issue, he now sent a letter to the editor of the *Liverpool Mercury*. This missive was published on 31 October, two weeks after news of the uprising had first arrived in the city. 'How indeed is it possible there can be two opinions,' Cropper asked rhetorically, 'that the slaves of the West Indies are degradingly driven like cattle, by the whip at their labour, that they are held and dealt with as property, and often branded as such with a hot iron?' From an economic point of view, he continued, it would be beneficial to the plantation owners if they freed the enslaved men and women, as an emancipated person was more likely to work harder than one in bonds. He went on to say that ironically, the sugar trade operated at a loss and only survived because it enjoyed reduced duties compared to the same product imported from India. In other words, the government, empowered by its voters, was subsidising the inhuman treatment of the enslaved people in the Caribbean.

Reading this article was too much for Gladstone, who immediately penned a response. Concealing his identity by submitting his dispatch under the alias 'Mercator', he described Cropper's letter as full of 'misstatements and exaggerations', and then addressed the issue of slavery head on. First, he said, he was in principle a supporter of gradual emancipation but that it must not come at a loss to the slaveholders, who must be fully compensated for their 'property'. Second, and contrary to Cropper's economic assertion, he declared that freed slaves were typically 'idle, indolent, slothful and too often become profligate'. Third, and on a wider point, how could it be immoral to own slaves if God allowed it 'in all ages, master and servant, bond and free'? Fourth, he hoped that the uprising in Demerara would awaken the government to the 'sense of extreme danger' that followed from their decision to ameliorate the conditions of slaves in the colonies, and that the 'well-meaning but mistaken man William Wilberforce' and his 'intemperate' friends would now take a pause. Finally, Gladstone concluded that Cropper was perhaps as guilty as anyone, for as a cotton trader he had bought and sold crops cultivated by enslaved people of African descent.

In reply, Cropper submitted another letter to the paper. He admitted that he had formerly purchased slave-produced cotton but that he had not done so for some time. 'Two things being wrong do not make one right,' he added. Then, clearly irritated by his opponent's personal attacks, he made an informed guess and publicly stated that Mercator was none other than the Liverpool resident John Gladstone: enslaver and owner of West Indian plantations, which, he proclaimed, was 'probably the worst form in which it [slavery] ever existed'.

Ignoring Cropper's attempted outing, Gladstone replied that the enslaved people in Demerara never worked after sunset, were 'supplied with more than they do or can consume' and were 'well provided with clothing'. Furthermore, their dwellings were 'roomy and commodious'. They had the Sabbath 'for the purposes of religion if so inclined', and 'ample spare time'. Families could not be separated and must be sold together, and 'no driver or overseer can punish beyond six lashes for offences'. He concluded this epistle by saying, 'When we compare their situation with that of the peasantry generally, it will be found that they possess serious and important advantages over them.' More than that, he added, the slaves 'were a contented and happy people'. If he was aware of the callousness, deception and cruelty of such statements, he did not profess it.

Back and forth went the argument, in print and all very much in the public domain. The exchange was widely known and commented upon. Copies of the letters were circulated around the country in coffee houses, private clubs and taverns. An anthology of the correspondence was published, and proved so popular that another edition had to be quickly printed. At one point the debate turned to the role of John Smith in the Demerara uprising. Gladstone wrote that he had closely followed the missionary's work with the enslaved people and seen their minds become 'corrupted and inflamed' with the doctrines of emancipation. He blamed John Smith and his supporters for the 'waste of life which attended the insurrection in Demerara', and stated that if the government should abolish slavery, and thereby take the slaveholders' property, 'they are bound to make *full* compensation'. He emphasised his meaning with italics.

Finally, weeks into their correspondence, Mercator at last responded to the earlier accusation that he was John Gladstone. Did Cropper 'not in this manner attempt to fix on a private individual all the slander, scurrility and abuse which he may put forth'? he asked. Attentive readers would note, however, that he did not deny the piercing of his identity, a fact that would be finally acknowledged when the West India Association published the full exchange in a pamphlet available for purchase by the public, and Gladstone permitted his alias to be uncovered.

Many believed that Gladstone had won the exchange with Cropper. Not only were his arguments clearer and less prone to factual errors, but his language was more succinct and quotable. And so, through October, November and then December, public opinion in Britain stiffened in favour of the colonists. The missionaries were viewed as traitors and troublemakers. Enslaved people were considered, at best, prone to manipulation and ill-prepared for emancipation; at worst, brutish ingrates who would seek vengeance if given half a chance. As to British abolitionists, they were anti-business naïfs whose folly endangered the economy of the Empire. It was perhaps unsurprising, therefore, that by the end of 1823, and in the glare of the Demerara uprising, the Anti-Slavery Society of Great Britain was struggling to survive. Its membership numbers were dwindling, whilst there were only half a dozen Members of

Parliament willing to associate with its cause, and the government was close to renouncing its pledge to ameliorate the conditions of slavery.

Yet – and this is one of the peculiarities of this story – the roiling debate gripping the parlours, taverns, church halls and drawing rooms of London, Edinburgh, Manchester and across the British Isles was taking place in a time delay. The press, the politicians, the traders and the public were all responding to news that was at least six weeks old, depending on the weather and the arrival of the post from Demerara. So it was not until Christmas Day 1823 – more than two months after the event had actually occurred – that *The Times* and other papers carried a much-anticipated news item from the colony: the trial of the missionary John Smith had begun.

While I'm in Guyana, I'm invited to lunch by Jocelyn Dow. It's going to be a real Guyanese meal, she tells me. Jocelyn is an activist working at both national and international level. She lives in Georgetown with her six dogs.

The meal includes a range of dishes: cook-up (a mixture of chicken, rice and vegetables), pepperpot (a stew of spiced meat), fish curry, roti, black pudding. It's delicious.

Over coffee, I ask Jocelyn about the legacy of the plantation system in Guyana. 'So few of the fundamentals have changed since slavery,' she says. 'There are the same means of robbing us of our wealth and our youth. We are not enslaved but we are certainly in bondage to financial mechanisms. Trade is still mostly to the benefit of the former colonisers.'

I ask her what we should do about this. 'First of all, Britain should acknowledge it,' she tells me. 'This needs to be meaningful. It would have to be some form of reparations. There must be some accounting of who benefited and who lost. When you apologise, you are saying to each other, "We have committed a wrong, we must acknowledge and be sorry." Unless truth is told within and amongst yourselves, there can be no healing.'

I ask her to explain what she means by this. 'The victims cannot be the beggars of your grace,' she says. 'The graciousness, the acknowledgement, the mea culpa has to come from the perpetrator.'

Later that evening, Elsie Harry, the youth activist with whom I attended the Atlantic slave trade commemoration, comes to see me at the Herdmanston Lodge.

We sit on the terrace. I drink a Banks beer, she a glass of water. I ask her what people in Britain should do, if anything, about the legacy of slavery. 'I would want British people to first learn about Guyana.' She laughs. 'It's not Ghana in Africa, it's Guyana in South America.'

She then becomes more serious. 'They should pay reparations,'
she says. 'Some people can trace their lineage back to the ownership
of enslaved people. But even those who can't, just living in a society
that was built on the backs of enslaved people means they benefited
from it. So yes, British people should pay reparations.'

I ask her if she thinks an apology should be part of the reparations
process.

She pauses for a moment, then says, 'I think an apology is only
important if it comes with something else. An apology is great.
But only if it comes with some sort of action to repair damage that
has been done.'

Again she waits a moment to collect her thoughts. 'Action speaks
louder than words. Britain needs to pay reparations.'

CHAPTER 19

John Smith, October 1823

Since their arrest at the end of August, John and Jane had been held in a cramped room in the attic of Colony House; the same building where Jack Gladstone had been tried. For whatever reason – tactics, compassion, prejudice – the authorities had chosen to keep the Smiths separate from the enslaved abolitionists arrested during the uprising.

Two guards from the Demerara militia were posted outside the Smiths' door. It would be their task to maintain security and control the flow of visitors in and out of the cell. There was little ventilation under the tightly shingled roof; the heat was unbearable. At night on the hard bed, they found sleeping close to impossible. John, already weak, deteriorated under these difficult conditions.

As the weeks progressed through the early autumn, the Smiths were kept apprised of what was going on at the court martial taking place three storeys below. By the first week of October, more than fifty abolitionists had been tried, including Jack Gladstone. Twenty-one had been sentenced to death, eight of whom were decapitated, with their heads fixed on poles in front of the Georgetown Fort. Ten had received prolonged floggings, with a minimum of three hundred lashes. Five had been assigned to hard labour in the workhouse. One had been banished and another was put in solitary confinement for two months. Notably, three of the ringleaders – Bristol, Paris and Seaton – had so far avoided punishment.

It was while the trials were taking place downstairs that a visitor arrived at John and Jane's attic room. It was Lieutenant Colonel

John Reed, aide-de-camp to Governor Murray and the owner of the Dochfour estate. Reed said that he had come to collect the two letters that his 'house servant' Jackey had sent to John Smith on the first day of the uprising. The missionary acknowledged that he had received both letters, but claimed that once he had read them, they had been destroyed. Reed said that he had a copy of John's response to Jackey. The missionary asked to read this, which he was allowed to do. He then handed it back to Reed, who, his business being complete, departed. John was left to ponder what had just happened. It seemed the prosecution was working hard to build its case against him, which was worrying.

On 13 October 1823, almost two months after his arrest, John was escorted down the stairs of Colony House to the ground floor and into the courtroom for the start of his trial. He was followed by Jane, who would be allowed to observe. Despite the missionary taking no active role in the uprising, the legal proceedings would be held as a court martial.

The hearing opened at 10 a.m. sharp, with the clerk calling the court to order. The proceedings were once again presided over by Lieutenant Colonel Goodman. Next to him were the twelve members of the court martial, all of whom had been active in quashing the uprising, and many of whom were themselves slaveholders. Five had taken part in Jack's trial, including Charles Wray, the head of the colony's justice system. Seven of them were new to the court.

If the trial of Jack Gladstone had been well attended by the public, that was nothing compared to today's hearing. Every seat in the swelteringly hot room was taken. The walls at the back and sides were lined with spectators willing to stand for long hours so that they could observe this courtroom drama. The local journalists were there in force, as were a multitude of witnesses who would be called later that day (there were no rules precluding them from hearing the testimony of other witnesses).

John Smith sat behind a small wooden desk on which he assembled his papers. Behind him sat Jane, along with Elizabeth Elliot, whose missionary husband Richard Elliot was still in custody. A few steps away was gathered the prosecution, also behind a wooden table. The team was once again headed by Victor Amadius Heyliger, the colony's fiscal, supported by two other junior lawyers. The president now asked the fiscal to begin.

Heyliger stood and read out the four charges against the defendant. First, that the missionary had promoted 'discontent and dissatisfaction in the minds of the Negro slaves towards their lawful masters, managers and overseers'. Second, that he had 'advised, consulted and corresponded with a certain Negro named Quamina, touching and concerning a certain intended revolt and rebellion of the negro slaves'. Third, that even though knowing about the uprising, he had not informed the proper authorities. And fourth, that he had failed to detain or stop Quamina when he visited on 20 August, even after knowing that the uprising had started.

When asked how he pleaded to the charges, John told the court, 'Not guilty'. Then, before the president could call for the proceedings to start, the missionary asked if the hearing could be adjourned. He wished to procure the assistance of a lawyer. As with Jack and the other accused abolitionists, and despite the trial already having commenced, he had not been given the opportunity to speak with counsel. The president granted the request, but cautioned that the defendant must be back in court in twenty-four hours.

Later that afternoon, John and Jane met William Arrindell in the cramped garret at the top of Colony House. The twenty-seven-year-old lawyer had been born in the Virgin Islands and had trained as a barrister at Lincoln's Inn, London. He also owned an estate in Essequibo to which belonged a number of enslaved people. On paper, therefore, the anti-slavery missionary and the slaveholding lawyer had little in common. Yet Arrindell was sympathetic to John's plight. He would later write, 'I do believe Mr Smith to be innocent,' adding that 'Nay, I will go further, and defy any minister, of any sect whatever, to have shewn a more faithful attention to his sacred duties.'

Over the next few hours, they discussed John's case at length. Arrindell explained how a court martial worked, how the proceedings were likely to unfold and which arguments Heyliger would probably make. He also explained that while he would be sitting next to his client in court, it would be John who would be asking questions. Arrindell's role would be as an 'advising advocate'. They talked about the witnesses the fiscal would call – the court had kindly provided a list – and who they in turn should ask to testify. It was clear to all of them that they were starting at a dramatic disadvantage. The prosecution had had weeks to prepare. There was no time to gather research, examine evidence, marshal their arguments, let alone prepare the defendant. The conversation continued late into the night.

Early the following day, 14 October, John and Jane awoke early, the sun's heat making it impossible to sleep under the burning roof. At 10 a.m., the court martial resumed once again. As first order of business, the defendant presented his new lawyer to the court. The president welcomed the barrister to the proceedings and then asked Heyliger for the second time to open his case. The fiscal started by introducing John Smith's diary into the proceedings. With the leather-bound journal in his hand, he called the estate manager Stewart to the stand and asked if he knew the prisoner. Stewart said he did. 'Do you believe this to be his handwriting?' Heyliger asked, passing the book to the witness. Stewart confirmed that it was. 'What reason have you to know it is his handwriting?' probed the fiscal. To which Stewart replied, 'He had frequently written letters to me to get up things by boat.'

At this point, it may have been expected that John, at his lawyer's urging, might challenge such a statement. After all, the witness was not a handwriting expert. But he did not. Neither was there any effort by the prosecution to prove chain of custody of the diary, nor why its content was pertinent to the trial, or how the journal had been seized (after all, no warrant had been given for the search of the Smiths' house). Instead, Smith was left to ask, 'Did you ever see me write?' To which Stewart said he had not. When Smith asked, 'How then can you swear that the contents of that book are in my handwriting?' he was told by the court that the question had already been answered.

With the bona fides of the journal established, at least in the eyes of the court, Heyliger began to read the first entry. It must have been excruciating for Smith to sit there, forced to listen in silence as his own words were used against him. Words that had been written in private, without intention of their being made public, let alone aired in a court of law. The missionary, however, was someone who could remain outwardly passive in the face of adversity. He had shown this when Lieutenant Nurse had sealed up his desk. He had done so again when Captain Simpson had returned to arrest him.

Heyliger started by reading out a series of passages that in his view proved the defendant's motive and state of mind. He began with an entry written in the autumn of 1817: 'The Negroes of Success have complained to me lately of excessive labour & very severe treatment. I told one of their overseers, that I thought they would work their people to death.' Then this one from March 1819: 'While writing this my very heart flutters at hearing the almost incessant cracking of the whip … It appears to me very probable that ere long they will resent the injuries done to them.' And then in November 1821: 'The people have scarcely any time to eat their food, they have none to cook it, eating for the most part, raw yellow plantains. This would be bearable for a time, but to work at that rate, and to be perpetually flogged, astonishes me that they submit to it.' Finally this from July 1823, just weeks before the start of the uprising: 'The rigors of Negro slavery I believe can never be mitigated. The system must be abolished.'

It is worth noting that Heyliger submitted this evidence in the ardent belief that it would help prosecute John Smith. The fiscal was confident that the descriptions of enslaved people being brutally treated would not have a negative impact on the members of the court martial, the president or others in the room. Instead, he believed that such evidence explained why the missionary – who clearly did not appreciate the methods required to run a sugar estate – supported the abolitionists.

Next, and fully aware that the members of the court martial were the governor's men, the fiscal quoted from a journal entry from 1822: 'O, that this colony should be governed by a man who sets his face against the moral and religious improvement of the Negro slaves!' Followed by another from the following year: 'Serious evils are likely to result from the measures which the Governor is adopting respecting the slaves attending chapel.'

The passages were delivered one after another in quick succession. The entries had been selected with intelligence and finesse; their impact was immediate. For her part, Jane Smith was outraged by the infringement of her husband's privacy. 'There is nothing in it to Mr Smith's dishonour,' she wrote, 'but it is too true to be relished by West Indians.' By the end of the trial's first day, the members of the court martial appeared to be persuaded that the accused had a clear objective: the overturning of the system of slavery in the colony of Demerara. All that was needed now was to show how he had converted his aspirations into action.

The next day, Wednesday, Heyliger called on Azor, who belonged to Van Cooten's plantation and was a member of Bethel Chapel. Azor explained how John Smith had often told the Bible story in which the Israelites had won their freedom. He must have heard it at least four or five times. 'When Moses had gotten over with the children of Israel,' he recalled, 'Pharaoh was drowned in the sea, and Moses built a temple and prayed to God.' The implication was clear: through his Bible readings, the accused had fostered hopes of freedom amongst his congregants and encouraged them towards rebellion.

At this, John took great umbrage. Once again, through innuendo and quotes taken out of context, his character was being tainted. He jumped up, eager to start the cross-examination. Had the witness ever heard him, John Smith, compare the condition of the enslaved people in Demerara to those in Egypt?

'No,' said Azor.

'Did I not always advise the Negroes from the pulpit and otherwise to do their own work and obey their master and all in authority under them?'

'Yes,' said Azor.

John took a breath and then asked Azor what he had said about working on the Sabbath. Azor recalled that the parson had interviewed each of the chapel members and asked them where they had been. Some said they had been working in their vegetable gardens, others said the managers made them work. 'John Smith said that we were fools for working on Sunday ...' He stopped, unsure whether to continue. John encouraged him to go on. Azor added, looking at the defendant, '... for the sake of a few lashes.' At this, there was much whispering and shaking of heads in the room.

John had made things harder for himself. The court had just been told that he had instilled ideas of rebellion in the minds of the enslaved people and had even encouraged them to endure whipping in return for their disobedience. He tried to move things on. When was this said? Who else had heard it? But he could see in the eyes of the members of the court martial that he was losing them. He understood that he had to do something to turn things around, but what? The odds were stacked against him. With a gesture from the president that his testimony was over, Azor walked away.

During the rest of that day and the next, Heyliger called three additional witnesses – Romeo, Manuel and Joe – each members of Bethel Chapel and each adding little to Azor's testimony. By Friday afternoon, the fifth day of the trial, the proceedings had become a little repetitive. Though the room remained full of spectators, the initial excitement had somewhat diminished. That was soon to change. Up next was Bristol, the prosecution's star witness. John knew him well: he lived at Chateau Margo on the other side of Success and was one of his deacons. He had also heard that Bristol had cut a deal with the court in return for adverse testimony.

'Did the prisoner advise you or others what to do in case of a complaint?' asked Heyliger. Bristol said John had told them to go and see the fiscal. Anything else? Heyliger persisted. 'That if the people ran away they must not allow themselves to be caught.' This again caused great displeasure in the courtroom. It was considered unconscionable for a colonist, no matter their profession or politics, to encourage runaways.

Seeing that the witness was willing to talk, Heyliger now asked about the Bible readings. 'Did the people apply any part of the history of the Israelites and the Jews to themselves?' Bristol said they did. The fiscal pushed harder. What made the people think this? Bristol considered this for a moment, then replied. 'Because they read it, and their own hearts make them say so.' Seeing he was almost there, the lawyer tried again. 'What was the reason the Negroes took it into their head to revolt?' Bristol replied easily, 'Because they had no other time to wash their clothes or do anything else.' This was not what the fiscal had wanted. He had hoped that he could lead Bristol into placing the blame squarely on the defendant. Sometimes a lawyer overreaches, picking too many times at the same thread. This was one such case. Sitting in his chair a few feet away, John Smith could only smile.

Hoping for a better result, Heyliger turned the questioning to timing. What did the parson know, and when? This would be crucial in proving that he had failed to alert the authorities about the uprising, a treasonable offence. Bristol stated that at 5 p.m. on Sunday 17 August, the day before the uprising, he and Quamina went to see John Smith at home. When they found him, Quamina asked if 'any freedom had come out for them', to which the parson said it had not. Quamina then said that Jack and others wanted to 'take it by force' and planned to drive the White people into town.

John was shocked when he heard this, as was Jane, who was shaking her head just behind him. The conversation did not happen like that at all. Quamina had not mentioned anything about force or driving White people anywhere. It was hard to see Bristol do this. John had taught him how to read; he had trusted him, come to rely on him as a colleague. But he knew that Bristol was facing his own problems. He was charged with taking part in the revolt, a capital offence. So John understood why he might have cut a deal with Heyliger. He would have to try and undermine his deacon's credibility. But before he could ask any questions, the president called for an adjournment. It was Friday evening; the court was dismissed for the weekend.

On Monday morning, Bristol was still in the dock and it was John's turn to cross-examine. He tried a rapid-fire approach to destabilise the witness.

JOHN: After you were examined on Friday night last, where did you go?
BRISTOL: I went back to jail.
JOHN: Have you at any time been instructed by anyone to say what you told in court?
BRISTOL: No, it came from my heart, and was not put into my head by anyone.

John hoped Bristol would admit to being coached by Heyliger or one of his assistants. He was disappointed that his former deacon was too smart to be caught out. He picked up some papers from the little wooden table and read through them, trying to think of what to do next. His lawyer gave him an encouraging nod. John needed to move on. He would now try and prove that he had never instigated dissent or rebellion in any way.

JOHN: Did I ever encourage any Negroes to run away?
BRISTOL: I never heard of it.
JOHN: Have you ever heard me apply the history of the Jews to the Negroes?
BRISTOL: No, sir.
JOHN: What did the people complain that they were licked for?
BRISTOL: Not doing the work on a Sabbath.

With that established, John moved on to the conversation on the Sunday night before the uprising. He asked the witness if there were any preparations made for war before they came to see him. Crucially, Bristol said he did not know of any. Did Quamina say when the colonists were to be driven to town? Again, Bristol said he did not know. Finally John asked what the purpose was of driving the managers and overseers to town. Bristol replied that they had hoped that their freedom would come about. With nothing more to add, he was dismissed.

John had done as well as could be expected for a man without legal training. He had established that even if he had been told about the uprising before it began – a fact he vehemently denied – he wouldn't have known when it would happen, how it would happen, where it would happen or with what resources. He hoped that the members of the court martial would see the obvious: that Bristol was lying when he said Quamina had told him about the revolt and that therefore there had been no reason for John to report the conversation to the authorities.

In the following days, Heyliger took a new tack and began to examine the finances of John's mission. He asked several witnesses how much money members were obliged to pay the church, what gifts the missionary received and what happened to the money raised. At one point, he asked a witness if any members of the church had paid for their psalm books or Bibles. Finally John had had enough. He stood up, red-faced. 'I am not tried for obtaining money under fraudulent pretences,' he declared, 'and therefore object to this question as being wholly irrelevant.' The president of the court martial was unmoved. He overruled John's objection and waived the fiscal to continue.

On the morning of 21 October, the eighth day of the trial, the president received a letter from Heyliger saying he needed some time away from court because of ill health. In his place, the prosecution would be carried out by his junior, the assistant judge advocate, who now called Michael M'Turk to give evidence.

After being sworn in, M'Turk was invited to share his memories of first meeting the missionary. He spoke about the closure of Bethel Chapel during the smallpox outbreak and his recollection that Smith had been 'violent' in his response. The assistant judge advocate then asked M'Turk how he had first learned of the uprising. The witness said he had been at his home in Felicity on 18 August when he was 'informed by a coloured man, about four o'clock, that the Negroes intended revolting that evening'. He was next asked when the unrest began. To which he replied, 'About 5 o'clock,' and proceeded to describe his role in the suppression of the uprising. He was then asked about the arrest of John Smith:

ASSISTANT JUDGE ADVOCATE: Did you give any orders respecting his papers?
M'TURK: I did.
ASSISTANT JUDGE ADVOCATE: What were they?
M'TURK: To seal them up.
ASSISTANT JUDGE ADVOCATE: What induced you to take this step?
M'TURK: It was a secondary step, in the event of his refusing to obey my orders.
ASSISTANT JUDGE ADVOCATE: Did he return to you with Lieutenant Nurse, in obedience to your orders?
M'TURK: He did not; Lieutenant Nurse reported he had refused to comply with my orders.

With that, the assistant judge advocate announced that he had no further questions for the witness. Throughout his testimony, M'Turk had come across as steady, reliable and objective; a man you could trust.

John needed to challenge this impression. He started his cross-examination by trying to make the witness confirm that he had closed the Bethel Chapel out of spite, rather than to protect against a smallpox outbreak, but M'Turk stuck to his narrative: that his priority had been preserving public health. John then attempted to show that his wife's honour had been put at risk during her husband's arrest, but M'Turk sidestepped this as well, saying that Mrs Smith had had the choice of 'every proper attention at my house' or 'a proper escort to town'. Frustrated by M'Turk's careful answers, John returned to the heated exchange during the smallpox outbreak. 'Did you not ridicule, or sneer, at the idea of the Negroes being instructed in Religion?' Before the witness could respond, however, the president declared the question invalid and told the defendant to move on.

Unsure what else to ask, but feeling that he needed to undermine the witness, John now enquired, 'How do you know that there were Negroes with Quamina when he was shot?' This was such a change in subject it took a moment for the witness to answer. M'Turk then said, 'From seeing them standing by him, and from the report of those that were there.'

'Were you with the expedition at the time Quamina was shot?' probed John Smith.

'I was,' replied the witness. And with that, the missionary said that he had no further questions.

John Smith had done well. In the minds of the members of the court martial, he had raised the possibility that M'Turk was little more than a hunter of runaway slaves, a man not of science but of prejudice. He had also elicited an important confession from his nemesis. M'Turk had admitted that he had been informed of the uprising prior to its outbreak. John would be able to use this to explain why he himself had not run to the authorities as soon as Quamina had informed him of the enslaved people's discontent.

Seeing that the assistant judge advocate needed help, the president stepped in. He asked M'Turk to again describe the 'violent' interaction with the missionary during the smallpox outbreak. 'The conversation was very desultory,' reported M'Turk. '[Smith] observed rather rudely, among other things, that it did not matter to him whether he preached to one or one hundred Negroes, "for I am not paid by the head, as you are". He used every kind of language to hurt my feelings.' With this final comment – and despite the defendant not being given the opportunity to respond – M'Turk was let go. His testimony had taken two days. It had left a clear impression of two men who despised each other. What this had to do with the charges before the court, or the evidencing of guilt, was less certain.

On 23 October, a Thursday, the fiscal was back in court. Apparently he had sufficiently recovered his health to take over from his assistant, whose performance over the preceding two days had been less than impressive. Heyliger now called Seaton, another of the abolitionists from Bethel Chapel, who, like Bristol, had so far escaped the gallows. Seaton confirmed that Jack and Quamina were the ringleaders, that it had all been agreed during the meeting at the Middle Walk after church service on Sunday 17 August, and that the plan was to drive the colonists to town, where the abolitionists would demand their freedom.

It was warm and humid in the courtroom, and those who had been following the proceedings had heard it all before. Already that morning, the heads of one or two of the members of the court martial had been seen to drop before the person sitting next to them kindly gave them a gentle nudge.

But then the witness said something that caught everyone's attention. The fiscal had just asked if the plan agreed at the Middle Walk meeting was made before or after Quamina had left the group and gone to see John Smith in his study. Seaton was clear in his memory. The plan had been made before. This was bad, John immediately realised, very bad. If the court believed that the plan had been settled before Quamina had spoken to him at his house, then it was hard to argue that the missionary was likely to know only vague details of the abolitionists' intentions. It was all too neat and convenient for the prosecution's case; Seaton must have also made a deal with the authorities. John stood, indicating that he wanted to cross-examine the witness. The president nodded; it would be allowed.

'Have you been instructed by anyone to say what you have just told the court?' John asked. Bristol had been quick on his feet when he answered this question, but Seaton might be caught unawares. The witness said he had not. The missionary wouldn't let it go. 'Have you ever told anyone before what you just have told the court?' The witness conceded that yes, he had spoken with the assistant judge advocate, who was at that very moment sitting in the courtroom next to the fiscal. 'It was put down in writing?' John asked, sensing an opportunity. He had no idea what the answer might be, but it was worth fishing. 'Yes,' said Seaton. The sound of people sitting up was like a gun going off. Everyone in the room was now wide awake. The witness had just confessed to being coached by the assistant judge advocate, a practice that was not only illegal in the British courts, but also deemed highly immoral.

Now it was the turn of the assistant judge advocate to get heated. He jumped to his feet and objected to the missionary's line of questioning. In an unusual step, the president of the court now swore him in and asked if he had prepared the witness. 'I have examined several of them,' the assistant admitted with disdain. 'The witness is one.' Behind her husband, Jane smiled. This was what they needed: a way to prove that John was the victim here, that the charges against him were part of a trumped-up conspiracy.

The president took a moment to let the court settle down and then asked the assistant judge advocate, 'Have you attempted to instruct or mislead the witness?' The assistant drew himself up to his full height and answered in the clear, clipped diction of Lincoln's Inn, 'As a witness here I am bound to answer, but as a professional man I should consider, on ordinary occasions, such a question degrading to be put to me.' Now, having asserted his moral superiority, he added, 'I answer no.'

No matter the assistant judge advocate's protestations, any clear-eyed observer could see that Seaton's testimony was at best coached, at worst totally unreliable. All things considered, the trial had so far gone well for the defendant. That was about to change.

*W*hilst researching Michael M'Turk, I find his biography on the website of his alma mater, the University of Glasgow. It says that he 'cared about the plight of the hundreds of slaves in the country and was knighted by Queen Victoria on 7 September 1839 for his efforts on their behalf'.

How on earth did this happen?

This is the same Michael M'Turk who 'owned' 130 enslaved people at his Felicity plantation. The same man who was compensated by the British government following abolition. The same person who hunted down, killed and then strung up Quamina and other abolitionists. Not to mention his preventing enslaved people from attending religious services.

But he was a tricksy character. One of those rare people who, with an eye to the future, attempted to manipulate how they are remembered.

By the early 1830s, in the run-up to the abolition of slavery, M'Turk could see the writing on the wall. So he did two things. First, he told a few of his enslaved men to write letters testifying that he was a wonderful man. Second, he organised it so that he was the person in the Court of Policy who, following the passage of the Abolition Act in London, proposed the motion that slavery be abolished in the colony. He then made sure that the governor informed his superiors back in England about these great acts in an effort to alert those close to the queen.

In my own experiment to see if it is possible to alter how history is remembered, I send an email to the university website suggesting they might correct the record.

A few days later, they write back saying they have revised the page to reflect the true legacy of Michael M'Turk.

Here's another example of how the legacy of slavery can be distorted.

In 2006, All Saints Church in Niagara Falls, Canada, published a history of their church. They recounted how, in 1833, John Murray, former governor of Demerara, settled in their town with his wife Ellen and their children. Twenty years later, in 1854, and after Murray's death, Ellen would donate land to All Saints to build a new church. Here's how the church's official record described Murray's time as governor:

> During the last year of his command in Demerara, the slaves, excited by the preaching of one John Smith, a Wesleyan missionary, rose in rebellion, massacred many of the colonists, burned their dwellings and committed many great atrocities. The rebellion was quickly suppressed by the prompt action of Lieutenant Governor John Murray and in gratitude, he was presented by the colonists with a handsome service of plate value at £2,000.

What they do not say is that John Murray 'owned' more than 540 enslaved men, women and children. That it was his refusal to enact London's instructions to ameliorate slave conditions (including ending the whipping of enslaved women) that led to the uprising. And that under his direct authority as commander-in-chief, the British militia brutally killed more than 500 enslaved abolitionists.

Today, two of the main streets in the city of Niagara Falls are named after John Murray: Murray Street and Murray Hill.

I track down the person who wrote the history of All Saints Church. His name is Jock Ainslie, the former church warden. We talk for half an hour or so. The following day I received an email from him. 'I realize that John Murray did bad things in putting down a rebellion, but I decry the habit nowadays of wanting to remove the names of people from streets or buildings in our more enlightened times,' Jock wrote, adding that 'I do not know if John Murray did anything of value, but his wife gave us the church ... and we were grateful for it!'

I call Sherri Darlene, organiser of the #JusticeForBlackLives group in Niagara Falls and member of the city council's anti-racism committee. She says she frequently walks up Murray Hill ('It's steep!' she says) and had no idea of the history of John Murray. 'There's going to be pushback,' she tells me, 'but we need to change the name.'

CHAPTER 20

John Smith, October 1823

The morning of 24 October 1823 ushered in the eleventh day of John Smith's trial in Demerara. Up till now, both the missionary and the fiscal had made strong arguments. For those monitoring proceedings, the decision was evenly balanced. Wanting to change this in his favour, Victor Amadius Heyliger now called Jackey Reed, an enslaved man from the Dochfour estate.

The fiscal asked Jackey to tell the court about the letters exchanged just before the start of the uprising. On Sunday 17 August 1823, Jackey recalled, he had received a note from Jack Gladstone. This letter had been lost, he said, but it went something like this:

> My dear brother Jackey,
> I hope you are well, and I write to you concerning our agreement last Sunday. I hope you will do according to your promise. This letter is written by Jack Gladstone and the rest of the brethren of Bethel Chapel, and all the rest of the brothers are ready, and put their trust in you; we hope that you will be ready also. We shall begin to-morrow night at the Thomas [plantation] about seven o'clock.

Jackey said that reading the letter had made him extremely anxious. He did not like to see his name associated with any action against the colonists, least of all in writing. So at first he did nothing, tucked the letter away and tried not to think about it. Then, the following morning, Monday 18 August, he realised that he couldn't ignore it any more. He belonged to the Bethel Chapel and so felt obliged to pass along Jack's letter to Parson Smith. To clarify his position, he added a note of his own. This letter had also been destroyed. At the fiscal's urging, however, he was able to remember the contents of this letter as well:

> Dear Sir,
> Excuse the liberty I take in writing to you, I hope this letter may find yourself and Mrs Smith well. Jack Gladstone presented me a letter which appears as if I had made an agreement upon some actions, which I never did, neither did I promise him anything, and I hope that you will see to it and inquire of the members whatever it is they may have in view, which I am ignorant of, and to inquire after and know what it is, the time is determined for 7 p.m. tonight.

Around 2.30 p.m., Jackey continued, he gave the two letters to Guildford, also of Dochfour, who went to John Smith's home and, around 6 p.m., handed them to him. It was after dinner, just near sundown. A few minutes later, the missionary sent back a reply.

The fiscal turned to the members of the court martial. Crucially, he told them, the defendant had received the two letters, with their warnings that 'the brothers are ready' and that they 'had made an agreement upon some actions', before – he emphasised this word – the uprising had started.

Heyliger now walked up to the witness and dramatically handed over a letter, asking if he recognised it. Jackey took the paper, looked at its contents and confirmed it was indeed the letter he had received from the missionary. He then folded it. 'It was like this,' he said, handing it back to the fiscal. Heyliger now read the letter to the court.

> To Jackey Reed,
> I am ignorant of the affair you allude to, and your note is too late for me to make an inquiry. I learnt yesterday that some scheme was in agitation; without asking on the subject, I begged them to be quiet. I trust they will; hasty, violent or concerted measures are quite contrary to the religion we profess, and I hope you will have nothing to do with them.
> Yours for Christ's Sake,
> J. S.

Once Jackey's testimony was complete, the fiscal called a twelve-year-old girl named Elizabeth to the stand. She said she 'belonged' to Industry, a plantation three miles west of Le Resouvenir, and had been staying with the Smiths for some time. On the night of the uprising, she recalled seeing Guildford deliver two letters to Mr Smith and then wait on the step for a reply. What about Quamina's visit? the fiscal asked. Elizabeth said that Quamina had come to see the Smiths on the third day of the uprising. She had been in the outside kitchen at the time, but could see through the back door, which was open. She observed that John and Jane were sitting close together on chairs, while Quamina stood near them. They spoke for about fifteen minutes, too quietly for Elizabeth to hear what they said. Then, when Quamina left, Jane had walked up to her. 'You must not tell anybody,' the missionary's wife had said, referring to the secretive meeting. 'If I told anyone,' Elizabeth remembered Jane saying, 'she would lick me.' After a few more questions about Quamina's visit, the witness was dismissed.

Over the course of the afternoon, the fiscal called several more witnesses. The last was Captain Simpson, who described arresting the defendant at his house and taking custody of his journal. Heyliger concluded by asking the soldier to read out the governor's proclamation of martial law, which he in turn had read to John Smith. The final words were 'God Save the King'. With that, the prosecution rested its case.

Once the fiscal had sat down, the president announced that the court would adjourn for a week. They would reconvene on Friday 31 October.

Over the next few days, John thought about what had happened in the courtroom. He must have realised he was in trouble. His letter to Jackey was a particular problem. It suggested he had known about the uprising before it had begun. 'I learnt yesterday that some scheme was in agitation,' he had written, even though he had been referring to Quamina, who had suggested talking to his manager about the king's letter, rather than rebellion. The second meeting with Quamina was also an issue. They had met after the uprising had begun, which made him look like a co-conspirator. And his wife threatening to beat the young girl made them out to be heartless, if not hypocrites. He had to turn things around. Fast.

When the court martial re-convened, on Friday 31 October, the president asked if John was ready to start his defence. The missionary said that he had not yet been able to complete his preparations but that by the next day he should be ready. He knew it was a big mountain to climb, but he had moral arguments on his side. And prayer. He hoped that would be enough.

At 10 a.m. the following day, Saturday, John Smith stood before the court. In his hands was the speech that he and Jane had been working on for weeks. It ran to more than a hundred pages. It was plain to everyone, including John, that it was probably too long, and that its arguments were circuitous, repetitive and even self-righteous. Yet this was his one chance to get his case across, in full and on the record. They felt he should err on the side of comprehensive rather than concise.

As to the charges, he freely admitted that he abhorred slavery. 'If it be a crime to cherish such an aversion,' he told the court, 'then I have as my associates in guilt the most liberal and best part of mankind.' He was particularly aggrieved that his journal had become part of the proceedings. It was meant for his private use only, never for public consumption. The contents of it were unknown even to Mrs Smith, he confided. Nevertheless, the journal demonstrated his innocence rather than the contrary. As an example, he cited the 8 August 1817 entry, in which he decided not to read the end of Genesis, which spoke of deliverance from slavery, because he did not want to 'make a wrong impression' upon his congregation.

Regarding the various witnesses, their testimony was often con-tradictory and appeared to have been tutored by the prosecution, which was prohibited in English courts. He vehemently denied being told about the uprising before it happened. And when he did finally learn of it from Jackey's letter, it was too late. He had just given his letter of reply to Guildford when he heard the uprising start on the adjoining plantation. But even if he had known in time, which he didn't, why was he the only person being charged with not reporting it, when many others – including Michael M'Turk – had known about it hours before him and had received no sanction? Finally, he addressed the accusation that he should have arrested Quamina on the third day of the uprising. He had a simple answer for that, he said: at the time he had had no idea of Quamina's role in the rebellion, and nobody had proved otherwise.

He now moved on to his frustrations with the governor. But before he could get into this in any detail, he was stopped by the president, who ordered the court to be immediately emptied. A phalanx of bailiffs ushered John out of the room, along with all the members of the public. The door was then locked. Thirty minutes later, they were invited back in. The president announced that the court was not sitting to try General Murray, and John's previous comments about him would be struck from the record. Clearly that line of enquiry wasn't going to get him anywhere.

So perhaps with an eye on who might eventually read the trial's transcript after it had been sent to London, copied and distributed to the supporters of the London Missionary Society, the accused now spoke about context. And maybe because he was no longer speaking of himself, he became more eloquent. If he was not the cause of the uprising, which he felt he had plainly proved, then what was? He offered four possibilities: the colonists' severe treatment of the enslaved people, the immoderate labour, the opposition to religious instruction, and the withholding of the new laws that would have ameliorated the slave conditions. It was these factors, he forcefully argued, that led to the uprising, not his Bible readings, not his conversations with his deacons, not his refusal to take part in the militia.

Over the next twelve days, John called eighteen witnesses, including Michael M'Turk, Colonel Leahy, John Stewart and Bristol. Each patiently answered his questions, and in some cases re-answered them, but little new was revealed that had not already been disclosed to the court. On a number of occasions, the president interjected, refusing to allow him to recite long quotations from the Bible or rejecting his line of questioning. On 13 November, the court allowed him to call his fellow missionary Richard Elliot, who was escorted from prison so that he could give testimony. It was John's hope that this might bolster his credentials as a man of theology rather than politics. Yet even this was not without its difficulty. For just as Elliot was saying that the estate owner Ben Hopkinson had spoken favourably about John Smith and his congregants, the president cut him short. The defendant must limit himself to evidence, he instructed. He must not encourage his witnesses to share hearsay. This despite the fiscal's case relying for days on numerous witnesses whose testimony was little more than repeating other people's words.

That night, John and Jane discussed their strategy. It was hard to know what other witnesses to call, what arguments to make. John was exhausted by the daily grind and emotional stress of having to represent himself. None of which was helping his already frail body. Jane, though, had a plan. She suggested one more roll of the dice.

The following day, Jane woke early to prepare. With the small bowl of water provided by the guards, she cleaned her face and hands as best she could and wiped the dust from her shoes. Then, having said goodbye to John, she rapped on the door. A few seconds later, she was walking down the stairs of Colony House and out into the open air. She did not have far to go. There on the other side of the street was the government building known as King's House.

Trying to hold on to her confidence, she walked up the steps and into the front hall. She was here to see the governor, she told the clerk. There was no need to explain who she was; her husband's predicament was known by everyone in the capital. The clerk would also have been aware that Jane had been living for weeks in the small attic room across the street. This had engendered much sympathy. Many felt sorry for her situation and impressed by her stoic resolve.

Did she have an appointment? he asked. No, she said, but she was ready to give a sworn statement about her husband, so long as the governor took her testimony personally. Realising the import of the moment, the clerk hastened inside and checked with a superior. A few minutes later, he returned and ushered Jane to a room upstairs. The governor would be in to see her soon. Perhaps John Murray was curious to meet Jane face to face. Or maybe he thought he might be able to obtain some confession from the missionary's wife where others had to date failed.

After a few minutes' conversation in which they exchanged pleasantries, they began; Jane sitting in a chair providing her account, the governor behind a large desk, a portrait of the king hanging behind him on the wall, taking down her every word. The facts she stated were an almost exact copy of what her husband had said in court just days before. What was different, was that the events were told from her point of view. She described John reading the note from Jackey, which made him 'distressed and uneasy'. How when she saw the abolitionists take charge of the Success plantation, she felt 'exceedingly alarmed' and 'terrified' and ran back home. How it had been her, and not John, who had called for Quamina on the Wednesday, as she wanted to find out what was going on with the enslaved people. The affidavit was two pages long and was a clear attempt by Jane to take some of the responsibility and, in so doing, shield her husband from the blame. After both she and the governor had signed their names at the bottom of the document, she thanked him and walked back to Colony House to join her husband.

On 14 November, John told the court he was closing his case. It had been a month since the trial had started; it was time to bring it to an end. 'Gentlemen, I have done,' he declared, his hoarse voice barely more than a whisper. 'To you my case is now confided, whatever may be your determination. I do as a minister of the gospel, in the presence of God, most solemnly declare my innocence.'

Five days later, the fiscal provided a summary of his case to the twelve men of the court martial. If John Smith's effort had been long-winded, this was even more so. No effort it seemed was made at brevity, let alone clarity of argument. It was laborious and excruciatingly boring to listen to, something even its messenger acknowledged at the end when he said, 'No one can be more sensible than myself of the inefficient manner in which this task has been executed.' Finally, though, he looked at the members of the court martial and concluded with the words 'I shall not detain you longer, but commit at once the case into your hands.' With that it was over.

The trial had taken twenty-eight days. In all, fifty witnesses had been examined; of these, twenty-one were White and twenty-nine were of African descent. John Smith was returned to the room in the attic above the courtroom. All they could do now was wait.

On 24 November, John was called back to the courtroom to hear the decision. The day was here at last. He was extremely nervous, his frail body struggling to cope with the adrenalin that coursed through him. After a few moments, he was told to stand. He pulled himself up and watched as the lead member of the court martial handed the decision to the president of the court, Lieutenant Colonel Goodman. Jane sat just behind her husband, anxious to learn his fate.

Having reviewed the verdict, the president read it out. The prisoner was guilty of all four charges. Goodman paused a moment, then continued. 'John Smith will be hanged by the neck until dead, at such time and place as his excellency the lieutenant governor and commander-in-chief may think fit to direct.' John and Jane were in shock. Their worst fears had come true.

But Goodman had not finished. 'The court, under all the circumstances of the case,' he continued, 'begs humbly to recommend the Prisoner to mercy.'

Perhaps there was hope after all. If Jack Gladstone, the leader of the uprising, had received clemency, maybe so too would John.

A few days later, Governor Murray sent a letter to the king in London requesting that the case of John Smith be reviewed, and that his sentence be reduced from execution to banishment from Demerara. Jane's affidavit may have made a difference.

When *The Colonist* – which was as pro-slavery as the other papers in Demerara – found out about this letter, it was outraged. A week after the trial's conclusion, the paper wrote that there was a 'universal feeling of distrust and dismay' at the governor's decision, and that it was 'a matter of deep regret to us all'. All they could hope for, they concluded, was that 'public apprehension will gradually subside – confiding in that watchful Providence which makes even the wickedness of the worst of traitors, subservient to the ultimate purposes of its justice'.

In other words, they hoped that His Majesty would make the right decision and the parson would be punished like the enslaved abolitionists. Indeed, as an expression of their feelings, a group of colonists erected a gallows, and while the crowd cheered and hollered, they hanged from its rough-hewn timbers an effigy of the missionary John Smith.

*W*hile I'm in Guyana I speak with Mark Phillips, the prime
minister. We're both attending an event at the State House
marking the launch of a postage stamp that honours the former
president, Janet Jagan.

From my research, I know that until recently Phillips served as
the chief of staff of the Guyana Defence Force. 'Do you think Britain
should pay Guyana for what happened during the enslaved period?'
I ask him.

'That is an interesting question,' he says, laughing. Then he adds
more seriously, 'What is important is that the discussion has started,
not only on this side, but also in England. My hope is that this could
lead to some conclusion that makes both sides happy. So, reparations
yes, but it should not be forced on to the British.'

So history is important? I ask. 'History is always important',
he says. 'We must always understand where we came from as we
chart our way forward into the future. But I am of the view we
can't be stuck in the past. We have to move forward. If reparations
are part of the process to move forward as a people then yes, let's
have that discussion. And I hope that we reach a conclusion that
is acceptable to both sides.'

Later, I have a call with Hew Locke, an award-winning visual
artist whose work sometimes includes themes of empire and history.
In one piece, he adorned a photograph of the slave trader Edward
Colston with gold coins, shells, beads and chains. Hew was born in
the UK, spent his formative years in Guyana, and has been living
in London ever since. His father was Afro-Guyanese, his mother
White English.

He tells me that his ancestors on his father's side came from
Barbados and were enslaved. He says that when he returns to
Guyana, he feels it is a 'blood-soaked' land. He is aware 'in the
back of my mind' of the brutal slavery that took place there.

He says that he 'feels it in the shadows'. If White people talk about slavery, he adds, they should do so sensitively; it shouldn't be all about 'me and my White guilt'.

CHAPTER 21

Cheveley, December 1823

On 6 December 1823, John Cheveley was back in Georgetown. The voyage from Liverpool had been rough; he had spent most of the time in his cabin trying not to be sick. The only consolation was the temperature, which gradually warmed as he approached South America.

Now walking along the street that ran away from the Demerara River and up to the parade grounds, he was reminded of what he had left back in September. The red flag of martial law still fluttered above Colony House. A detachment of militia marched by, and from their shuttered windows, it seemed that the majority of warehouses and stores remained closed. Then, as he turned a corner and onto the road that ran up to the parade ground, he saw at least a dozen decapitated heads stuck on the ends of tall wooden pikes: the would-be free men.

It had been hard to avoid the topic of the uprising during his trip home. As soon as he had stepped off the *Glenbervie* in Glasgow and onto the overnight steamer to Liverpool, he had heard people talking about the news from Demerara. When they found out that he had been a participant, they had bombarded him with questions. What was it like? Did you see action? Was the missionary responsible? He found himself the centre of attention. After a while, a well-dressed man took his arm and escorted him to the cabin of the Duke of Athol, who happened to also be on board. Again he was interrogated, and was careful in his answers. At one point, the duke looked him up and down and, observing his skeletal and much-sunned physique, remarked that Demerara 'must be a wretched place to live'.

As soon as he arrived in Liverpool, he went to see William Pattinson's brother, John, who questioned him closely about the uprising. Why did it start? Who was involved? How would it impact the economy? They also spoke about the business back in Demerara, and Cheveley assured Pattinson that he would turn things around.

Next, he took a coach to Prescot to see his old friend Thomas Driffield, the man who had originally set him up with the job in Demerara and who was like a second father to him. Once more he was asked about the uprising, the troubles having by now been widely reported in the newspapers. He told his mentor that he believed, like most others, that the missionaries were 'the authors of the mischief' in Demerara and that they were inspired by the anti-slavery groups in Britain. Encouraged by Reverend Driffield, he then attended a meeting convened by a local missionary society. Their focus was Africa, but inevitably people asked him about what had just happened in Demerara. For the fourth time, he shared his views and experiences.

Before he set sail once more, he just had time for a quick visit to see his parents, who were still living in Essex. His father was 'jolly and happy' to see him, and his mother 'given up to delight'. He hugged the younger siblings still living at the house, and soon they were catching up on the news. His stay, though, was a 'pleasurable yet painful time as my days were numbered'. His father asked if he really had to return to the colony. He replied that he must; there were business matters to resolve, financial obligations to meet.

The following day, he tried to put on a brave face as he said his goodbyes. It was raining hard. They were all crying as he walked away, umbrella held up against the tumult. All in all, his stay in Britain had lasted only a month, but he had achieved much. Despite his homesickness, he felt rested and re-energised.

*

Soon after Cheveley's arrival back in the colony, the governor issued another proclamation. This time, Murray declared that where the enslaved population had proved 'faithful to their lawful masters' during the recent 'unhappy disturbances', they would not be obliged to work on Christmas Day or the day after. However, those who lived on the east coast plantations at the centre of the uprising – such as Success, Bachelor's Adventure and Nabaclis – would not benefit from such relief. Some of the enslaved people at Nabaclis declared they would ignore this latest proclamation and that they intended to take the day off and drink and dance. When he heard this, the head of the militia dispatched a company of troops to quell the revellers. According to the *Guiana Chronicle*, the object was to 'keep the Negroes in awe till the holidays are over'. At least thirty-nine people were placed in the stocks. In other words, the spirit of the uprising, if not the scale, was still very much alive.

Over the next few days, Cheveley learned that a great deal had happened while he had been away. Following his guilty verdict, the missionary John Smith had been moved from the attic of Colony House and placed in a jail cell, where he awaited execution. The manager of Le Resouvenir, John Hamilton, had been judged as having encouraged the abolitionists. He had been expelled from the colony and told never to return. The Bethel Chapel had been set on fire, though only partially damaged. Most believed that some local planters were behind the arson, and there was a general agreement that no more missionaries should be allowed into Demerara. There was even a book to be published about the uprising. It had been written by local resident Joshua Bryant and included a number of plate sections that captured the key moments of the revolt. Both the *Gazette* and *Chronicle* were carrying advertisements announcing that Bryant was accepting subscriptions and the book would be available the following year.

But that was not all. During Cheveley's absence in England, there had been much discussion of another topic: John Cheveley.

Since his return to Georgetown, he had quickly discovered that rumours had been widely circulating that he supported the abolitionists' cause. The evidence for this, apparently, was that he had failed to fire his gun at Bachelor's Adventure and that he let a prisoner escape rather than doing his duty. More than that, he had then fled the colony fearing charges of treason and desertion, and that he had done so without permission from his commanding officer. Finally, and perhaps most traitorously, whilst in England he had attended missionary meetings, where he had taken the side of John Smith and 'abused the planters'. Many, he was informed, believed that he should now be brought before the court martial. This was a 'pretty catalogue of crimes', Cheveley later recalled, 'some degrees of truth mixed with a large quantity of malicious falsehood'.

Realising that his reputation was now at stake, if not his freedom, he set about correcting the record. A few days after his return to Georgetown, he headed rifle in hand to the military headquarters and made an appointment to see Captain Croal, his commanding officer. After listening to Cheveley's concerns, Croal said that he 'did not believe half of these reports'. When Cheveley asked if he believed any, Croal hesitated. Now worried that he might be in real danger, Cheveley showed Croal the rifle that he had used at Bachelor's Adventure, demonstrating the weakness of its lock, which had prevented him from firing despite his best efforts. He said that it was true that he was thankful he had not taken anyone's life, but that this in itself was not a crime. At this, Croal seemed less than impressed, but commented that he had checked with Lieutenant George Rainey, who confirmed that he had given permission for Cheveley to leave the colony.

Seeing that Croal remained suspicious, Cheveley suggested that his superior conduct an inquiry to get to the bottom of the matter. The captain agreed that this was a sensible way forward, and said that until the investigation was completed, Cheveley would be suspended from the militia. This came as a shock to the young Essex man. He walked away realising that the colonists were not only looking for someone to blame, they were wilfully blind towards evidence presented to them.

This understanding led him to re-examine his beliefs about what had happened during the uprising. John Smith had been sentenced to death, but what was the evidence that the missionary had encouraged the enslaved abolitionists? All he had done was preach the gospel. It was 'undoubtedly a mistake', Cheveley believed, to fail to alert the authorities to what a few of his parishioners were planning, but this was hardly a hanging offence. Also, why did the governor not publicly declare the amelioration measures that had been sent out from London? And perhaps most importantly of all, why had the militia deployed such brutal counter-insurgency measures against the local population? When he asked these questions, in the store, in the taverns, at the docks, he was met with either stony silence or anger. They said that John Smith had put 'mischief into the slaves' heads' and that he had 'concealed knowledge of their guilty intentions'. Cheveley no longer found these arguments persuasive.

Wanting to get out of town for a few hours, he decided to go for a ride along the east coast. He had a commercial justification if anyone asked – Pattinson had asked him to deliver a package to one of the managers – but the real reason was to get away from the rumour mill and the broiling accusations of Georgetown. He needed some time to think. To clear his head.

It was a bright and cheery day as he made his way along the public road. He rode past one estate and then another: Thomas, Kitty, Blygezight, Bel Air. This was the same route he had taken with the militia just weeks before, when they had marched out to crush the rebellion. He tried to put this out of his mind. After about half an hour, he approached Wittenburg plantation, the eleventh estate. Here, at the estate entrance next to the public road, he saw a head on a spike. It was disgusting. He kept going. A few estates further along, there was another. And then another. So when he reached Success, he was half expecting to find the same thing.

Instead, as he came closer, he saw a body hanging from a wooden gibbet by the roadside directly across from the entrance. It was Quamina, still strung up weeks after he had been killed in the bush. Cheveley approached to take a better look. He noticed that the flesh had been eaten away and a colony of wasps had built their nest inside the abdominal cavity. They were flying in and out of Quamina's jaw, which gaped 'frightfully open'.

He was still staring, transfixed, when two women approached from the opposite direction. The elder was in her fifties, the other in her twenties. When they reached the body, which was now swinging back and forth in the ocean breeze, they covered their faces and started screaming. 'Never had he heard a cry so full of anguish,' he later recalled. After a few moments, the girl pulled at the woman and guided her away down the road.

Cheveley was horrified. Turning his horse, his pursuit of equanimity now forgotten, he galloped back to Georgetown.

A few days later, word arrived in the colony that Reverend Wiltshire Stanton Austin had turned against the planters. Austin was in charge of St George's, the church Cheveley attended in Georgetown. He had written a letter to a colleague in England sharing his concerns about the governor's failure to implement the amelioration order, and the militia's ruthless suppression of the uprising. These thoughts, which were intended as private, had been read out at a public meeting, then reported in the British newspapers, copies of which were sent back to Demerara.

Things now went from bad to worse. In a front-page editorial, the *Guiana Chronicle* proclaimed that Reverend Austin 'vilifies his fellow colonists in the dark', and called him 'that advocate of sedition and murder, the Evil Genius of Demerara'. They demanded his immediate expulsion from the colony. Next, a public meeting was held to discuss the matter. Austin and his supporters were mockingly labelled as 'saints' and openly described as 'enemies' and 'traitors' who threatened the colonists' way of life. Many speeches were passionately given decrying the 'sufferings of the white people'. Such lack of self-awareness was lost on the majority of those present. 'The colony resembled a hive of bees which has been disturbed and cannot resettle,' wrote Cheveley, 'armed and ready to sting all comers who strive to cope with their determination to have their own way, and such ill feelings and suspicions and quarrels among the white people was most odious.'

Wanting to show his support but fearing the anger of the mob, he went to see Austin under cover of darkness. Like Cheveley, the reverend had at first firmly believed that John Smith had instigated the uprising, but now, he said, he was having second thoughts. During the tumult, he had visited one of the plantations and met with thirty or forty abolitionists on the road, including Sandy, whom he knew from before. Sandy said, 'I have been slave long enough' and complained of 'hard usage'. A principal reason for their upset, he added, was the governor preventing them from attending church – not any instigation by John Smith. In addition, the abolitionists assured Austin that they had no intention of causing physical harm to any managers or plantation owners. This was in sharp contrast, as Cheveley very well knew, to the brutal violence deployed by the British militia during the days of suppression. Cheveley said that he was shocked by how the reverend was being treated and would do anything he could to lend support.

The following day, he heard that some planters intended to march into that Sunday's morning service and grab the preacher whilst he was giving his sermon from the pulpit. Luckily, Austin also became aware of this plan, and someone else gave the address. Soon after that, a small group arrived outside Cheveley's door demanding he sign a petition that called on the governor to expel Austin. Pattinson signed the document but Cheveley refused. When he was asked why, he said that he did not feel he had to give a reason. Not happy with this reply, the petitioners pushed him further. 'Well,' said Cheveley, 'it is because of private friendship.' With that, the bearers withdrew.

Several days later, Governor Murray announced that Austin and his wife had to leave the colony immediately. When they departed soon afterwards, they took with them a letter of introduction from Cheveley to his friend Thomas Driffield, explaining the injustice of what had happened and asking him to provide assistance to the Austins.

Cheveley was beginning to realise the truth. When he had travelled back to Britain in September, he had been 'impressed as to the guilt of Smith and others from what I had heard ex-parte'. And though he 'abhorred the slaughter of the Negroes' at Bachelor's Adventure, he had 'thought it necessary'. Now he was starting to think otherwise, 'to see how fearfully the pro-slavery feeling turned with savage unreason on all who dared to think differently'. More than this, he now understood that on the basis of a 'few interested white people and the most ridiculous evidence', John Smith had been condemned to be hanged. This was, he concluded, a 'mockery of justice'. It was 'military tyranny'.

*T*o hear the view of Her Majesty's Government, I visit Greg Quinn, the British High Commissioner in Guyana. He greets me at the front door of his residence in Bel Air Gardens, a large two-storey colonial-style house surrounded by razor-wire fencing. He's in his black socks and asks me to remove my shoes. A few moments later we are sitting on the cream-coloured sofas that are organised in a U-shape in his living room. He offers me a tonic water, which I think colonially apt.

Greg grew up in Northern Ireland, and has been in the Foreign Service for more than a decade and in Guyana for five years. His posting ends in a few weeks. I start by asking about Britain's role in slavery in Guyana. 'There is still stuff to be done within the UK to understand the bad bits of our history,' he says. 'There is a fundamental lack of understanding in your average man and woman in the UK about what happened.'

So, should Britain apologise for slavery? 'That's a huge political question,' he says. 'I think there is concern partly that if you apologise for one thing, does that then create a legal precedent. An obligation.'

Then, to my surprise, the British High Commissioner adds, 'I'm not saying we would not get to that point. And certainly, Tony Blair got [to that point] when he talked about the potato famine in Ireland.' He is referring to the statement made by the former British prime minster in 2011 when he said that 'Those who governed in London at the time failed their people.'

I move on to the next logical question: should Britain pay Guyana reparations? 'It's a hugely emotive subject here,' he says, and then sighs. 'Even though I'm a historian and I love looking at history, I think sometimes you need to look forward and not back too much. And in fact, the problems in Northern Ireland were caused by too many people looking too far back.' He continues, 'That doesn't mean we are trying to say that slavery was not abhorrent, that wrongs were not committed. Clearly they were.'

I tell him that many people in Guyana have said to me that if the Jews were paid reparations after the Holocaust, why not the descendants of slavery? He nods. 'It's a hard argument and I fully agree,' he says. 'I think it's a hugely difficult question and there is no easy answer for it.' I tell him that I feel very sympathetic to those who ask this question. Again he nods his head. 'It's extremely hard to see why that should not happen.'

CHAPTER 22

John Smith, December 1823

John Smith was now being held in a small cell in the colonial jail. This was the same facility that had held Jack Gladstone and the other abolitionists. His was a dark, low-ceilinged, cramped room on the ground floor, which hung over a pool of stagnant water. The fetid damp air rose up through the wide gaps between the floorboards. It was hard to imagine worse conditions for his fragile lungs.

Unable to accompany her husband, Jane had returned home. She had spent the last three months with John in the attic room of Colony House. She was exhausted, disorientated and eager to put on some fresh clothes. But as soon as she was back in their house on Le Resouvenir, and before she did anything else, she wrote to the secretary of the London Missionary Society. 'You have no doubt heard of the trouble which has befallen Mr Smith and myself,' she began, 'and the temporary ruin of the missionary cause in this colony, in consequence of the revolt of the Negroes on the east coast.' She explained that on 21 August they had been arrested at their house in a 'forcible and brutal manner' and had been unable to write sooner because they were both in prison.

She said that the causes of the uprising were twofold: the 'innumerable grievances' endured by the enslaved people, along with their being disallowed from taking part in religious services. 'Many of the planters, I think I may say the colonists generally, apprehended that the religious instruction of the slaves was incompatible with their condition in life, and that as soon as they became a little enlightened, they would revolt.' She continued, 'It is alleged that most of the people that attended our chapel were engaged in it [the uprising]. That many of them were implicated is, I am sorry to say, too true.' She went on to say that her husband had nothing to do with the uprising and in fact 'endeavoured to persuade them to desist from their purpose', adding that it had been started by Jack Gladstone, who was 'a dissolute, gay young man, very irregular in his attendance at the chapel. Religion, it is to be feared, he had none.' As to his father, Quamina, he was no more than 'a runaway, although he was shot and gibbeted'.

Now, she wrote, her husband had been sentenced to death. 'How the Court-Martial could justify a conviction on such evidence, must, I think, be a wonder to every unprejudiced person.' She believed that it was her husband's journal that had caused the worst enmity against him. It contained 'many reflections on the evils and iniquity of slavery' and some remarks on the governor's opposition to the instruction of the enslaved people. Desperate and isolated, Jane ended: 'I must, therefore, close this letter, earnestly entreating that the Directors will use every exertion in behalf of Mr Smith, whose greatest crime was his devotedness to the object of his mission.'

A week later, on 12 December, John wrote a letter of his own to the directors of the London Missionary Society.

Dear Sirs,
You will have heard, ere this comes to hand, of the trouble that has befallen me, and of the desolated state of the Demerara Mission, both which are occasioned by the revolt of the Negroes on the East Coast. Of my own personal sufferings, I shall say nothing further, than that the close and solitary nature of my imprisonment, with the disease under which I labour and have laboured for more than twelve months, have pressed very heavily upon me. I have, however, much consolation from the consideration of my innocence of the crimes with which I have been charged, and of which I now stand convicted.

Like his wife, John affirmed that he had done nothing to embolden or support the enslaved men and women in their uprising. 'Notwithstanding what the Negroes say,' he wrote, 'if they had kept to what they were taught by me, they never would have acted as they did; yet, because two or three of them, who were deeply concerned in the revolt, chose to pervert and misrepresent what I had said to them about working on Sundays, it is therefore settled, in the judgment of the people here, that the revolt is to be attributed to me.' Also like Jane, at the end of his letter, he pleaded for help: 'I trust the directors will seriously consider the hardship of my case, and make every effort on my behalf.'

By the first week of January 1824, John's health had worsened. He was attended by a Dr Chapman, who was appalled at the cell's terrible conditions and said that unless the floor and the windows were sealed, the prisoner's ailments would deteriorate. But no change was made to his situation. In a letter to the London Missionary Society sent on the 12th of that month, John spoke of his 'fatigue' and 'emaciated frame'. He added that his 'close imprisonment, with its innumerable privations … has brought me to the borders of the grave'. He ended:

> It grieves me, dear Sirs, that I am now a useless burden upon the Society. I have endeavoured from the beginning to discharge my duties faithfully. In doing so, I have met with the most unceasing opposition and reproach, until at length the adversary found occasion to triumph over me. But so far have these things been from shaking my confidence in the goodness of the cause in which I was engaged, that if I were at liberty, and my health restored, I would again proclaim (all my days) the glad tidings of salvation amidst similar opposition; but of this I see no prospect.

Tired by the effort to write legibly and with coherence, John handed the letter to his wife. She would find a way to have it taken on the next possible mail packet to England.

*

If the missionary was still dealing with the consequences of the uprising from inside his prison cell, the same was true for many of the enslaved abolitionists who had been tried the previous summer. Whilst more than twenty had faced immediate execution, another thirty were still being held in the colonial jail awaiting implementation of their sentence.

Amongst these number were Cudjo, Quabino and Sammy, who had escaped with Jack and Quamina to the bush in the days after the Bachelor's Adventure massacre. On 18 January 1824, they were taken from their cells and escorted to the barracks on the edge of the town. Around them stood a brigade of the militia, to witness the punishment and ensure the peace. Quabino was the first to be beaten. He was thrown to the ground, his arms tied to stakes, and then thrashed with a tamarind switch, made from three tamarind rods that had been braided and oiled. He had been sentenced to a thousand lashes – which some euphemistically called 'stripes'. Somehow he managed to live through the whole amount. Next was Sammy, who received nine hundred lashes before becoming insensible. Finally it was Cudjo's turn. He was tied to the stakes and the whipping began. One hundred, two hundred, on and on. By eight hundred he had stopped crying out for the torture to end and the commanding officer called it off.

The three bodies were left out in the sun. If the men survived, which was doubtful, they would be taken to the workhouse, where they would spend the rest of their lives in chains.

As January neared its end, John's health declined still further. He woke up feverish and suffered bouts of diarrhoea. He found it increasingly hard to speak and struggled to swallow. He had lost a considerable amount of weight; his body appeared gaunt and skeletal. Outside, the rain seemed unending, flooding the ground beneath, filling his cell with malodorous air. At last, and only after repeated appeals from his physician, John was moved to a higher room in the prison, away from the dank ground. Given her husband's rapidly failing health, Jane was allowed free access to him, and spent most of the day and night at his side. 'I fondly hoped for a few days he was getting better,' she wrote to friends back home, 'but soon found the hope delusive.'

Finally, at 1.20 a.m. on 6 February 1824, John Smith drew his last painful breath. He was thirty-four years old. Jane was with him when he died. Also present in the prison cell were Elizabeth Elliott (the wife of the missionary Richard Elliot), whose high temper and animosity had been forgotten, and Mary Chisholm, Jane's friend from Success. Mr Padmore, the keeper of the jail, was immediately informed of the parson's death and left to tell the governor. A few hours later, a funeral director and his assistants arrived and placed the body in a coffin, leaving the top open. All the while, Jane and her friends waited, saying prayers and wondering what would happen next.

That afternoon, Victor Amadius Heyliger walked into the cell. Without a word of condolence, or any sign of compassion, he demanded that Jane grant him an interview. He instructed her that she must testify as to the cause of her husband's death, right then and there. When Elizabeth protested that it was too soon, the fiscal replied that 'It must be given today.' Jane said that she would speak but asked that she remain in the room where the corpse lay. 'If you can command your feelings, madam, you may,' Heyliger said. Ignoring his insensitivity, Jane said she would do her best.

A few minutes later, a dozen more people crowded into the tiny cell, including two members of the Court of Policy, two colonial secretaries and two doctors, Dr Chapman and a Dr Webster. The fiscal asked the physicians to examine John Smith's body. As they proceeded, a clerk wrote down his findings. Dr Chapman acknowledged that the cause of death was pulmonary, and said that the prison's appalling conditions had accelerated the dead man's illness. The lowness of the room in which he was confined, in particular its dampness, worsened by the heavy rains, plus the water flowing under it, which seeped through the open floorboards, had contributed to the rapid progress of the disease. Dr Webster confirmed this opinion. But when Dr Chapman's deposition was read back to him, it was found to be so different from the statement he had made that he repeatedly refused to sign it. Exasperated, the fiscal announced that the doctor's findings should be ignored.

Heyliger then asked what Jane thought had caused her husband's death. She said John had been ill for some time, but that the false accusations that had been brought against him, the cruel persecutions he had endured and his long imprisonment had no doubt hastened his death. The fiscal and other officials reacted angrily to her words. It was not Mrs Smith's opinion they wanted, but the cause of his death.

Heyliger then turned to Elizabeth, who said she had nothing to say. 'Madam,' insisted the fiscal, 'you must give your evidence.' To this she replied calmly, 'I do not consider this a legal meeting, and do not feel bound to answer any questions.' Now infuriated, Heyliger retorted, 'Do not you know that I have the arm of power, and can oblige you to speak?' Elizabeth Elliot was not to be bullied. 'I should be sorry to oblige you, Sir, to do anything repugnant to your feelings,' adding bravely, 'but if you did, I should still resist.' Realising that he would be unable to get his way, Heyliger ended the encounter and stormed out, followed by his retinue. A year earlier, Jane had been offended by Elizabeth's wilful manner. Now she was grateful for her support.

A short while afterwards, Michael M'Turk walked into the cell. Seeing her husband's adversary at this time must have filled Jane with considerable anger. After all, it was M'Turk who had ordered John's arrest, which had led to his sordid confinement and ultimate death. M'Turk explained that he had also been asked to examine the corpse, which he did briefly, agreeing that the cause of Smith's death was pulmonary.

After M'Turk's departure, Jane had a few hours to mourn in peace before she was disturbed yet again. This time it was the second head constable. He told her that he would collect the body at four the next morning and take it away for interment. Elizabeth asked whether they would be allowed to attend the burial. The officer said that would not be possible and the order had come directly from the top, adding that 'It is probable there will be soldiers there and something unpleasant may occur; and, therefore, I advise you not to go.' To this Jane, who was still sitting by her husband's corpse, exclaimed loudly, 'General Murray shall not prevent my following my husband to the grave, and I will go in spite of all he can do.'

Just before sunrise, the coffin carrying John Smith was carried out of the prison and loaded onto a small wagon. Despite the constable's threat, Jane and the others followed the desolate cortège through the quiet streets, their way lit only by a lantern held by a free Black man, and out to a cemetery on the edge of town. There, after a brief few words were spoken, the coffin was lowered into the ground.

It's coming to the end of my trip to Guyana and I'm sitting with Eric Phillips under a tree in the garden of the Herdmanston Lodge. A short, energetic, charismatic bald man, he is the chairman of the Guyana Reparations Commission. Above us, parakeets chirp and tweet. In the distance, someone is using a power washer.

'The history is there, the evidence is there,' he says, yet so far no British prime minister has given an outright apology for the country's role in slavery. Tony Blair came closest when he spoke of 'regret'. The problem, Eric continues, is that when a perpetrator denies a crime, it retraumatises the victim. And for those of African descent in Guyana, this has resulted in 'psychological disadvantage, the feeling of inferiority and anger'.

I tell him that during my research, I have heard one point made again and again: even if we agree that reparations are necessary, what would this look like? Who would pay? Who would receive the money? How much?

Eric looks at me patiently; he has clearly been asked this many times before. He knows his stuff, for in addition to leading his country's reparations efforts, he is also vice president of the Reparations Committee for the Caribbean Community (CARICOM), representing fifteen states and dependencies throughout the region. This group demands reparations for the enslavement of Africans and genocidal actions upon indigenous communities.

In 2014, Eric tells me, CARICOM published what it called a 'Ten-Point Plan for Reparatory Justice'. The action points included Britain, France, the Netherlands and other countries making a formal apology, cancelling the debt owed to them by Caribbean countries and paying for the repatriation of people who wish to return to Africa.

More recently, the CARICOM Reparations Committee proposed that the European countries that were owners and traders of enslaved

Africans contribute $50 billion into an investment development fund. This fund would not make payments to individuals but would, with the agreement of a regional and international management committee, pay for health, education and infrastructural projects across the Caribbean.

Such a concept is not new, Eric reminds me. A similar approach was deployed after the Second World War to rebuild western Europe. It was called the Marshall Plan. 'It's a question of priorities,' he says. 'The money is there if you want it.'

At the end of our conversation, I ask Eric why someone in Britain today should care about atrocities that took place in Guyana and other Caribbean countries two hundred years ago.

'I can understand that question,' he replies, 'because they have a sense that "I have my own problems, my own struggles, and this happened so long ago". But the society they live in, the society they are benefiting from – materially, spiritually, economically – that society has a historical platform. And that historical platform impacted others negatively. It has created a global hierarchy of race that impacts everything we do, from the pandemic to debt relief.'

Finally, I ask if he believes that Britain will actively engage with reparations in his lifetime. He tells me that he does. Perhaps not in the next five years, but maybe in the next ten. He adds, 'I am hopeful.'

CHAPTER 23

Gladstone, February 1824

In the first week of February 1824, John Gladstone read in the papers that John Smith had been found guilty by the court martial in Demerara. The politician was relieved. The parson more than deserved to face the consequences of his ill-thought actions.

A few days later, just after lunch on 10 February, he and forty fellow plantation owners, merchants and others with interests in the West Indian trade gathered at the City of London Tavern. Their purpose was to respond to the growing attacks in the press. These, the group quickly agreed, had misrepresented 'the condition of the Negroes' and calumniated the characters 'of their masters to inflame the public mind'. It was also agreed that the group's ultimate aim was the protection of their 'sacred property', and if this was interfered with, they should be awarded compensation for their loss. At the meeting's end, punctuated by much cheering and cries of 'hear, hear', those assembled signed a petition that would be submitted to the government. Part of it read as follows:

> We beg to leave humbly to state to you, Majesty, that we hold our plantations in your Majesty's colonies by grants or purchase from the Crown. That those grants and purchases were made in some cases under the stipulation, in all upon the understanding, that the lands so acquired were to be cultivated by Negro slaves. That Negro slaves were brought by your Majesty's British subjects from Africa to your Majesty's West India colonies and sold by them to planters under the sanctions of acts of the British Parliament, giving to British subjects the exclusive privilege of carrying on that trade, confining

it to British ships and prohibiting the planters from trading with the merchants of any other country.

If nothing else, this petition was a testament to how the Caribbean slave societies and slave business were intrinsically linked to Britain.

Over the next few weeks, Gladstone worked hard to furnish his colleagues in the Tory Party with the 'facts'. In particular, he corresponded with the foreign secretary, George Canning. A colourful character who had been shot in the thigh during a duel a decade earlier, Canning was one of the leading politicians of his day. Though six years younger than Gladstone, he played the role of mentor. In Liverpool, Gladstone had organised Canning's parliamentary election campaign. In London, he and his associates supported Canning's efforts to bolster international trade. He considered the foreign secretary to be a personal friend. Gladstone's son William later wrote that 'I was bred under the shadow of the great name of Canning. Every influence of that name governed the politics of my childhood and of my youth.'

Gladstone now sent Canning several reports he had received before the uprising. 'You will see,' he wrote, 'that these letters when written were not intended to meet any Eyes but those of my partner and myself.' Amongst them was the letter from his agent, Frederick Cort, which stated that the enslaved people were so well taken care of that when they attended church the men wore nankeen trousers and the women were dressed in muslin frocks accented by blue silk handkerchiefs. Gladstone hoped that such evidence would encourage the foreign secretary to take a firm stand against the British abolitionists.

In Great Britain, the spring of 1824 was unusually wet and windy. A gale on 3 March brought chaos across southern England. Roofs were blown off several hundred houses in south London. Boats were overturned in Portsmouth and Southampton harbours. Several people were killed by falling tree limbs.

While the weather wreaked havoc on England's infrastructure, three things happened that dramatically altered the course of the slavery debate. The first was that the king, or more likely his advisers, had at last made a decision on the fate of John Smith. It was good news for the prisoner in Georgetown. 'His Majesty has been graciously pleased to remit the sentence of Death against John Smith,' the statement began. Instead, the missionary was to be banished from the colony on pain of a stiff fine of £2,000 if he ever returned. The tragedy, of course, was that John Smith died before the order would arrive in Georgetown. He never knew that his sentence had been commuted. Nor did he have the chance to leave Demerara and recover from his illness somewhere less hateful and more conducive to his health. Perhaps because of this apparent injustice, someone leaked news of the king's decision to the press.

Then the second thing happened: the arrival of a thick bundle of documents on the doorstep of the London Missionary Society. This had been sent by Jane and included the full transcript of the trial, which had been annotated by John Smith before he died, along with a copy of the missionary's journal, various letters written by the Smiths, and copies of the governor's proclamations. These documents were now indexed, collated and then forwarded to newspapers. Over the next two weeks, periodicals around the country, from *The Star* in London to the *Courier* in Inverness, published verbatim sections of the proceedings, often taking up more than half a page.

All the while, Gladstone and his allies prepared for the inevitable showdown in Parliament. At first, Gladstone felt the wind continue to blow in his favour. In one early skirmish on 16 March, for instance, Canning stood up in the House of Commons and decried the behaviour of the 'enthusiasts' – by which he meant the members of the Anti-Slavery Society – declaring his support for the rights and property interests of the plantation owners and sugar traders. While slavery was 'in theory' to be seen as 'evil' and 'abhorrent', he boomed, emancipation – if it was to happen – must be gradual. Why was this? he asked. Because the enslaved people were not ready for emancipation. 'In dealing with the Negro,' Britain's foreign secretary explained, 'we must remember that we are dealing with a being possessing the form and strength of a man, but the intellect only of a child.' Hearing Canning's remarks, Gladstone was reassured. It was clear that the government had no intention of taking drastic action any time soon.

Four days after Canning's appallingly racist speech in the House of Commons, the third thing happened. Gladstone found out about it when he read a copy of the *Barbados Mercury* that had just arrived in Liverpool on the *Lancaster*. The paper reported that John Smith had died in prison six weeks earlier. 'We are happy to state, by personal inquiry and inspection,' the writer reassured his readers, that 'his apartment was airy and commodious and he had always had at his command every comfort which his taste fancied'. Gladstone was secretly pleased. 'I was not sorry to hear of Smith's death,' he would later write, 'as his release would have been followed by much cavil and discussion here.'

Despite Gladstone's glee, when the three events were put together – the king's commutation, Jane's bundle of documents, plus the missionary's death – the story of the Demerara uprising was suddenly reframed. Relying on the sovereign's edict, pamphleteers, street-corner orators and columnists now declared that John Smith had suffered a gross injustice. From the bundles of court transcripts, newspaper editors began to print page upon page of colourful detail. Meanwhile, the British abolitionists had been delivered a royally certified martyr. With quotes taken from John Smith's journals that proved the missionary's peace-loving nature, they now mobilised their supporters to sign petitions and used these to lobby members of Parliament.

By mid-April, public opinion was turning against the West Indian traders and in favour of John Smith and the enslaved abolitionists. One of the first indications of this shift was an article published in *The Times* on the 15th of that month. In contrast to its jingoistic coverage the previous autumn, the paper now took issue with the proceedings of the court martial. In particular, it focused on the fiscal's use of John Smith's private diary. 'The mere fact of the smallness of the number of passages selected in a journal of such length of busy life, is a strong presumption in favour of Mr Smith,' they opined. 'In reality, the passages which are produced prove nothing against him, unless it be a crime to be zealous and humane, and to feel some degree of horror at the oppression of one's fellow-beings.' There was some value in the journals, the paper continued, for their 'throwing light on the slave system of the colonies'. *The Times* then quoted at length various sections in which John Smith described the brutal treatment of enslaved people. They next lauded his decision not to read the Bible story about the Israelites escaping Pharaoh, which might have provoked his congregation. 'This only shows,' concluded the paper, 'the desire which Mr Smith felt to avoid inflaming the minds of the Negroes.' In an ironic twist, the very same evidence used by the colonists to prove the guilt of the missionary was now being used in London to demonstrate the guilt of the slave-holding colonists.

On the same day that *The Times* article was published, Sir James Mackintosh MP presented a petition to the House of Commons on behalf of the London Missionary Society. He pointed out that unlike other slave rebellions, 'little or no injury was done to any property' during the Demerara uprising, and 'the life of no white man was voluntarily taken away by them'. Mackintosh and his fellow petitioners now asked the House of Commons to consider the evidence and declare 'not merely a remission, but a reversal' of John Smith's sentence and his 'thorough aquitment from all guilt'. The missionary was not only 'an innocent and unprotected victim', he said, but also a 'martyr'.

In reply on behalf of the government, Robert Wilmot-Horton (who served as George Canning's under-secretary) said that he 'regretted' that the petition had been presented ahead of the official transcript of the trial being submitted to Parliament. He added that though he would make no further comment on the petition at this time, this must not be understood to preclude him from exposing on future occasions 'the extreme inaccuracies with which it abounded'. He continued, spitefully, that he doubted those behind the petition had 'exercised a sound discretion in the course which they had pursued'. With that, the petition was read in full and ordered to lie on the table, pending a full debate in the House. This gave Gladstone a few more days to lobby and cajole MPs. Quiet lunches and dinners in which favours were exchanged, pressure points were pressed. On balance, the sugar trader was pleased. The government's response had remained unified and robust.

Public opinion, however, was less susceptible to the influence of John Gladstone. What had started as a conversation about slavery and abolition now became a discussion about the British Empire, Christianity and the role of its missionaries. 'We for our part hold the spreading of civilisation and religion among our foreign dependencies to be our National Duty,' wrote the *New Times* in a widely syndicated opinion piece. 'To reduce the savage natives by gentle and just manners to the love of civil society and Christian Religion,' the writer continued, was 'the very condition of our dominion over those territories'. Missionaries, clergy and other members of the Church were 'entitled to peculiar encouragement from Parliament and from the public and more especially ought they to be protected against all injustices on the part of the colonists'.

It had been almost a year since the first tremors had started in the far-flung colony of Demerara, but like some slow-moving tsunami, the shock waves were now being painfully felt in London. Each camp had marshalled its arguments and supporters; the stakes were now set. On one side was positioned God, morality and duty;

on the other, money, power and British exceptionalism. Or to put it another way, was the legacy of one good man, John Smith, and the freedom of hundreds of thousands of enslaved people to be sacrificed on the altar of the Empire's business interests?

So it was that on 1 June 1824, well aware of the growing public disquiet and eager to bring about some national reconciliation, the House of Commons met to discuss the John Smith trial and the Demerara uprising. Given the public interest in the issue, the chamber was full. On the front benches perched George Canning, the foreign secretary and John Gladstone's friend. Next to him was the attorney general, Sir Robert Gifford. A grocer's son who married a rector's daughter, Gifford was known as a hard-liner following his recent prosecution of protestors, radicals and parliamentary reformers. On the other side, the debate would be led by William Wilberforce and Fowell Buxton, the long-time proponents of abolition. John Gladstone was there as well, sitting on one of the green back benches, maintaining a low profile, but keeping a watchful eye.

The speaker of the house, Charles Manners-Sutton, called forward Henry Brougham, Whig and MP for Winchelsea in Sussex. From his seat at the centre of the back benches, Brougham rose to his feet and read out the motion in a loud, clear voice: that the members of Parliament contemplate the trial of John Smith in Demerara 'with serious alarm and deep sorrow' and deem those 'unexampled proceedings' as being in 'violation of law and justice'. Furthermore, the motion called on the king to secure 'a just and humane administration of law' in Demerara, including protecting both the enslaved people and their instructors from 'oppression'. It was a carefully worded motion. Soft enough to avoid antagonising the plantation owners, but clear enough, they hoped, to encourage His Majesty to exonerate John Smith.

Brougham now opened the debate, galvanising his supporters with the following words: 'It will be my duty to examine the charge preferred against the late Mr Smith, and the whole of the proceedings founded on that charge.' He continued, 'And in so doing, I have no hesitation in saying, that from the beginning of those proceedings to their fatal termination, there has taken place more of illegality, more of the violation of justice – violation of justice, in substance as well as form – than in the whole history of modern times.'

The MP now moved on to demonstrate how the legal proceedings were biased against Smith. The defendant did not have access to his own counsel prior to the trial, hearsay evidence was permitted for the prosecution but not the defence, 'proof' was substantiated only by a single witness testimony (civil courts required two) and there was no right to appeal. Perhaps most astonishingly, Stephen Arthur Goodman, the president of the court martial, also held the position of vendue master in the colony. Waving a copy of a gazette from Demerara in his hand, Brougham pointed out that a slave auction had been advertised just days before the insurrection, and upon each 'lot' was attached the signature of one S. A. Goodman. 'There was one sale of fifty-six of these hapless beings,' he proclaimed, 'who were to be torn from the place of their birth and residence, and perhaps separated for ever from their nearest and dearest connections.' Another announcement spoke of several 'prime single men'. Another 'lot' consisted of a woman and her three children. A third offered a young pregnant woman. Clearly, concluded the MP, neither the president nor his court martial was impartial.

Henry Brougham was incensed. 'There was never exhibited a greater breach, a more daring violation, of justice, or a more flagrant contempt of all those forms by which law and justice were wont to be administered,' he thundered to his colleagues, 'and under which the perpetrators of ordinary acts of judicial oppression are wont to hide the nakedness of their injustice.' His comments were greeted with roars of approval and shouts of 'Hear! Hear!'

After Brougham concluded his statement, the debate began in full. Given the long list of MPs who wished to speak, it would last two days. The MPs began by rehearsing the facts of the case and repeated many of the arguments that had been stated during the court martial. The timing of when John Smith was alerted to the uprising was carefully examined, as were passages from his journal and their alleged inflaming of enslaved people's feelings. There was much chest-thumping about safeguarding the rights of the colonists to protect their property, and as much that it was well past time to abolish slavery in Demerara and across the rest of the Empire.

Predictably, perhaps, given that many of those present had previously worked as barristers or judges, there arose new legal arguments and opinions. Around mid-afternoon, a powerful discussion was had about the jurisdiction of the court. One member of Parliament pointed out that under British law, a treasonous offence could not be punished by the death penalty. Someone else pointed out, however, that Demerara was still governed by Dutch law, which did allow for hanging. To which a third member responded that the laws of Holland did not countenance the proceeding by court martial. This seemingly crucial paradox remained unresolved, confounding many of the spectators watching from the balcony.

At one point, the proceedings were interrupted by a commotion just outside the main chamber. The motion's sponsor, Henry Brougham, had been walking through the lobby when a young man named Robert Gourlay ran up to him and asked him for his name. When the MP gave it, Gourlay struck him several times on the shoulder and head with a penknife. A man who happened to be standing nearby stepped in to prevent serious injury. Still in shock, Brougham asked, 'Who is this man, I don't know him, what does he want?' Gourlay responded, 'Let the dead bury the dead, but do your duty by me.' Before he had the chance to say anything more, he was bundled off to custody by the sergeant-at-arms. There he was asked what he meant by his comment. He said it was in reference to the missionary John Smith whose case was being discussed. He added that the dead didn't need attention, but the living did.

Meanwhile, back in the chamber, the debate was continuing. Dr Stephen Lushington, a Whig from Ilchester, rose to speak. He declared that if the motion was defeated that night, then 'the persecutors of Mr Smith will rejoice' and the 'severity exercised to the Negroes, will be increased one hundred-fold, the cause of religion will fall to the ground, government will lose its authority, and all the hateful and degrading passions of man will be brought into full and unrestrained action'. To this more than fifty MPs jumped to their feet, waved their papers and shouted, 'Hear! Hear!' Lushington added, 'I call, then, upon every man who hears me, not to vote until he has read the evidence, and fully sifted the grounds upon which the question stands. I hope the decision to which we shall come will be in unison with the voice of the country, and that we shall, by our vote this night, mark, as it deserves, an act alike repugnant to British justice and British feeling.' This was received with more cheers.

Now it was time for William Wilberforce to speak. The great abolitionist, famed around the world for promoting the law in 1807 that had banned Britain's Atlantic slave trade, was now sixty-four-years old and in failing health, but he remained a force in Parliament. 'Mr Smith had maintained through life the character of a truly amiable and good man,' Wilberforce proclaimed. 'It was not against Mr Smith only, and the particular body of religionists with which he was connected, that the resentment of the colonial population was pointed; it was against all who were endeavouring, by religious instruction, to raise the condition of that degraded class whom we have taken under our protection.' After reciting various legal arguments that others had raised, he concluded with a rallying call. They had a dilemma, he said. They could either leave John Smith under a stigma of having been wrongfully convicted, or condemn the proceedings and conduct of the court martial. 'I shall indeed regret,' he continued, 'if we can suffer such proceedings as those on which we are now called upon to pronounce our sentence, to pass, without expressing our strong and decided reprobation of them.'

It was well past midnight on the second day of the debate, 11 June, and still more members wanted to speak. One MP stood up and denounced the system of slavery and its immorality; another rose and condemned the anti-slavery politicians and their lack of care for the economy. On and on they went. Finally it was the turn of the attorney general, Sir Robert Gifford, who spoke on behalf of the government. He confessed that he might not have come to the same conclusion as the court martial, but it was important to consider the issue from the viewpoint of those living in the colony at Demerara, to remember 'the terror which surrounded the inhabitants . . . The whites had to protect everything that was most dear to them – their wives and families; their own lives and properties,' he continued. 'And, could it be expected, that they would expose themselves naked to the barbarians who were armed for their destruction, instead of resorting to the most vigorous means which were presented to them, for averting the evils by which they were threatened?' He went on to articulate the greatest fear of the colonists, the fear that was always at the back of their minds: that if the enslaved people won their freedom, they would avenge themselves on their former masters. Had his colleagues 'forgotten the horrors which accompanied the revolt of the Negroes in the neighbouring island of St Domingo'?

It was almost 3.30 a.m. when the debate finally finished. After more than twenty hours of relitigating the John Smith case, arguing over the necessity and pace of abolition, discussing back and forth whether the colonial government or Parliament should have the final power, the speaker of the House called on the motion's proposer to give his concluding remarks. An exhausted Henry Brougham rose to his feet and briefly summarised the main arguments. He then gave his opinion about those who described John Smith as a martyr: 'For my own part, I have no fault to find with it; because I deem that man to deserve the name, as in former times he would have reaped the honours of martyrdom, who willingly suffers for conscience,' adding, 'If theirs is a holy duty, it is ours to shield them, in discharging it, from that injustice which has persecuted the living and blasted the memory of the dead.'

Brougham, however, was no revolutionary. Though anti-slavery, he believed in a slow process of reform; one that, most importantly, took care of the financial needs of the slaveholders. With that in mind, he made this point. 'It is for the sake of the blacks themselves, as subsidiary to their own improvement, that the present state of things must for a time be maintained. It is because to them, the bulk of our fellow subjects in the colonies, liberty, if suddenly given, and, still-more, if violently obtained by men yet unprepared to receive it, would be a curse, and not a blessing; that emancipation must be the work of time, and, above all, must not be wrested forcibly from their masters.' On both sides of the house, his colleagues erupted with approval.

And with that, the debate was over. The speaker called out, 'Division, lock the doors!' It was time to vote. Those in favour of Brougham's motion to ask the king to exonerate John Smith walked towards the 'aye' door, those against headed to the 'no' door. It would then be up to the tellers to make the count and report to the speaker, who would announce the result to an expectant chamber.

On Saturday 12 June 1824, the people of London woke up to read their morning paper. On the front page of *The Star*, contractors were invited to submit offers to build a reservoir for the navy near Plymouth. A notice stated that the Theatre Royal, Covent Garden, would be performing Shakespeare's *Comedy of Errors* the following Tuesday, featuring the actors Miss Paton and Miss Tree. The property Norwood House, along with fifty-one acres of fine arable land, was offered for sale in Surrey. And in the bottom-right corner, Barrow Cliffs Manufactory on Regent Street, Piccadilly, invited the public to purchase mattresses filled with white goose feathers, and several four-post beds, both new and soiled. These announcements and others similar made up the paper's front page. The rest of the periodical, three pages in all, or 75 per cent of that day's total, covered the Demerara debate in the House of Commons.

The Star's multi-page coverage was repeated in other papers, including *The Sun*, the *British Press,* the *Evening Mail* and *The Times*. It was an indication of the importance the editors gave to this issue and their perception that the British public considered it of enormous interest. Each of the stories ended with the vote count and the result: 146 for, 193 against. Henry Brougham's motion had been defeated. Somehow John Gladstone and his allies had pulled victory from the jaws of defeat. Despite the public outcry over the treatment of the Demerara enslaved people and the shock of the death of John Smith, the status quo had been maintained.

But if those who won the debate saw this as a victory, as having achieved success, they were misguided. The impact of the two-day parliamentary debate upon the abolitionist cause was profound. Following extensive coverage in both regional and national papers, the horrors of the slave system had been exposed, as had the corruption of the colonial regime. This public awakening was then built on by missionary and other anti-slavery organisations, who widely circulated the full speeches of the key abolitionist parliamentarians. John Smith's name became a rallying cry.

As one commentator put it, though the iniquities of slavery had long been the topic of comment, 'this single case of a persecuted individual falling victim to those gross perversions of law and justice which are familiar to the colonial people, produced an impression far more general and more deep than all that had ever been written or declaimed against the system of West India slavery'. Or as the biographer of John Gladstone wrote, 'The death of the Demerara missionary was an event as fatal to slavery in the West Indies as the execution of John Brown was its death blow in the United States.'

It was just a matter of time for this decisive shift in public opinion to be reflected in law.

*I*n my various discussions, I have found that the term 'reparations' is a loaded phrase. One that can provoke heated debate, sometimes fear and shame, occasionally anger. Some see it as insulting, others as impractical or a distraction. Even for those supportive, the prospect of reparations raises a series of challenging questions. Who will pay? How much will it be? Who receives the money? And who gets to decide?

In the USA, public discussion of reparations has become common in recent years. At the federal level, presidential candidates are routinely asked during their campaigns if they support reparations, and there's currently a bill before Congress that seeks to explore the need for government reparations. At the local level, numerous institutions are engaging in reparative projects. For instance, the city council of Asheville, North Carolina, unanimously voted to pro-vide financial reparations, and students at Georgetown University in Washington DC voted to add a levy to their tuition fees to subsidise scholarships for descendants of slavery. Reparations efforts are also taking place at an individual level. There's a Facebook page where descendants of slavery post their financial needs – a car repair, a medical bill, a plane ticket – which are paid by contributors wishing to engage in reparative justice. And there are television stories about descendants of slaveholders providing financial support directly to descendants of those enslaved.

In the UK, I have found fewer examples of those making reparation for slavery. Perhaps the best known is the University of Glasgow, which has committed to transferring £20 million to the University of the West Indies. Besides that, various institutions have committed to exploring their legacy of slavery, including the University of Bristol, the University of Cambridge, the brewer Greene King and Lloyds of London. And partly because there are fewer examples, there is an awkwardness about the subject.

I know of one instance where a well-known company offered a substantial sum to an academic institution only to be rejected for fear that they might be seen as whitewashing history. Was the company wrong to offer the money? Was the institution wrong to reject it? Such questions are fraught and provoke much anxiety.

Even within my own family we had a version of this. After learning how the family had benefited from slavery, I wrote to my relatives and asked if they wanted to engage in a conversation about our family's history and possibly support a reparative justice project. A handful said they did not wish to be involved (we mustn't apply the values of today to the nineteenth century, they said; we mustn't damage the family's reputation). But the majority said that it was vital that the family's legacy of slavery be acknowledged and that a reparative justice project was important, timely and necessary. In the end, more than thirty family members agreed to make a financial contribution. These funds were used to support a Black British student to study a PhD at a UK academic institution.

But then came the question of anonymity. Both the institution that received the funds and the family members who contributed were keen to keep the project away from the public gaze. The institution did not want to be seen as laundering our history. My relatives did not wish to appear self-aggrandising or to put their heads above the parapet.

I understand this reflex for privacy. But the problem with keeping such projects behind closed doors, even a modest one such as our family's, is that there's no accountability. No chance for open debate. No opportunity to learn from other people's successes or mistakes. This instinct for anonymity not only underscores the complexity and messiness of reparations, but also its necessity.

EPILOGUE

Ten years after the start of the Demerara uprising, almost to the day, the House of Commons passed the Abolition of Slavery Act. The act came into effect a year later, on 1 August 1834. Newspapers declared that 665,000 enslaved men and women in the British Caribbean and more than 100,000 in Britain's other colonies, were now free. In Georgetown and elsewhere around the British Empire, people took to the streets and celebrated.

Emancipation was not, however, immediate. Nor was it universal. Children under the age of six were freed at once, as were enslaved people in the Bahamas and Antigua. But all others were bound as apprentices to their former slaveholders. Agricultural workers were obliged to work for another six years. They were required to work 40½ hours per week without pay, and were provided with rations and accommodation. Household labourers, who worked longer hours, were required to apprentice for four years. Many were deeply disappointed by the false promise of emancipation. On one sugar plantation in Essequibo, more than seven hundred former slaves went on strike. The revolt was promptly suppressed, and its leaders captured, tried and executed.

The apprentice scheme did not, however, last the full six years. Following numerous investigations that proclaimed the new arrangements akin to slavery, political pressure mounted in Britain, and following persistent campaigning by anti-slavery groups, the system was deemed unworkable. So it was that on 1 August 1838, the apprentice scheme was annulled and full emancipation was finally declared throughout the British Empire. Tens of thousands of formerly enslaved people in Demerara now found themselves without jobs or homes. Many banded together and, using their carefully stored-up savings, purchased abandoned sugar estates, such as Ithaca, Victoria and Friendship. Within a short while, more than 14,000 former enslaved people owned over 2,900 lots. These villages became the backbone of the colony.

For more than a century, historians have argued about what brought about the British abolition of slavery. Some, for example Eric Williams in his book *Capitalism and Slavery*, emphasised the economic forces, such as the financial collapse of the sugar, cotton and coffee plantations. Others have said that the anti-slavery humanitarians in Britain – William Wilberforce, Fowell Buxton, Elizabeth Pease and Anne Knight – were able to convince their peers as to the immorality of the system. Still more, including C. L. R. James in his book *The Black Jacobins*, have credited slave rebellions with triggering emancipation. The uprisings that are most often cited include the Haiti Revolution (1791–1804), Bussa's rebellion in Barbados (1816), and Sharpe's rebellion in Jamaica (1831–2), which was also known as the Christmas rebellion or the Baptist war. These insurrections, the argument goes, shook the British establishment into understanding that the enslavement of African people was untenable, since they would continue to fight for their freedom through organised resistance. That they were highly aware and conscious actors, agents of change. That they were human beings with natural rights and the commitment to demand those rights.

To this list of key rebellions, I would add the Demerara uprising of 1823. There is something special about this insurrection. After Britain banned the transatlantic slave trade in 1807, public support for the anti-slavery movement underwent a massive collapse. The success of the 1807 act took the wind out of the British abolitionist cause. The argument became one of economics. How would the Empire survive if emancipation was enacted? Who would compensate the slaveholders, and how much? This is why the Demerara uprising was so significant. The year 1823 marks the reinvigoration of the anti-slavery movement in Britain.

Why was this? First, the death of John Smith captured the imagination of the British public. That a White missionary had died for the cause of abolition was in itself sensational. More than this, through his journal entries and courtroom testimony, he provided a bridge to those unfamiliar with slavery, a way in for the public to understand what was going on in the colonies. Then came the inquiries into the condition of the enslaved people, which truly appalled the residents of London, Manchester, Edinburgh, Cardiff and beyond. Certainly, news of the disgracefully high mortality rates on the plantations and the abhorrent conditions the enslaved people endured shocked many into joining the anti-slavery cause. In addition, people were impressed by the enslaved abolitionists' careful planning and their efforts to limit violence during the uprising. Meanwhile, Governor Murray's refusal to implement the instructions sent from London calling for amelioration, followed by the militia's horrendous brutality, turned many against the slaveholders. Perhaps more than anything, those living in the British Isles wanted to put distance between themselves and the colonists.

To put it simply, enslaved abolitionists in the Caribbean – including both the Demerara uprising, Sharpe's rebellion in Jamaica and other insurrections – played as important a role as humanitarians in Britain in bringing about the end of slavery.

What happened to the main characters in this story?

On 16 February 1824, Jane Smith posted a notice in the *Guiana Chronicle* that she was planning to leave the colony within two weeks with her friend Elizabeth Elliot. 'All persons having any claim against either of us,' went the advertisement, 'to render the same for settlement.' Six weeks later, she arrived in Portsmouth, desperate to put distance between herself and the traumas of Demerara.

Within a few days of her arrival, a fund was created by several British churches to provide her with money to live on. She spent the next months and years supporting the London Missionary Society's effort to clear her husband's name, before moving to the village of Rye in Sussex. Here she became ill, remaining in bed until she died at 8.30 a.m. on 10 February 1828, aged thirty-two. According to one of those present, she expired with 'serenity' in her mind, a 'lovely expression in her eyes' and 'without a sigh or the least symptom of convulsion'. Five days later, she was buried in the Protestant Dissenters' cemetery, in the same grave as Mary Smith, perhaps her mother-in-law. Next to her death record was added a hand-written note declaring her to be 'Widow of John Smith missionary for London Society who died in prison at Demerara 1824'.

Throughout the 1820s and early 1830s, John Gladstone continued to expand his sugar plantations in Demerara. Meanwhile, back in Britain, he led the campaign to prevent the amelioration of conditions for those enslaved. When he realised that this was likely to fail, he joined with other slaveholders to persuade the British government to compensate them for the loss of what they called their 'property'. So it was that following the passage of the Slave Abolition Act in 1833, it was the British slaveholders, rather than the enslaved people themselves, who were paid compensation. Indeed, more than 60,000 slaveholders received payments from the Slave Compensation Commission. In total, Britain handed out £20 million to these slaveholders, equivalent to 40 per cent of that year's government expenditure. In today's money, the compensation would be worth around £17 billion, when calculated according to the value of wages. According to a tweet released by Her Majesty's Treasury, the debt that was taken out by the British government to make these payments was only paid off in 2015.

At the time of abolition, John Gladstone was registered as personally 'owning' 1,778 enslaved people across his plantations, and jointly 'owning' 1,134 others. For these enslaved people, he was paid more than £100,000 – today that is the equivalent of more than £80 million. This was one of the largest of all the compensation payments. For Gladstone, the timing could not have been better. Four years earlier, he had finally purchased his dream Scottish estate at Fasque in Aberdeenshire. He would use the compensation money to improve the elegant stately home and its more than six thousand acres of farmland.

Abolition did, however, present Gladstone with a problem. He no longer had free labour to work his plantations in Demerara. Which is why, on 4 January 1836, he wrote to Gillanders, Arbuthnot & Co. of Calcutta asking them to send indentured labourers to replace the emancipated people of African descent on his plantations. In return for their labour they would receive clothes, food and shelter, and after five years they would be free to stay in Demerara or return to India. To reassure his colleagues in Calcutta, Gladstone painted a rosy picture of life on a Demerara plantation: 'Labour is very light … They are furnished with comfortable dwellings and abundance of food … A school for the children … They have likewise an annual allowance of clothing sufficient and suitable for the climate … it may be fairly said they pass their time agreeably and happily … They have regular medical attendance whenever they are indisposed, at the expense of their employers.' By return, the Calcutta traders said they saw no problem complying with Gladstone's request, particularly given that 'the Natives being perfectly ignorant of the place they agree to go to, or the length of the voyage they are undertaking'. On 15 May 1838, the ships *Whitby* and *Hesperus* arrived in Georgetown carrying 407 men, women and children from India. A quarter of these were transported to plantations owned by Gladstone; the rest were distributed to other estates.

Worried that indenture was a new form of bondage, in 1840 the Anti-Slavery Society sent a team to investigate. They found terrible living conditions, long hours at work, frequent floggings and widespread sickness. More than a hundred indentured Indians had died in the first year. The report included interviews from a number of witnesses, including Elizabeth Caesar, who said the indentured people 'were locked up in the sick house and next morning they were flogged with cat-o-nine tails. The manager was in the house, and they flogged the people under his house. They were tied to the post of the gallery of the manager's house. I cannot tell how many licks; he gave them enough. I saw blood. When they were flogged at the manager's house, they rubbed salt pickle on their backs.' Between 1838 and 1918, more than 340,000 indentured labourers from India were imported into British Guiana, far more than any other colony. At the time of this book's writing, those of Indian descendant made up more than 40 per cent of the population of Guyana.

On 18 July 1846, John Gladstone was created a baronet by the outgoing prime minister, Robert Peel. Over the next five years, he continued his work, including minding his railway investments and winding up the estates in Demerara, but towards the end of 1851, he grew feeble. By early December, he had become so infirm that his children were called to his bedside. He died just before 9 a.m. on the seventh day of that month, aged eighty-six. He was buried a few days later in the crypt beneath the small St Andrew's Episcopal Church on the family estate in Fasque.

The obituaries remembered Gladstone kindly. The *Illustrated London News* called him a 'merchant prince' and described his commercial skill as 'unprecedented'. According to the *Morning Advertiser*, Gladstone was 'a fine example of the union of Scottish thrift and caution with English largeness of view, commercial correctness and stainless probity in all trading transactions'. The *Edinburgh Evening Courant* was similarly effusive: 'He took rank with the largest and most successful merchants' and 'amassed great riches by his enterprise, industry and skill'. As a sign of respect, the flag on Liverpool town hall remained at half-mast from the time of his death till the day after his funeral.

Over the next half-century, Gladstone and his family were memorialised around the country. A white marble monument was erected inside St Andrew's declaring that John Gladstone was an accomplished merchant. The Liberal Club in Leith, his home town, erected a plaque on the corner of Great Junction Street and King Street celebrating him as the father of William, the four-times prime minister. The University of Liverpool named one of its student accommodation blocks Gladstone Hall. On none of these was it mentioned that John Gladstone had made his money on the slave plantations in the Caribbean or that his son William inherited significant funds from his father.

That is, until the murder of George Floyd in May 2020. Students at the University of Liverpool had campaigned for years to change the name of Gladstone Hall, but after Floyd's death, resistance crumbled. The university announced it would rename the building due to John Gladstone's links to slavery. A spokeswoman said: 'We share in the shame that our city feels because its prosperity was significantly based upon a slave economy.' She added, 'We have an important opportunity to ensure that the name of this new hall reflects our values of equality and respect while sending a clear message about the commitments we have made to our Black, Asian and minority ethnic staff and student community.'

Towards the end of my research, I connected with Charlie Gladstone, the four-times great-grandson of John Gladstone. With his wife Caroline, Charlie lives in Hawarden Castle in Flintshire, Wales. In addition to managing the estate, they run a number of large cultural events under the banner of The Good Life Society, operate two farm shops, a gastropub, a wedding venue, a holiday cottage and cabin business in Scotland and a homeware and interior retail business called Pedlars.

'John Gladstone was an awful man,' Charlie told me, 'I am profoundly ashamed to be his relative.' He then added, 'There have been lots of times when I have wished that I did not share the surname.' The one building that he inherited from John Gladstone was Fasque in Scotland, Charlie continued, which had for a long time felt like a 'millstone for me'. When he sold it at a loss back in 2008 he believed that it was 'karma'. He said that he had really started exploring the family history only after the Black Lives Matter protests had erupted around the world. That was when he had first heard about the Demerara uprising and that it had started at Success. This had also been the moment when he had learned that the rebellion had been led by an enslaved man called Jack Gladstone, who was given his surname because he was 'owned' by Charlie's four-times great-grandfather, John Gladstone.

John Cheveley left Demerara in 1825, a year after John Smith's death. Faced with bankruptcy, he closed down the Pattinson business, packed his bags and fled. According to the law, he was meant to issue a two-week notice in the local paper to alert any creditors of his departure. Luckily, his brother George was in town with his ship the *Anna*, and the two of them set sail without anyone being the wiser. In his memoirs, Cheveley wrote that 'I had nearly wasted five years and was in worse plight than when I began, for I had liabilities out of which I saw no way.'

Once back in England, he regrouped. Within a short time, he married Frances Barry, the sister-in-law of his former Demerara business partner, and took a job as a bookkeeper in Liverpool. The couple moved into a small cottage overlooking a meadow and a line of elm trees, and soon had three children. Cheveley described himself as being 'settled' and his new life as 'paradise'.

Following abolition in 1834, Cheveley submitted a claim to the Slave Compensation Commission for fourteen enslaved people. These comprised a tradesman, four 'domestic servants', two 'inferior domestics', three 'inferior people of the same description', and four children under six years of age. John Cheveley was not himself a slaveholder, the 'ownership' appears to have been passed down through his marriage to Frances Barry. The Cheveleys received £479, or £415,000 in today's money. The enslaved people, once again, received nothing.

After an idyllic start, for Cheveley the next forty years back in England were filled with tragedy. His wife Frances died during a complicated childbirth. Seven years later, he married a Scottish woman named Emily. Their first child, Stephen, died aged three months. Two other children would die over the next few years. Then John's brother Henry drowned in a Brazilian river, then two others, George and Richard, died soon after. In 1864, at the age of sixty-nine, John embarked on his memoirs. Five years later, he was still writing when he stopped mid-sentence. The topic at hand was the patenting of copper smelters. Presumably he was too ill to continue. He died of chronic heart disease in Hastings on the south coast of England on 9 April 1870. He was buried five days later in West Norwood cemetery, London, next to his children.

How about Jack Gladstone? In his letter to Lord Bathurst of 14 February 1824, Governor Murray recommended that Jack be sent to the British colony of Bermuda. Starting in 1823, over 9,000 convicts were transported from Britain to this island to serve out their sentences. Most ended up in task gangs, working at the naval dockyard breaking and carrying stones, and housed on the *Antelope*, a prison hulk anchored offshore. It would have been a grim, exhausting, punishing existence.

Yet according to Keith Forbes, who manages a historical website in Bermuda, it is doubtful that Jack ever made it there. The island was more than two thousand miles from Demerara, and at the time, there was no direct shipping service between the two colonies. Keith believes that Governor Murray's request was never implemented. 'It may not have been practical to the governor's bosses in London,' he told me. So what did happen to Jack?

I found a clue in the archives of the University of Florida, which houses digitised copies of various Caribbean newspapers. There I discovered a letter dated 3 May 1824 published in the Demerara pro-slavery rag the *Colonist*. In this, an unnamed writer reports that Jack had a girlfriend, to whom he was later married by John Smith, and 'by her had four children'. No more information is given. The next mention I found is contained in Joshua Bryant's book about the uprising; Bryant reports that on 9 September 1824, Jack was still being held in the colonial jail in Georgetown, a year after being sentenced.

The final piece of the puzzle emerges from a letter sent by Robert Wilmot-Horton (under-secretary of state for war and the colonies) to John Gladstone dated 16 March 1825: 'In case you should not have already received information from your Agent in Demerara with respect to the fate of the Slave Jack, I think it right to inform you that he has been removed from Demerara and enrolled as a Military Labourer in St Lucia.' St Lucia was a small island that lay five hundred miles north of Demerara. As a 'military labourer', Jack likely provided manual work to the British garrison stationed on the island, perhaps employed in the kitchens or building fortifications. Was this where he spent the rest of his life? How young was he when he died? I like to think that he lived long enough to obtain his freedom. That he was able to savour the fruits of his abolitionist campaign. Perhaps even to have a family, his children born free. But, when I ask the national archives in St Lucia to see if they have any records for him, they tell me they have none.

Nevertheless, traces of Jack and his family remain. In 1984, on the 150th anniversary of the emancipation of slaves in British colonies, the government of Guyana renamed one of Georgetown's main streets. Up till then it had been called Murray Street, after the governor who had brutally suppressed the insurrection. Now it was to be called Quamina Street. Almost thirty years later, on 5 August 2013, former president Donald Ramotar unveiled a statue commemorating the 1823 rebellion next to the Georgetown sea wall and opposite the Guyana Defence Force headquarters. It was carved showing a man of African descent wielding a cutlass with a chain attached to its end. He stands erect, legs apart, conveying strength and defiance. Each year, on the anniversary of the uprising, Guyanese gather around the memorial and retell the story of how Quamina and Jack Gladstone led the fight for freedom. Parents name their children after them; there are numerous Gladstones still living in the country today.

When I was in Guyana, I visited the Bethel Congregational Church in the village of Beeter Verwagting ('Better Expectation'). After the service, I spoke with the presiding minister, who told me with a smile that the walls, beams, roof and floorboards of the church came from John Smith's church at Le Resouvenir. Then she pointed to the picture of Quamina on the wall and a plaque to John Smith on the other side of the aisle. Every year, she continued, the church commemorates the 1823 uprising with a service and a parade. At the church, I also met Genevieve Allan, who said she was descended from Quamina. 'Whenever we talk about emancipation,' she told me, 'I proudly say I have the blood of the late Quamina flowing through my veins. I owe it to him to celebrate the legacy so many years after.'

The spirit of Quamina and Jack lives on.

POSTSCRIPT

*O*n my last day in Guyana, I meet with Kibwe Copeland, the
twenty-eight-year-old president of IKEMBA, the first youth
reparations organisation in the Caribbean.

It's early, just after sunrise, and we are standing in the middle of
the parade ground in Georgetown, an area of scrubby grassland the
size of four football fields. This is the place where more than fifty
abolitionists were executed in the autumn of 1823. At the far edge,
a group of men play basketball. Other than that, the place is empty.
We are here to remember those who took part in the uprising.

We take off our shoes and stand barefoot on the damp earth.
We talk for a few minutes about the uprising, the trials and how
those found guilty were marched through the streets to this ground.

Kibwe then reads out the names of those who were executed
here: 'Allick, Attila, Bethney, Billy, Damas, Daniel, Evan, France,
Hamilton, Harry of Good Hope ...' After each name, he pours a few
drops from a bottle of water onto the ground, paying respect to the
ancestors, and then says 'asè', or 'and so it is'. He kept going '... Harry
of Triumph, Louis, Murphy, Natty, Nelson, Philip, Pickle, Quamina
of Noot en Zuyl, Quintus, Scipio, Tom.'

After he has finished, we stand silent for a few minutes.

Then Kibwe says, 'If it wasn't for them, I would not have the
freedom of speech that I have. I would not be able to walk as a free
man. Because of their sacrifices, I can.'

Later, as we are heading home, I ask him what British people should
do about this history. 'Slavery happened so long ago,' he says, 'but we

are still living with the side effects today. So many problems that we face today exist because we never properly dealt with that issue.'

'So, reparations?' I ask him.

'If you are against crimes against humanity,' he says softly, 'then you must support reparations. If this had happened to your family, you would want to be compensated. Why not the descendants of Africans who were enslaved?'

I think about being British and growing up in a country whose wealth was partially built on slavery. I think about finding out about my family's particular link to slavery. And I think about what I have learned in Guyana. Yes, the Slavery Abolition Act was passed two centuries ago, but from all my conversations, it is clear that the legacy of slavery is still being felt today. People affect history, but history affects people too. History is personal.

In the months and years since the killing of George Floyd and the Black Lives Matter protests that followed, there has been an upsurge in interest in Britain's colonial history. There have been discussions about the way that subjects are taught in schools, including more of a focus on Black and Asian writers and events told from a non-European perspective, which some have called 'decolonising the curricula'. Corporations, media outlets, sports federations and other groups have made public commitments to increase the diversity of their recruitment and representation efforts. Various police forces and other government agencies have announced new programmes to address their historically unequal treatment of the Black population. But though such efforts are laudable, many say they do not go far enough or fast enough.

And while it is hard to prove a direct link between Britain's role in slavery and the social conditions today – given the passage of time and the large number of events and forces that have occurred in between – the link, nevertheless, exists. That the picture is complex is a truism. As is the argument that there were individuals who acted in good faith during the time of slavery, and many, including some

White people, whose efforts resulted in social good. Yet any objective reviewer of history must surely conclude that the roots of today's systemic racial inequality are found buried in Britain's colonial past.

Therefore I agree with Kibwe. Reparations should be made to the descendants of those enslaved by the British. If we don't confront our history now, we will just pass the burden on to future generations. This is not about feeling guilty for what our ancestors did before we were born, it is about addressing the legacy of slavery that still impacts people today. Harm has been done, repair must be made. And while it is true that the debt can never be fully repaid – the atrocity of slavery cannot be erased from history – that shouldn't be an excuse for inaction.

It is up to all of us, therefore, all of us who benefited from slavery – individuals, families, companies, institutions and governments, those who have established direct links to slavery as well as those who have generally profited from the wealth that was generated during the time of slavery, to get involved.

We are in this together. We need to acknowledge and take responsibility for the White Debt.

APPENDIX

List of the abolitionists punished following the Demerara uprising of 1823*

Executed

1. Allick of Coldingen +
2. Attilla of Plaisance
3. Bethney of Success +
4. Billy of Ann's Grove +
5. Damas of Plaisance
6. Daniel of Foulis
7. Evan of Good Hope
8. France of Porter's Hope +
9. Hamilton of Success
10. Harry of Triumph +
11. Harry of Good Hope
12. Louis of Plaisance
13. Murphy of Foulis
14. Natty of Enterprise
15. Nelson of Golden Grove
16. Philip of Foulis
17. Pickle of Le Bonne Intention +
18. Quamina of Noot en Zuyl +
19. Quintus of Beeter Verwagting +
20. Scipio of Bachelor's Adventure +
21. Tom of Chateau Margo +

Other punishments

22. Achilles of Beeter Verwagting (death in chains)
23. Adonis of Plaisance (death sentence commuted, deported, worked as convict)
24. April of Le Bonne Intention (prison)
25. Alexander of Lusignan (flogged up the coast)
26. Austin of Cove (flogged and in the workhouse two years)
27. Britain of Success (death, respited)
28. Cato (freeman) of Success (banishment)
29. Cobus of Beeter Verwagting (prison)
30. Cudjoe of Lusignan (flogged and in the workhouse for life)
31. Cudjoe of Porter's Hope (death sentence commuted, deported, worked as convict)
32. David of Le Bonne Intention (in prison)
33. David of Beeter Verwagting (death, respited)
34. Duke of Clonbrook (death sentence commuted, deported, worked as convict)
35. Edward of Good Hope (flogged on the estate)
36. Field of Clonbrook (flogged and in the workhouse for two years)
37. Fingal of Triumph (flogged on the estate)
38. Frank of Success (flogged on the estate)
39. George Morrison of Enmore (500 lashes/too sick to receive punishment)
40. Gilbert of Paradise (death sentence commuted, deported, worked as convict)
41. Hugh of Noot en Zuyl (released and sent to plantation)
42. Ingliss of Foulis (death sentence commuted, deported, worked as convict)
43. Jack of Success (death sentence commuted, deported, worked as convict)
44. Jemmy of Bachelor's Adventure (death in chains)
45. Jessamine of Success (flogged and in the workhouse for life)

46. John Smith of Le Resouvenir (sentenced to death, died before execution, later commuted)
47. Kate of Chateau Margo (two months' solitary confinement)
48. Kinsale of Bachelor's Adventure (death sentence commuted, deported, worked as convict)
49. Lindor of Le Bonne Intention (death in chains)
50. Louis of Porter's Hope (flogged and in the workhouse for one year)
51. Mercury of Enmore (700 lashes)
52. Maximilian of Success (700 lashes)
53. Nelson of New Orange Nassau (death sentence commuted, deported, worked as convict)
54. Paris of Good Hope (in chains)
55. Paul of Friendship (in chains)
56. Primo of Chateau Margo (death sentence commuted, deported, worked as convict)
57. Profit of Le Bonne Intention (in prison)
58. Philip of Le Bonne Intention (in prison)
59. Quabino of Chateau Margo (1000 lashes, worked in chains)
60. Quacco of Success (death sentence commuted, deported, worked as convict)
61. Quacco of Chateau Margo (death sentence commuted, deported, worked as convict)
62. Quamine of Haslinton (death sentence commuted, deported, worked as convict)
63. Ralph of Success (death sentence commuted, deported, worked as convict)
64. Sam William of Coldigen (in prison)
65. Sammy of Lusignan (flogged and in the workhouse for seven years)
66. Sandy of Non Pareil (in chains)
67. Smith of Friendship (death sentence commuted, deported, worked as convict)

68. Telemachus of Bachelor's Adventure (death in chains)
69. Windsor of Success (flogged on the estate)
70. Zoutman of Beeter Verwagting (death sentence commuted, deported, worked as convict)

Other
1. Dick of Success (acquitted)
2. Jack of Le Bonne Intention (released)
3. Trim of Chateau Margo (sentenced to 300 lashes then pardoned for 'endeavouring to trace the rebel Richard')

* The list of names and punishments comes from Joshua Bryant's book *Account of an insurrection of the Negro Slaves in the Colony of Demerara* appendix titled: 'List of the Insurgent Negroes Who were Tried by Court-Martial, held at the Colony House, Georgetown, with their Sentences etc.' Additional information for those deported, like Jack Gladstone, taken from Governor John Murray's letter to Earl Bathurst 14 February 1824.

+ According to Bryant, these abolitionists were 'decapitated after being down from the gallows. Their heads were affixed on poles within the Fort.'

ENDNOTES

INTRODUCTION

4 *'not only Black and Brown, but also White ...'* Following the lead of the Associated Press and other media outlets, I have capitalised 'Black' in the context of race and culture, so Black men, Black communities and Black culture. And in line with the advice of the National Association of Black Journalists (USA), I have also used uppercase when using colour to describe race, including White and Brown. The exception to this rule is when I have quoted from historical sources, in which case I have retained their usage of upper- or lowercase.

4 *'they had sold tobacco from plantations ...'* According to the 1844 parliamentary select committee report from 1844 on the UK tobacco trade, more than 95 per cent of all tobacco imported to the UK came from the USA. In this same report, it was acknowledged that this tobacco was cultivated on plantations worked by enslaved people.

6 *'I had never heard of Demerara. That is, beyond the brown crystallised sugar ...'* On 30 June 1913, a grocer on King's Cross Road in London was accused of falsely selling 'Demerara sugar' that did not come from Demerara (then British Guiana). Instead, it was white cane sugar from Mauritius, with added brown dye. The magistrate dismissed the case (Anderson v. Britcher), finding that 'Demerara sugar' was a 'generic term applicable to any sugar of the substance, kind, and colour of the sugar in question wherever produced, and that therefore the said sugar was of the nature, substance, and quality of the article demanded by the appellant, the purchaser'. When the case was appealed to the King's Bench court, the judges found that Demerara sugar 'does not mean sugar grown only in Demerara', but refers to sugar of 'a particular colour'. Today, Demerara sugar is mostly produced in Mauritius. It is also produced in Barbados, India, Malawi and Guyana.

PROLOGUE

10 *'On one side of the platform stood the auctioneer ...'* The source for this passage is John Cheveley's memoirs, republished as *No Messing: The Story of an Essex Man*.

10 *'Capital slave, gentlemen, ...'* The original quotation includes the N-word instead of 'slave'.

CHAPTER 1

13 *'approximately the same size as Great Britain ...'* Today, the area of the Cooperative Republic of Guyana is 83,000 square miles, whereas Great Britain is 80,823 square miles, making Guyana slightly larger. The population figure of 7,000 Indigenous people comes from Schomburgk (1840) and was used in the 1878 census; the real number may have been higher.

14 *'the Dutch colonists had reclaimed this area of wetland ...'* According to the British government's Venn Commission (1948), the enslaved Africans in Guyana 'cleared, drained and reclaimed 15,000 square miles of forest and swamps. This is equivalent to 9,000,000 acres of land. In short, all the fields on which the sugar estates are now based were cleared, drained and irrigated by African labour forces.'

14 *'According to the colony's meticulously kept slave register ...'* In his seminal book, *Slave Population of the British Caribbean*, Barry Higman wrote that 'slave registration was meant to identify slaves brought to the West Indies in the illicit Atlantic slave trade that continued after the British abolition of 1807'. Trinidad was the first British colony to introduce registration of enslaved people in 1813. Demerara started in 1817. These registers are kept at the National Archives in Kew, London (file number T71/ 395, pages 2139 and through 2146). The entry for the Success plantation in the slave register, dated, 26 August 1817, records that the information was provided by 'Fred R. Cort, attorney to John Gladstone'. On the left-hand side of the page are the names of the enslaved men, women and children, each penned in neat brown ink. To the right of the names are five columns, separated by thin red vertical lines, memorialising the following data: 'colour', 'age', 'country', 'employment', and 'condition' (eg: 'healthy', 'able', 'sickly' and 'invalid').

14 *'more than 80 per cent of those over sixteen years old had been born in Africa ...'* Demerara had the highest number of enslaved people born in Africa in the British Caribbean. According to Barry Higman's *Slave Population of the British Caribbean*, in 1817 the proportion of the enslaved population (including children) born in Africa was: Demerara-Essequibo (55 per cent), Jamaica (37 per cent), Bahamas (21 per cent), St Lucia (21 per cent), St Kitts (16 per cent), and Barbados (7 per cent).

15 *'His mother had died shortly after giving birth to him ...'* According to John Smith's journal, Peggy was a free woman who had been with Quamina for 'nearly 20 years' when she died on 22 October 1819, therefore they had become partners at the earliest in 1799. The slave registry has Jack as being 22 years old in 1817, so he must have been born in 1797 or 1798, before his father got together with Peggy. John Smith also reports that Peggy was Quamina's 'wife' and Quamina was Jack's 'father', but it does not say Peggy was Jack's mother. This all suggests that she was not his mother, otherwise he would be free. The most likely explanation for why his mother disappeared around the time of his birth is that she died during labour or soon after. Alternatives would be that she was sold to another slaveholder or ran away, both unlikely without Jack going with her.

15 *'Since she was enslaved when Jack was born ... he was also enslaved ...'* The legal doctrine that children of an enslaved woman were born into slavery and that children of free women were born free was called *partus sequitur ventrem*. This was typically applied by both Dutch and British colonies. Jack was born around 1798, when Demerara was controlled by the British but governed by Dutch law.

15 *'he was charismatic and widely considered handsome ...'* In the court testimony and subsequent histories, there are multiple mentions of Jack's sexuality. I have avoided such references, given the problematic trope of the aggressively sexual Black man.

15 *'At an early age, Jack ...'* The description of Quamina's time as a houseboy comes from John Smith's diary, 9 May 1817. According to the slave registers held at the National Archives in Kew (T71/395, beginning at folio 2139), Quamina was 46 years old in 1817. This means that Tonisen is likely to have been at least 60 when she died. The register recorded his place of birth as 'Demerary', his position as 'carpenter', and his health as 'weakly'. The same page in the register has Jack as being 22 years old, 'able' and a 'Cooper'.

15 *'kidnapped from her village in West Africa ...'* According to Barry Higman, the majority of enslaved people across the Caribbean came from the Bite of Biafra and Central Africa. There is little specific for Demerara, but the figures for the neighbouring British colony of Berbice in 1819 are as follows: Central Africa (22.5%), Bite of Benin (22.2%), Bite of Biafra (16.5%), Gold Coast (14.8%), Senegambia (10.1%), Sierra Leone (8.1%), Windward Coast (5.7%) [Higman, Slave Populations of the British Caribbean].

18 *'Jack had witnessed his father undergo something of a transformation ...'* On 14 December 1817, Quamina wrote a letter to Reverend Burder, the head of the London Missionary Society ('Letter from the Negroes of Demerary', Council for World Mission). It was also signed by Seaton, Bristol and Aasar (who presumably was a deacon at the Bethel Chapel like the others). It was transcribed by Moses Chisholm. 'Dear Master,' they wrote, 'we bless God for his goodness in enabling [thee] to send out a minister to us.' They were referring to John Smith. They added, 'Our masters and managers says that they have no objection of our attending to the teaching of the catechism but we find they try every means to stop it in working us so late at night through all our distress we try to oblige them as far as we can. They are more strick now than ever they was for they are watching us as a cat would for a mouse.' This is the only source I have found where we can hear Quamina's voice, at least in part.

19 *'They taught him some of the local words ...'* For a list of terms used on the plantations, see Bryant's book.

19 *'According to Wray's reports ...'* For more on John Wray and Hermanus Post, see the biography by Thomas Rain. Post died in 1809. His wife remarried Johannes Van der Haas soon after. Hendrik Van Cooten was a good friend of the Posts and was their attorney for affairs involving Le Resouvenir plantation. Johannes Van der Haas died in 1813. His brother Adrianus Van der Haas managed Le Resouvenir until he was let go and replaced by Hamilton.

20 *'the doors of Bethel Chapel were locked ...'* For a brief period in 1814, Richard Elliot took charge of Bethel Chapel, before being assigned to the west coast (*The History of the London Missionary Society, 1795–1895*).

21 *'A short while later, Tonisen took her last breath ...'* According to John Smith's journal entry of 30 June 1817, when he spoke to her in the minutes before her death, Tonisen 'lifts up her hands & eyes to heaven bursts into tears and exclaims, "Oh, my blessed Jesus! What am I, but a poor old dying slave, who knew nothing" & she seems almost overwhelmed with a sense of the love of Jesus, insomuch that she can hardly speak, until she is relieved by a flow of tears.'

22 *'British companies ran slave plantations in the Caribbean ...'* There is some confusion about which region Guyana belongs to. Geographically, Guyana is located in South America. Culturally, Guyana sees itself as part of the wider Caribbean and politically it belongs to the Caribbean Community (CARICOM). In the nineteenth century, Demerara was typically referred to as being part of the West Indies by the British. Today, Guyanese cricketers play for the West Indies.

22 *'I look up some statistics ...'* Arrest, unemployment, wealth and birth information from Commission on Race and Ethnic Disparities report, 31 March 2021; incarceration figures from *The Times* article 'Is the criminal justice system racist against Black people?' 14 June 2020; poverty information from the *Guardian* article 'Nearly half of BAME UK households are living in poverty', 1 July 2020.

CHAPTER 2

24 *'They belonged to the Independent Church ...'* This is now the United Reformed Church.

29 *'John Murray ... according to one of his descendants ...'* The information in this paragraph comes from *All Saints Church History, Niagara Falls* (2006). The 'descendant' was Canon John Crowe who visited Niagara Falls in 2005, John Murray's great-great grandson. According to their wedding certificate, Ellen and John Murray would not marry until 27 November 1827 in London (by then they already had a number of children together). There is some confusion about the number of John Murray's wives and how many children he had and by who. According to John Crowe's cousin Margaret Crothers, who extensively researched their mutual family, Murray had 22 children, 16 of them by Ellen. In a letter dated 2 February 1992, Margaret wrote that the 'family was shocked' when Murray ran away with Ellen. As to the first six children, it appears that at least two of them were with Elizabeth Hume, who appears to have died around the birth of Augusta Hume Murray in 1807 in St John's Newfoundland, perhaps during or soon after childbirth.

29 *'he was proprietor of three sugar estates ...'* According to the Centre for the Study of the Legacies of British Slavery at UCL, John Murray owned three plantations including: Buses Lust (152 enslaved people) and De Resolutie (133 enslaved people), both in Berbice, and Huis T'Dieren (226 enslaved people), in Demerara-Essequibo. One of John Murray's early 'purchases' of an enslaved person took place in Pointe-à-Pitre, Guadalupe on 10 September 1815. The receipt from the seller, a local barrister, stated that: 'I have sold to General Murray, my negro cook called Bernendet, of Creole nationality, aged around 30 years, for the sum of 600 gourds which the General has paid me in full.' [Receipt dated 14 September 1815, courtesy Caroline Jones.]

31 *'Then came Blygezight, followed by Bel Air, Sophia ...'* For a complete list of plantations on the east coast in 1823, and for their spellings, see Joshua Bryant's book, *Account of an Insurrection of the Negro Slaves in the Colony of Demerara*. For 1798, see Thomas Walker's map, 'A Chart of the Coast of Guyana', with detailed legends including plantation names and their owners.

31 *'the twentieth plantation, Le Resouvenir ...'* The estate's former owner and sponsor of Bethel Chapel, Hermanus Post, had died in April 1809. The plantation was inherited by his widow, who lived in Leyden, Holland. Hermanus Post was buried on 30 April near the chapel under a mango tree. The site is still maintained and fairly easy to see.

33 *'"We're very glad to see you, master," Gringo said ...'* The original entry in John Smith's diary reads 'You no so glad we massa' and 'Massa glad, we glad much.'

CHAPTER 3

39 *'Kingston Stelling ...'* The name of these waterside buildings is Dutch in origin and is recorded in numerous contemporary maps and letters. Later, a stelling was known as a wharf. Such name changes are common in Guyana. For example, according to Joshua Bryant's book, in 1823 three of the plantations near Georgetown were known as Chateau Margo, Beeter Verwagting and Leliendaal. Today, these have slightly different spellings: Chateau Margot, Beterverwagting and Liliendaal. I opted for the 1823 spellings as the story takes place at this time. Then, for the sake of consistency, I stuck with these for the contemporary narrative.

39 *'He walked along Water Street ...'* For a map of Georgetown from this time, see Bryant's book.

40 *'Cheveley later recalled in his memoirs ...'* These were republished in two volumes as *No Messing: The Story of an Essex Man*.

46 *'Robert Edmonstone ...'* According to the family memorial in Holy Rude Kirkyard, Stirling, Scotland, Robert died in Edinburgh on 8 March 1834 aged 43 years. His brother Charles died in Demerara on 1 September 1822 aged 29. His other brother, Archibald, died aged 69 in Glasgow in 28 January 1856. According to the Centre for the Study of the Legacies of British Slavery at UCL database, Robert Edmonstone and Archibald Lapslie, as partners in Archibald Edmonstone & Co.,

claimed compensation of £6,734 for the 122 enslaved men and women registered to their plantation on Waratilla Creek.

CHAPTER 4

51 *'William Ewart Gladstone ...'*   As a young man, William Gladstone's generous allowance, education and half of the cost of his Newark parliamentary seat was paid for from his father's income, reports Peter Francis in his book *The Widening Circle of Us*, adding 'we know that a considerable amount of that income derived from the plantations and from slave labour'. According to *Hansard*, during the debate about abolition in 1833, William defended the interests of the West Indian slaveholders (like his father) and argued that if slavery was abolished then they should be compensated. A few years later, he argued that the apprentice scheme, which many described as another form of slavery, should not be abolished. After John Gladstone's death, William inherited about £120,000 (according to the family biographer S. G. Checkland), worth between £12 and £90 million today. Later in life, William was a staunch opponent of slavery. On 19 March 1850, for instance, he declared in parliament that 'I can find no words sufficiently strong to characterise its enormous iniquity. I believe the slave trade to be by far the foulest crime that taints the history of mankind in any Christian or pagan country.' He became known as a humanitarian and a liberal defender of oppressed peoples such as the Armenians. William's racism persisted, however, until his old age. As Roland Quinault pointed out in an essay on this subject, William pronounced in another parliamentary debate on 13 June 1873 that 'Whites' were the 'superior race' and 'Negroes' were 'the less developed and less civilized race'. Then in 1877, in a pamphlet entitled 'The Sclavonic provinces of the Ottoman Empire', he compared the treatment of Bulgarians to Africans enslaved by Britain which was 'worse in this respect, that in the case of Negro slavery, at any rate, it was a race of higher capacities ruling over a race of lower capacities'. As a result of this legacy, some institutions are reexamining their commemorations of William Gladstone. The family name has been removed from a hall of residence at the University of Liverpool, whilst in London the William Gladstone Primary School has been renamed The King's Church of England Primary Academy. On the other hand, Gladstone continues to be appreciated by many. In April 2021, for example, in a debate sponsored by the *Economist*, subscribers voted William Gladstone as Britain's greatest liberal prime minister, while in June 2021 BBC's *History Extra* magazine included him in their list of Britain's eight most successful prime ministers.

51 *'he acquired a one-half interest in the Success plantation ...'*   This comes from S. G. Checkland's book *The Gladstones*. According to Checkland, John Gladstone converted the estate to sugar. 'There is no doubt that the gains from [Success] much affected Gladstone's outlook,' wrote Checkland, 'making him anxious to go further.' Previously, in 1798, Success was owned by Charles Hamilton and Duncan Campbell.

51 *'Which was why Quamina's son ...'* The historian Davis Alston told me that Quamina was not likely to have used this last name 'Gladstone' as, unlike his son Jack, he did not grow up on an estate owned by John Gladstone.

52 *'Frederick Cort ...'* According to Davis Alston's website Spanglish, around 1831 Frederick Cort returned to Liverpool, where he established a trading company with his brother-in-law, John Wilson. According to his will, he had two legitimate children, William and Frederick, along with Eliza Ann, whose mother Ann had been his servant at Everton between 1832 and 1833. Cort received compensation for the emancipation of twelve enslaved people.

CHAPTER 5

56 *'complain about ill-treatment to what was known as the fiscal ...'* The Fiscal Reports for Demerara and Berbice are contained within 24 volumes kept at the National Archives in Kew, London. Overall they contain more than 10,000 pages of information. As historian Trevor Burnard points out in *Hearing Slaves Speak*, the complaints brought before the fiscal are a 'rare example of slaves speaking for themselves'. They report brutal floggings, sexual assaults, stabbings, underfeeding and general neglect.

60 *'Jack heard about other rebellions ...'* In his book *Tacky's Revolt*, Vincent Brown described the earlier revolts that spread across the region during the seventeenth and eighteenth centuries – in Cartagena, de Indias, Suriname, St John, New York, Antigua and Jamaica – as an 'archipelago of insurrections'.

62 *'several romantic portrayals of the plantations ...'* Joshua Bryant, for example, produced a series of oil paintings of Demerara from this time. These are highly stylised and sanitised portrayals of life in the colony.

CHAPTER 6

70 *'The other paper was the* Guiana Chronicle *...'* The *Guiana Chronicle and Demerara Gazette*, to give it its full title, had one of the largest subscriber bases in the Caribbean, with 700 subscribers out of a total colonist population of 6,000. The paper was published by Alexander Stephenson and his brother John, until Alexander drowned in the Orinoco River on 25 August 1823.

70 *'It was an approach supported by Governor Murray ...'* According to Governor Benjamin D'Urban, who replaced Murray, the provocative articles published by the *Guiana Chronicle* were partly to blame for the 1823 uprising. 'I can have no doubt,' he said, 'that this was a great combining cause, and this very paper, a principal agent in it, of the revolt of 1823' (National Archive, London. C.0.111/116, D'Urban to Goderich, 15 August 1831).

73 *'an unattractive side to John Smith ...'* The woman referred to in this entry is Susannah, who was the enslaved housekeeper for John Hamilton.

CHAPTER 7

75 *'As Cheveley remembered it ...'*   This and much of the chapter comes from Cheveley's memoirs.

76 *'thirty-six-year-old Ben Hopkinson ...'*   Cheveley says he first met Hopkinson on the boat from England.

81 *'The most recent effort ...'*   According to the book's index, Jack is listed 23 times, Quamina 25 times, whilst John Smith has 75 entries.

81 *'notably Olaudah Equiano ...'*   When he died in 1796, Equiano left half of his money to the 'Society instituted at the Spa Fields Chapel on the twenty second day of September one thousand seven hundred and ninety-five for sending Missionaries to preach the Gospel in Foreign Parts', later the London Missionary Society that sent John Smith to Demerara. The first name included in the list of subscribers to Equiano's book was the Prince of Wales, later George IV, who was on the throne during the Demerara uprising. Equiano was also known as Gustavus Vassa. He was a key member of Sons of Africa, a group of twelve Black men in London who campaigned for the abolition of slavery.

CHAPTER 8

83 *'Buxton had the audacity to bring a resolution ...'*   From Parliamentary Papers and Hansard.

86 *'A few days later, he convened the Court of Policy ...'*   Originals of minutes are in the National Archives in Georgetown.

84 *'more than 390,000 signatures ...'*   For an exploration of the anti-slavery petition campaigns, read Mark Jones' PhD thesis, 'The mobilisation of public opinion against the slave trade and slavery'.

CHAPTER 9

91 *'Jack went into town to speak with his friend Daniel ...'*   It is not clear what happened to Daniel. Beyond his brief provision of evidence on 6 September 1823 in which he confirmed Jack's story, he does not appear amongst those tried or sentenced. It is hard to believe, however, that he was allowed to return to his job working for the governor.

91 *'at Camp House, the governor's residence ...'*   In 1855, Camp House was washed away when the sea dam was breached following the Kingston Flood. It prompted the building of the sea wall in 1858.

91 *'Manumission was a rare occurrence in Demerara ...'*   In 1820, the number of enslaved men and women who were manumised per thousand was as follows: Trinidad (6.6), Bahamas (4.5), St Lucia (1.6), Antigua (1.5), Jamaica (1.0) and Demerara-Essequibo (0.2). Figures quoted from *Slave Populations in the Caribbean* by B. W. Higman. In his book, Higman explained that the reasons for manumission are complex and can be understood 'only in part by differences in economic and political structure.'

91 *'increasing the 'price' of enslaved people ...'* According to the ranking of colony by average 'compensation payment per slave 1834', at £58.50 Demerara was the second highest, and twice as much as Barbados (£24.90) and Jamaica (£22.90) and more than three times Bahamas (£15.90) [Higman, Slave Populations of the British Caribbean].

92 *'He had already heard that an overseer from New Orange Nassau ...'* This came to Jack via York, who worked in the field gang at Success.

97 *'John Murray and the other colonists typically used ...'* For instance, in his letter to Earl Bathurst, dated 24 August 1823 (five days after the start of the uprising), Governor Murray wrote, 'Wherever these detachments came up with bodies of the insurgents, they endeavoured to persuade them to lay down their arms and return to their allegiance; nor were forcible measures resorted to, until expostulation had failed, or the rebels had given the first fire.'

98 *'I pull my* Oxford English Dictionary ...' This definition comes from the Concise Edition, 1979. The first volume of the first *Oxford English Dictionary*, then called *A New English Dictionary on Historical Principles*, was published in February 1888. This was for letters A to B. It included a similar definition of 'abolitionist'.

CHAPTER 10

101 *'The following morning, a Monday, the missionary was visited ...'* This and much of the chapter comes from John Smith's journal.

102 *'they found the group engaged in an urgent discussion ...'* The quotations from this chapter come from testimony given by various enslaved men and women during the trials held after the insurrection (*The London Missionary Society's Report*, 1824).

CHAPTER 11

107 *'Jack and his father were in the cooper's shed ...'* From Murchieson's and other people's testimony at trial (*The London Missionary Society's Report*, 1824).

108 *'The search was led by Richard, Bethney and Jessamine ...'* In his court testimony, Stewart said that 'Richard was the most desperate and dissolute; Bethney and Jessamine were very active.' In his statement, Jack said that Richard 'has been a runaway for several months, is extremely violent, and will do harm yet if left at large'. Murchieson said that 'The Negro Bethney appeared to be very active to get at us.' (*The London Missionary Society's Report*, 1824)

114 *'Her name was Amba ...'* This description of Amba comes from 'Demerara Further Papers' (1824), p. 58. The only woman to be found guilty of taking part in the uprising was Kate (enslaved at Chateau Margo) who was sentenced to two months in solitary confinement, see 'Demerara Further Papers' (1824), p. 58.

CHAPTER 12

118 *'As they spoke, a crowd of men and women carrying the recently seized rifles ...'* Testimony by Hamilton during John Smith trial. (*The London Missionary Society's Report*, 1824)

119 *'There was also Elizabeth, a teenage girl ...'* During the trial of John Smith, Elizabeth was asked by the judge advocate 'Where do you belong to?' and she replied 'Industry'. This suggests that she was enslaved to the owner of the Industry plantation, ten estates to the east of Le Resouvenir. It is likely that John and Jane Smith, or at least the mission, paid this owner a fee for Elizabeth's domestic work. In her testimony, she also said that she was living with the Smiths at the time of the rebellion.

119 *'"In the next place," Jane later remembered ...'* From Jane Smith's letters to the London Missionary Society.

123 *'governor's proclamation of martial law ...'* Since the Petition of Right of 1628, there was no possibility of martial law in Britain. However, the declaration of martial law and the use of court martial had been used in its colonies, following the rebellions in Barbados in 1805 and 1816, and in Ceylon in 1817. According to G. G. Phillimore, who reviewed the use of martial law in British colonies (*Journal of the Society of Comparative Legislation*, 1900), courts martial are 'not courts at all, or court martial properly speaking, they are merely committees formed for the purpose of carrying into execution the discretionary power issued by the government. On the one hand, they are not obliged to proceed in the manner pointed out by the Mutiny Act and Articles of War, on the other hand, if they do so proceed, they are not protected by them as the members of a real court martial might be.'

124 *'Captain Alexander Simpson ...'* According to the Centre for the Study of the Legacies of British Slavery at UCL database, along with William Shand of Liverpool, Simpson owned Ogle and Montrose plantations, to which were registered 249 and 260 enslaved people, for which he was compensated £13,075 and £14,154 respectively. He also had interests in Le Reduit and other estates in the colony. His birth date is unknown; he died in 1837.

CHAPTER 13

129 *'John Cheveley was in bed ... when he heard the sound of the bugle ...'* This and much of the chapter comes from Cheveley's memoirs.

129 *'Captain John Croal ...'* According to the Centre for the Study of the Legacies of British Slave-ownership at UCL database, Croal served in British Guiana as Commissioner of Compensation (Slavery Bill) in 1835. A year after, he was the first mayor of Georgetown; later a major street was named after him.

133 *'as many as four thousand men and women ...'* Bryant reported that at least

2,000 took part in the battle. In his letter of 22 August 1823, Governor Murray reported the number to be 'considerably above 1,500'. Cheveley in his memoirs said it was between 3,000 and 4,000.

CHAPTER 14

136 *'At least twelve thousand people were taking part ...'* The size of the rebellion is a matter of some debate. According to an early report published by *The Times* on 13 October 1823, 'thousands of enslaved women and men had taken part in the uprising'. In his book, Joshua Bryant reported that 'about forty plantations' were involved. In her PhD thesis, 'Quamina, do you hear this?', Janet Mills concludes that somewhere between 3,472 and 4,166 enslaved people participated in the insurrection. In his book *Testing the Chains*, Michael Craton says that the figure was more like 12,000. In her book, *Crowns of Glory, Tears of Blood*, Da Costa estimates figures ranging from 9,000 to 12,000. Finally, the official numbers submitted as 'Schedule A' by Governor Murray to Lord Bathurst on 24 November 1823 has the total number of abolitionists as 9,015. However, a note is added to this saying that it is 'impossible to identify all those who were engaged in the revolt'.

139 *'He needed to find his father, Quamina ...'* Jack's court testimony and other matters related to Jack's trial taken from Parliamentary Paper: 'Demerara: Further Papers viz Return to an Address by the House of Commons dated 13 April 1824 for copies or extracts of Correspondence with the Governors of the Colonies in the West Indies respecting Insurrection of Slaves from 1st January 1822 to the present time, with Minutes of Trials'. (Printed 21 May 1824)

CHAPTER 15

142 *'"Well done, Rifles!" Colonel Leahy proclaimed ...'* The source for this quote and much of the chapter comes from Cheveley's memoirs. Joshua Bryant's book contains an illustration of the battle along with a map giving the locations of those who took part.

145 *'"Mr Buckra Massa, I'm innocent, truly" ...'* These words are given in the vernacular by Cheveley.

CHAPTER 16

153 *'a meadow of razor grass ...'* To establish the flora and fauna of this period, I contacted Kaslyn Holder at the University of Glasgow and read contemporary books *A Voyage to the Demerary* by Henry Bolingbroke and *A Description of British Guiana, Geographical and Statistical* by Robert Schomburgk.

153 *'The ground was swampy ...'* To understand the bush, I visited the areas behind Chateau Margo with John Piggott, former agronomist for GuySuCo. He also took me out on the conservancy behind Uitvlugt estate on the west coast.

154 *'in their trunks could be found tacoma worms ...'* This description of how to

survive in the bush comes from Major General Joseph Singh, an expert in survival skills in the Guyana Defence Force.

158 *'The only person ... Robert Edmonstone ...'* According to Joshua Bryant, Edmonstone acted as aide-de-camp to the court president Goodman and was 'sworn in as an interpreter, to explain to the prisoner in the Negro dialect, the nature of the Charge, the evidence, to ask any questions, by way of cross-examination, and to assist the Prisoner with his Defense'. He was not, however a lawyer.

CHAPTER 17

163 *'The success of such advocates ...'* The Prisoner's Counsel Act was finally passed in 1836. For more on this, see 'Scales of Justice' by J. M. Beattie, in *Law and History Review* Vol. 9, No. 2 (Autumn 1991).

164 *'Many of those supporting such legislation were also abolitionists ...'* Including Stephen Lushington and Sir James Mackintosh.

165 *'the recently founded* Colonist *...'* The first issue of this paper was published on 13 October 1823. It was four pages long, and according to the note on the bottom of the final page was printed and published by William Towart every Monday and Thursday evening.

174 *'Gladstone should be compensated by the government ...'* In his letter dated 18 August 1824, Wilmot-Horton reveals that Gladstone had previously requested that Jack should not be returned to the estate. 'I have no doubt that Lord Bathurst will authorise Sir Benjamin D'Urban [the new governor of Demerara] being informed of your wish that your Slaves should be returned, with the exception of Jack: but the question will be, what is to be done with *that* slave; & of course this will be for the consideration of the Governor.' In another letter, dated 30 March 1825, Wilmot-Horton wrote that Gladstone's intervention had been critical to saving Jack's life and that he requested compensation: 'I have laid before Lord Bathurst your letter of the 19 inst. on the subject of your Slave Jack and I am directed by His Lordship to observe that Jack's life was forfeited to the State but at your intercession the Sentence was commuted. Lord Bathurst is of opinion that you may be entitled to the compensation which you would have received if the original sentence had been executed.' These letters are found in Gladstone's Library (Flintshire Record Office, Hawarden, Glynne-Gladstone MSS, G-G MSS 272). I was unable to visit the library given the COVID pandemic; my thanks to Michael Taylor for their transcription.

176 *'Salmon & Gluckstein also sold Cuban cigars ...'* These included cigars with names such as 'Queen Habanas', 'Caliope', 'Havannah Reinas', 'El Cielo' and 'El Cervantes'.

CHAPTER 18

179 *'Gladstone had never visited Demerara and had no intention of going there ...'* Gladstone never did visit his plantations. In 1838, he sent his son Robertson to investigate. During this trip, Robertson reported that the agent Cort was incompetent (Gladstone later fired him) but reported that the ill-treatment of the enslaved people was exaggerated. For more on this, see Morley's *Life of Gladstone*.

181 *'a handful of "stragglers" had been killed ...'*   In his memoirs, John Cheveley said that three colonists were killed during the rebellion: two during the skirmishes at Nabaclis and one at the Battle at Bachelor's Adventure. According to 'Schedule B' sent by Governor Murray to Lord Bathurst, 24 November 1823, and entitled 'The number of white persons put in the stocks during the revolt', at least 63 proprietors, estate managers, overseers and others were imprisoned in stocks.

182 *'The Church of England, for one, was deeply enmeshed with slavery ...'*   In June 2020, the Church of England put out a statement saying that 'While we recognise the leading role clergy and active members of the Church of England played in securing the abolition of slavery, it is a source of shame that others within the Church actively perpetrated slavery and profited from it.' This followed reports that the Centre for the Study of the Legacies of British Slavery at UCL had found that 96 of the Church's clergymen had profited from the transatlantic slave trade. See also *Britain's Black Debt* by Hilary Beckles on the Church and slavery.

182 *'By the 1820s, Liverpool had become ...'*   In her book *The Economic and Social Development of Merseyside*, Sheila Marriner reported that 'By 1857, Liverpool was responsible for 45 per cent of the UK's export trade and also for a third of her imports.' Other figures quoted in this paragraph come from this book.

CHAPTER 19

189 *'Colony House ...'*   This building was replaced in 1887 to house the High Court. In 1894, a statue of Queen Victoria was erected in front of it. During the struggle for independence in the 1950s, the statue was attacked with dynamite and its head and left hand were blown off. Later, it was removed from public view. In the 1990s, it was brought out again in time for a royal visit. In 2018, it was daubed with red paint (the assailant was never caught). The statue is still missing its left hand.

191 *'he had not been given the opportunity to speak with counsel ...'*   The right for defendants in felony cases to have access to a lawyer did not become established until 1836 in Britain. The role of the defence counsel, however, had become relatively common before this, starting in the 1800s.

191 *'John and Jane met William Arrindell ...'*   Arrindell was later appointed fiscal in Demerara, and then became chief justice in the colony.

192 *'"Do you believe this to be his handwriting?" ...'*   Another non-expert witness called to corroborate handwriting was the merchant Robert Edmonstone. On 12 November 1823, he examined eleven letters, including those from Cort and Stewart. According to the trial record, 'The whole of these documents were papers or licenses from the persons named, allowing the Negroes to be baptised.'

199 *'the assistant judge advocate ...'*   Confusingly, his name was also John Smith.

205 *'In 2006, All Saints Church in Niagara Falls, Canada ...'*   In 1833, John Murray and his family arrived in Drummondville, Ontario, Canada (later called Niagara Falls). Two years later, Murray was made Lieutenant-General (*Gentleman's Magazine*, Vol. 172, 1842). The *All Saints Church History* (2006) reports, euphemistically, that Murray 'made his money from his West Indian sugar plantations in the old slave holding days'. They also say that 'when slavery was abolished', John Murray received an 'indemnity' from the British government of £100,000. It is not clear where this figure comes from. According to the Centre for the Study of the Legacies of British Slavery at University College London, between 1835 and 1836, John Murray received over £20,000 compensation from the British government for the more than 540 enslaved people he 'owned'. Today that figure is valued at £20 million (according to measuringworth.com). Murray invested 'much' of this compensation money in Drummondville, including the failed 'City of the Falls' land development project and used the same funds to build 'a fine home' on Main Street facing Robinson Street (Niagara Falls *Evening Review*, 22 April 1967). He also invested in the Pavilion Hotel, the area's largest hotel. In 1837, Murray returned to Europe with his family 'to give them a European education'. John Murray died on 16 September 1841 in Paris, France, aged 64. This was after a 'protracted illness' (Dublin *Evening Packet*, 23 September 1841). Later, his wife Ellen Murray and children moved back to Drummondville. In 1854, she donated land to the community upon which All Saints Church was built and she donated additional land for a rectory in 1872 (*All Saints Church History*, 2006). Ellen and other family members worshipped and were later buried at this church (Niagara Falls *Evening Review*, 22 April 1967). The church was deconsecrated in 2004, and is currently being used by the Solid Rock Assembly parish. Today, two of Niagara Falls' main thoroughfares are named after John Murray: Murray Street and Murray Hill.

CHAPTER 20

215 *'When* The Colonist *found out about this letter ...'*   For its provocative coverage of the 1823 insurrection, amongst other things, the *Colonist* was shut down by Sir Benjamin D'Urban, the new governor of Demerara, in September 1824. Its editor, Towart, moved to Barbados. There he set up a new paper, the *Barbados Colonist and Sentinel*, which included many articles that attacked the authorities in Demerara. He died in June 1826. For more on the role of the press in the 1823 uprising, see Andrew Peter Lewis' *The British West Indian Press in the Age of Abolition*.

215 *'a group of colonists erected a gallows ...'*   David Chamberlin mentions this in his book *Smith of Demerara*, and gives as a reference page 130 of Captain Studholme Hodgson's book *Truths from the West Indies*. Wallbridge repeats this in *The Demerara Martyr*, and da Costa also refers to the effigy in *Crowns of Glory*. Yet the only reference on page 130 of the Hodgson book I could find was the following note: 'Before the court martial by which he was tried, had come to a decision, a gallows was prepared for the prisoner.'

CHAPTER 21

216 *'If reparations are part of the process…'* On 1 August 2021, Emancipation Day, Guyana's president Mohamed Irfaan Ali went further, saying 'It is therefore fitting that on this day, we as Guyanese recommit to the goal of gaining international reparations for the crime of African enslavement. Reparative justice must include a full and unconditional apology from those responsible and/or who benefited from the transatlantic trade in captive Africans and their consequent enslavement. Reparative justice, however, cannot be confined to such an apology. It must go further. Guyana will continue to support the efforts being made within the Caribbean Community to press for the convening of an international summit to demand reparative justice for the victims of the transatlantic slave trade, African enslavement, and its enduring effects.'

CHAPTER 22

228 *'being held in a small cell in the colonial jail …'* A joint project between the University of Guyana and the University of Leicester has been set up to explore the history of the prisons in Guyana. Called 'History and Security Sector Reform: Crime and Punishment in British Colonial Guyana, 1814–1966', it includes early documents relating to the jail, available at the National Archive in Kew (CO 111/150/367).

229 *'John wrote a letter of his own …'* Included in the *London Missionary Society's Report*, 1824.

231 *'Amongst these number were Cudjo, Quabino and Sammy …'* From Joshua Bryant's book. Note that Primo who had fled with them to the bush, but had given testimony during the trials, was 'respited', according to Bryant's list of sentences printed at the back of his book.

234 *'the coffin was lowered into the ground…'* In *The Demerara Martyr*, Wallbridge writes that after John Smith was buried, 'two negro workmen, a carpenter and a bricklayer, who had been members of his congregation' added bricks and rails to mark the edges of his grave. But when the fiscal heard of this, 'he ordered the bricks to be taken up, the railing to be torn down and the whole frail memorial of gratitude and piety to be destroyed'. The site of John Smith's final resting place remains unknown to this day.

CHAPTER 23

238 *"'I was bred under the shadow …'"* Quoted in Morley's *Life of Gladstone*.

240 *'I was not sorry to hear of Smith's death …'* Letter from Gladstone to Wilton-Horton, quoted in Checkland's *The Gladstones*. Checkland gives the date of this letter as 9 December 1823, but John Smith would not die for another two months.

EPILOGUE

253 *'Tens of thousands of formerly enslaved people in Demerara ...'* In 1831, Demerara, Essequibo and Berbice merged into the new colony of British Guiana. Demerara remained the name of the region that included the estates on the East Coast and the capital Georgetown.

255 *'Jane ... died at 8.30 am on 10 February 1828, aged thirty-two ...'* In his journal entry dated 22 September 1819, John said 'This day completes Mrs Smith's 24th year. May the Lord spare her have 24 more.' This suggests she was born on 22 September 1795.

255 *'In today's money, the compensation would be worth around £17 billion ...'* According to the *Guardian*, 12 February 2018. This figure is frequently cited by academics and the media. It is based on relative labour value (or labour earnings) but is only one of several different ways of measuring the changing value of money, goods and services. An alternative approach focuses on the retail price index as a measure, giving a figure of £2 billion. A third way relies on 'economic share' (a measure of share of GDP), resulting in £96 billion. These figures come from the website measuringworth.com.

256 *'today that is the equivalent of more than £80 million ...'* According to the Centre for the Study of the Legacies of British Slavery at UCL, John Gladstone received compensation both solely and as part of a group. As a sole awardee, he received £78,402.75. As a joint awardee, he received part of £34,319.08. It is therefore possible to say he received at least £80,000. Today's figure is based on 'labour value' and is in the middle of the possible range. The low end, based on retail price, would be around £10 million, and the high end, based on economic share, would be more than £500 million (measuringworth.com).

259 *'Cheveley received £479, or £415,000 in today's money ...'* According to the Centre for the Study of the Legacies of British Slavery at UCL, Cheveley's brother Charles was awarded the compensation for a group of enslaved people in British Guiana as the trustee of the marriage settlement of John Castelfranc Cheveley and Frances Barry. The source for the contemporary figures is the website measuringworth.com.

260 *'His wife Frances died during a complicated childbirth ...'* John married Frances Barry on 8 September 1826. According to John's memoirs she died aged 33 on 21 October 1831 (the register at Walton On The Hill has her buried on 19 October). John married Emily Pellatt on 20 April 1838. She died in 1878.

261 *'Jack ... "had four children" ...'* Another figure is provided by a pamphlet entitled 'No. VII. Negro Slavery: Insurrection of slaves in the West Indies particularly in Demerara', which reported that Jack 'had been united, indeed, by one of the Missionaries, to a young woman on a neighbouring estate, by whom he had two children.' (Ellerton and Henderson printers, 1824)

261 *'Now it was to be called Quamina Street ...'* There is a monument to Quamina on Carmichael Street in Georgetown. He is also included in a mural in the dome of the Guyana Bank for Trade and Industry building on Water Street. Yet there are no memorials for Jack Gladstone in Georgetown. When I asked people why Quamina was remembered in Guyana more than Jack Gladstone, I was given different answers. One person said it was because Quamina was more of an 'African-sounding' name than Jack Gladstone and therefore more attractive to those trying to celebrate African culture. Another told me that Quamina was important because he argued against the violence being used in the uprising. A third person suggested it was because those in power just didn't know their history.

POSTSCRIPT

264 *'then you must support reparations ...'* Elsie Harry, a youth activist in Guyana, told me that it is 'important' that people take action at the government and family level. 'There's something more personal than at level of state when people-to-people conversations are happening and it will help to build the consciousness of young generations, which is critical.' But, she added, she would also like to see families like mine lobby their governments to engage with reparations, as state action can have a widespread effort. If people on both sides lobby, she said, 'there will be a united force that could move us along'.

BIBLIOGRAPHY

I have compiled the following reading list as an introductory guide. It is not meant to be comprehensive. I have included books that I found helpful in my understanding of these subjects and in writing this story.

BRITAIN, SLAVERY AND REPARATIONS

Akala, *Natives: Race & Class in the Ruins of Empire* (Two Roads, 2018)

Araujo, Ann Lucia, *Reparations for Slavery and the Slave Trade* (Bloomsbury, 2017)

Andrews, Kehinde, *Back to Black* (Zed, 2018)

Beckles, Hilary, *Britain's Black Debt* (University of the West Indies Press, 2013)

BLM, *Reparations Now Toolkit* (2019)

Browne, Randy, *Surviving Slavery in the British Caribbean* (University of Pennsylvania Press, 2017)

Burnard, Trevor, *Hearing Slaves Speak* (The Caribbean Press, 2010)

CARICOM, *Ten Point Plan for Reparatory Justice* (2014)

Coates, Ta-Nehisi, 'The Case for Reparations' (*Atlantic* magazine, 2014)

Coupland, Reginald, *The British Anti-Slavery Movement* (Cass, 1964)

Cugoano, Ottobah, *Thoughts and sentiments on the evil and wicked traffic of the slavery and commerce of the human species* (1787)

Draper, Nick, *The Price of Emancipation: Slave-Ownership, Compensation and British Society at the End of Slavery* (Cambridge University Press, 2010)

Eddo-Lodge, Reni, *Why I'm No Longer Talking to White People About Race* (Bloomsbury, 2017)

Equiano, Olaudah, *The Interesting Narrative of the Life of Olaudah Equiano* (1789)

Francis, Peter, *The Widening Circle of Us* (University of Chester, 2021)

Fryer, Peter, *Staying Power: The History of Black People in Britain* (Pluto Press, 1984)

Higman, B. W., *Slave Populations of the British Caribbean 1807-1834* (University of West Indies, 1997)

Hirsch, Afua, *Brit(ish): On Race, Identity and Belonging* (Jonathan Cape, 2018)

James, C. L. R., *The Black Jacobins* (Penguin, 1938)

Livesay, David, *Children of Uncertain Fortune: Mixed-Race Jamaicans in Britain and the Atlantic Family, 1733–1833* (University of North Carolina Press, 2018)

Marriner, Sheila, *The Economic and Social Development of Merseyside,* (Croom Helm, 1982)

Olusoga, David, *Black and British: A Forgotten History* (Macmillan, 2016)

Prince, Mary, *The History of Mary Prince* (Penguin Random House, 1831)

Sanghera, Sathnam, *Empireland: How Imperialism Has Shaped Modern Britain* (Viking, 2021)

Stephen, James, *The Slavery of the British West India Colonies* (Joseph Butterworth, 1824)

UN Basic Principles and Guidelines on the Right to a Remedy and Reparation (2005)

Walvin, James, *Black Ivory: Slavery in the British Empire* (Blackwell, 1992)

Williams, Eric, *Capitalism and Slavery* (University North Carolina, 1994)

DEMERARA, GUYANA AND THE CARIBBEAN

Bahadur, Gaiutra, *Coolie Woman, The Odyssey of Indenture* (C. Hurst, 2013)

Bolingbroke, Henry, *A Voyage to the Demerary* (Richard Phillips, 1809)

Brown, Vincent, *Tacky's Revolt: The Story of an Atlantic Slave War* (Harvard University Press, 2020)

Bryant, Joshua, *Account of an Insurrection of the Negro Slaves in the Colony of Demerara* (self-published, 1824)

Burnard, Trevor, *Hearing Slaves Speak* (The Caribbean Press, 2010)

Burnard, Trevor, *Mastery, Tyranny, and Desire: Thomas Thistlewood and His Slaves in the Anglo-Jamaican World* (University of North Carolina, 2004)

Buxton, Charles, *Memoirs of Sir Thomas Fowell Buxton* (John Murray, 1849)

Chamberlin, David, *Smith of Demerara: Martyr-Teacher of the Slaves* (Colonial Missionary Society, 1923)

Checkland, S. G., *The Gladstones: A Family Biography* (Cambridge, 1971)

Cheveley, John, *No Messing: The Story of an Essex Man. Volume One*, ed. C. C. Thornburn (Spennymoor, Co. Durham, The Memoir Club, 2001)

Cheveley, John, *No Messing: The Story of an Essex Man. Volume Two*, ed. C. C. Thornburn (Chichester: Crosswave Publishing, 2012)

Craton, Michael, *Testing the Chains: Resistance to Slavery in the British West Indies* (Cornell University, 2009)

Dalton, Henry, *The History of British Guiana* (Longman, Brown, Green and Longmans, 1855)

Dabydeen, David, *Johnson's Dictionary* (Peepal Tree Press, 2013)

da Costa, Emilia Viotti, *Crowns of Glory, Tears of Blood* (Oxford University Press, 1994)

Gibbons, Arnold, *The Legacy of Walter Rodney in Guyana and the Caribbean* (University Press of America, 2011)

Granger, David, *The Emancipation Movement: The pursuit of dignity and liberty* (Free Press, 2020)

Hodgson, Studholme, *Truths from the West Indies* (William Ball, 1838)

Horne, Charles, *The Story of the L.M.S. 1795-1895* (1894)

Jagan, Cheddi, *The West on Trial* (Hansib, 1994)

James, C. L. R., *A History of Pan-African Revolt* (Independent Labour Party, 1938)

Jones, Mark, *The mobilisation of public opinion against the slave trade and slavery* (University of York, 1998)

Kars, Marjoleine, *Blood on the River: A Chronicle of Mutiny and Freedom on the Wild Coast* (New Press, 2020)

Kirke, Henry, *25 Years in British Guiana* (Sampson Low, Marston, 1898)

Lean, J. H., *The Secret Life of Berbice Slaves* (University of Canterbury, 2002)

Lewis, Andrew Peter, *The British West Indian Press in the Age of Abolition* (University of London, 1993)

London Missionary Society, *Report of the Proceedings against the late Rev. J. Smith of Demerara* (Westley, Ave-Maria Lane, 1824)

Lovett, Richard, *The History of the London Missionary Society* (Henry Frowde, 1899)

McDonnell, Alex, *Considerations on Negro Slavery With Authentic Reports Illustrative of the Actual Condition of the Negro in Demerara* (Longman, Hurst, 1825)

McGowan, Winston, *A Survey of Guyanese History* (Guyenterprise Advertising Agency, 2018)

Mills, Janet, *"Quamina, do you hear this?" Revisiting the Demerara Slave Rebellion, 1823* (Dalhousie University Halifax, 2018)

Morrison, John, *Fathers and Founders of London Missionary Society* (Fisher, 1844)

Morley, John, *Life of Gladstone* (Macmillan, 1903)

Northcott, Cecil, *Slavery's Martyr* (Epworth Press, 1976)

Rain, Thomas, *The Life and Labours of John Wray: Pioneer Missionary in British Guiana* (John Snow, 1892)

Raleigh, Sir Walter, *The Discovery of Guiana* (1848)

Rodney, Walter, *Guyanese Sugar Plantations in the Late Nineteenth Century* (Release, 1979)

Rodney, Walter, *How Africa Underdeveloped Europe* (Bogle-L'Ouverture Publications, 1972)

Rodway, James, *The History of British Guiana* (Thomson, 1891)

Schomburgk, Robert Hermann, *A Description of British Guiana, Geographical and Statistical: Exhibiting Its Resources and Capabilities* (1840)

Smith, Matthew, *Liberty, Fraternity, Exile: Haiti and Jamaica After Emancipation* (University of North Carolina Press, 2014)

Streather, George, *Memorials of the Independent Chapel at Rothwell* (Rothwell United Reform Church, 1994)

Taylor, Michael, *The Interest: How the British Establishment Resisted the Abolition of Slavery* (Bodley Head, 2020)

Thompson, Alvin, *A Documentary History of Slavery in Berbice* (Free Press, 2002)

Titus, Noel, 'Reassessing John Smith's Influence on the Demerara Slave Revolt of 1823', in: Alvin Thompson, *In the Shadow of the Plantation* (Ian Randle, 2002)

Wallbridge, Edwin Angel, *The Demerara Martyr, Memoirs of Rev. John Smith, Missionary to Demerara* (Charles Gilpin, 1848)

Waterton, Charles, *Wanderings in South America* (Cassell and Company, 1891)

Webb, Jack, and Westmaas, Rod, *Memory, Migration and Decolonisation in the Caribbean and Beyond* (University Press London, 2020)

SLAVERY, RACE AND AMERICA

Baldwin, James, *The Fire Next Time* (Dial Press, 1963)
Baptist, Edward, *The Half Has Never Been Told: Slavery and the Making of American Capitalism* (Basic Books, 2014)
Berry, Mary Frances, *My Face Is Black Is True* (Vintage, 2005)
Degruy, Joy, *Post Traumatic Slave Syndrome* (Uptone Press, 2005)
DiAngelo, Robin, *White Fragility* (Allen Lane, 2018)
Fields, Karen, *Racecraft: The Soul of Inequality in American Life* (Verso, 2012)
Hooks, Bell, *Ain't I a Woman: Black Women and Feminism* (South End Press, 1981)
Jacobs, Harriet, *Incidents in the Life of a Slave Girl* (Dover Publications, 2001)
Kendi, Ibram, *How to be an Antiracist* (Penguin Random House, 2019)
Kendi, Ibram, *Stamped From the Beginning* (Nation Books, 2016)
Morrison, Toni, *Playing in the Dark: Whiteness and the Literary Imagination* (Vintage, 1993)
Procter, Alice, *The Whole Picture* (Cassell, 2020)
Row, Jess, *White Flights: Race, Fiction and the American Imagination* (Graywolf Press, 2019)
Saad, Layla, *Me and White Supremacy* (Quercus, 2020)
Styron, William, *The Confessions of Nat Turner* (Jonathan Cape, 1988)
X, Malcolm, and Haley, Alex, *Autobiography of Malcolm X* (Grove Press, 1965)

TOBACCO

Alford, B., *W. O. & H. O. Wills and the Development of the UK Tobacco Industry* (Methuen, 1973)
Tanner, Arthur, *Tobacco: From the Grower to the Smoker* (Pitman, 2012)
Tille, Nannie, *The Bright Tobacco Industry* (1948)

ACKNOWLEDGEMENTS

I could not have written this book without visiting Guyana. So thank you to the Guyana Civil Aviation Authority for arranging my flight to Georgetown during the COVID-19 lockdown, to Eastern Airlines for flying me in and out of the country, and to everyone at the Herdmanston Lodge Hotel who took such amazing care of me during my stay. Most of all, a huge thank you to Vishani Ragobeer, who helped me navigate Guyana and is a truly great journalist, and Alissa Trotz, who has been such a good friend and ally throughout this project; and Juanita Cox and Rod Westmaas, for opening up their remarkable network of contacts.

Thank you to all those who helped me with my research: Jock Ainslie, Vibert Alexander, David Alston, Clare Anderson, Drew Armstrong, Richard Atkinson, Anthony Balniel, Tikwis Begbie, Patrick Bernard, Ras Blackman, Ulele Burnham, Hamley Case, Denis Chabrol, Gabriella Chapman, Rodney van Cooten, Kibwe Copeland, Juanita Cox, Sarah Cox, Canon John Crowe, Christina Crowe, Josephine Crowe, Peter Cruchley, David Dabydeen, Euton Daley, Jenny Daley, Jocelyn Dow, Lotte Lieb Dula, Amantha Edmead, Orealla Felix Smith, Stephen Foster, Peter Francis, Gao Gao, Dee George, Charlie Gladstone, Drew D. Gray, Stanley Greaves, Ruth Hecht, Justin Holder, Kaslyn Holder, Bram Hoonhout, Vikki Jackson, Caroline Jones, Hanan Lachmansingh, David Lammy MP, Hew Locke, Chris Lowe, Cecilia McAlmont, Winston MacGowan, Elton MaCrae, Keith McClelland, Suzanne Moase, Craig Morrissey, Stephen Mullon, Gert Oostindie, Sir Geoffrey Palmer, Diana Paton, Deo Persaud, Rani Persaud, Eric Phillips, John Piggott, Denita Prowell, Nazima Raghubir, Gavin Ramnarain, Cathy Roy, Greg Quinn, Olive Samson, Clem

Seecharan, John Schultz, Richard Stone, Michael Taylor, Bruce Tomkins, Suzanne Urwin, James Walvin, Nigel Westmaas, Rod Westmaas, Keith Williams, Simba Williams, Thomas de Wolf and Hazel Woolford. There are others, I would also like to thank, whose names I either changed or omitted, for reasons of anonymity. And a special thanks to Rodney Van Cooten, for his numerous research efforts.

Thanks also to the staff at the various archives who helped me, especially given the difficulties posed by the pandemic: British Library, Centre for the Study of the Legacies of British Slavery (UCL), Library of Congress, National Archives in Kew, National Archives in Georgetown, Museum of African Heritage in Georgetown, Gladstone's Library, SOAS, University of Florida, and all those who maintain *The Times* and *New York Times* archives and the British Newspaper Archive.

To my family members, who agreed to talk with me about our shared legacy of slavery and engaged in discussions about how we might repair this historical harm.

Thank you to Darren Bennett for the superb maps, to Barrington Braithwaite and Errol Brewster for their artwork, and to Tim Oliver for the internal illustrations.

Thank you to my readers: Lucy Baring, Zam Baring, Niall Barton, James Dawkins, Amanda Harding, James Harding, Kate Harding, Elsie Harry, Rupert Levy, Gayle Lucka, Keith McClelland, Lulu McConville, Lynn Medford, Sebastian Meyer, Matthew Smith, Alissa Trotz and Amelia Wooldridge. And to Sonny Marr for believing.

Thank you to my agents, Sarah Chalfant and James Pullen at The Wylie Agency, and to my editors Alan Samson and Jenny Lord. Publishing a book is a team effort. So a massive thank you to Steve Marking who designed the stunning cover, Natalie Dawkins for excellent picture research, and Clarissa Sutherland the project editor for brilliantly managing the production. Also Tom Noble for marketing and Elizabeth Allen for publicity for their excellent work. Along with everyone at W&N who worked on the book.

Finally, to my daughter Sam and wife Debora – thank you both, for your belief, your tolerance and for making me laugh.

INDEX

Grovesting, Baron, 148
Guadalupe, 29
Guiana Chronicle, 70–1, 79, 165, 220, 223, 254
Guildford, 117, 208, 211
Gun, Mr, 118
Guyana, 114–16, 126–8, 134–5, 140–1, 150–1, 175–7, 187–8, 216–17, 226–7, 235–6, 263–4
    demographics, 114, 257
    geography, 266, 273
    see also, British Guiana
Guyana Bank for Trade and Industry, 286
Guyana Defence Force, 261
Guyana Reparations Commission, 235

Haiti Revolution, 59–61, 97, 247, 253
Hamilton, 263, 268
Hamilton, John, 65, 67–8, 93, 117–19, 165, 220
Hampton Court estate, 49
Harris, John, 45
Harris, Lorenzo, 61
Harry, of Triumph, 263, 268
Harry, of Good Hope, 158, 263, 268
Harry, Elsie, 115, 187, 286
Hawarden Castle, 258
Herbert, Charles, 169–72
Herdmanston Lodge, 114, 187, 235
Hesperus, 256
Heyliger, Victor Amadius, 56, 69, 86, 165, 168, 192–7, 199, 201, 207–8, 232–3
Higman, Barry, 271
Hill, Alec, 65
Hinds, David, 140
Hodgson, Captain Studholme, 283
Holder, Kaslyn, 280
Holocaust, 4, 227
Holy Rude Kirkyard, Stirling, 274
Hopkinson, Ben, 76–7, 130, 144–5, 212
Hopkinson, Johanna, 76–7
Huis T'Dieren estate, 274

Imperial Tobacco, 176
indentured labour, 256–7
Industry estate, 209, 279
Irish potato famine, 226
Ithaca estate, 253

Jackey, 190
Jagan, Janet, 216
Jamaica, 14, 26, 37, 57, 83, 91
    Sharpe's rebellion, 253–4

James, C. L. R., 12, 253
Jefferson, Thomas, 74
Jenkinson, Charles, 243
Jessamine, 108, 278
Jews, 48, 54, 89–90
Joe, 168–9, 195
Johnson, Boris, 3
Joseph (Bachelor's Adventure), 96, 155, 158
Joseph (Nabaclis), 111–12
Joseph, Sir Keith, 48, 274–5

Kendi, Ibram X., 73–4
Kerman, Lieutenant Owen, 148
King's Black Regiment, 77
King's House, 212
Kingston Stelling, 39
Kitty estate, *xiii*, 31, 222
Knight, Anne, 253

La Bonne Intention estate, *xiii*, 109, 147
La Reconnaissance estate, 139
La Reduit estate, 168–9
Lammy, David, 22–3
Lancaster estate, *xiii*, 136, 143–4, 155
Laretio, 128
Le Resouvenir estate, *xiii*, *xv*, 18–21, 31–6, 93, 107, 126, 209, 220, 228, 262
    improved conditions, 65–6
    punishments, 34–5
    uprising, 119–25, 136
    see also Bethel Chapel
Leahy, Lieutenant Colonel Thomas, 81, 137–8, 142–6, 168, 212
Leliendaal estate, 31
Liddle, Rod, 54
Liverpool, Lord, 243
Liverpool, 15, 26, 42–3, 46, 49–50, 75, 83, 174, 178, 180, 182–4, 218–19, 238, 240, 243, 257–9, 282
Liverpool Mercury, 183–5
Lloyds of London, 250
Locke, Hew, 216–17
London Missionary Society, 18, 21, 24–5, 28, 36–7, 63–4, 121, 181, 211, 228–9, 239, 241, 255
Lord's Prayer, 33
Louie, 109
Louis, 158, 263, 268
Louverture, Toussaint, 59, 61
Loveless, 44
Ludin, Hanns, 89
Lushington, Dr Stephen, 246